THE NEW
BREAD LOAF
ANTHOLOGY
OF CONTEMPORARY
AMERICAN POETRY

Bread Loaf Anthologies

The New American Poets: A Bread Loaf Anthology,
edited by Michael Collier , 2000

The New Bread Loaf Anthology of Contemporary American Poetry,
edited by Michael Collier and Stanley Plumly , 1999

Touchstones: American Poets on a Favorite Poem,
edited by Robert Pack and Jay Parini, 1995

American Identities: Contemporary Multicultural Voices,
edited by Robert Pack and Jay Parini, 1994

Poems for a Small Planet: Contemporary American Nature Poetry,
edited by Robert Pack and Jay Parini, 1993

Writers on Writing,
edited by Robert Pack and Jay Parini, 1991

The Bread Loaf Anthology of Contemporary American Essays,
edited by Robert Pack and Jay Parini, 1989

The Bread Loaf Anthology of Contemporary American Short Stories,
edited by Robert Pack and Jay Parini, 1987

The Bread Loaf Anthology of Contemporary American Poetry,
edited by Robert Pack, Sydney Lea, and Jay Parini, 1985

The New BREAD LOAF ANTHOLOGY of Contemporary American Poetry

Michael Collier

and

Stanley Plumly, *editors*

Bread Loaf Writers' Conference and
Middlebury College Press
Published by University Press of New England
Hanover and London

Middlebury College Press
Published by University Press of New England, Hanover, NH 03755
This collection copyright © 1999 by Bread Loaf Writers' Conference/Middlebury College
All rights reserved
Printed in the United States of America
5 4 3 2
CIP data appear at the end of the book

Copyright to poems in this volume is held by the individual authors, with the few exceptions noted below. The editors gratefully acknowledge permission from the poets and/or their publishers to reprint the poems in this collection.

David Baker's "Ohio Fields After Rain" first appeared in *Poetry*, was copyrighted in February 1998 by the Modern Poetry Association, and is reprinted by permission of the Editor of *Poetry*.

Marvin Bell's "The Book of the Dead Man #35" and "The Book of the Dead Man #61" appeared in *Ardor: The Book of the Dead Man, Volume 2,* © 1997 by Marvin Bell. Reprinted by permission of Copper Canyon Press, P.O. Box 271, Port Townsend, WA 98368.

Stephen Berg's "In a New Leaf" and "Legacy" are from *Shaving*, Four Way Books, 1998.

Wayne Dodd's "October Notes" appeared in *The Blue Salvages,* Carnegie Mellon University Press, 1998.

Tess Gallagher, "Owl-Spirit Dwelling," "Laughter & Stars," and "Urgent Story" © 1995, Tess Gallagher, *My Black House,* Blood Axe Books, Newcastle upon Tyne.

"Vita Nova (You saved me)" "Formaggio" "The Burning Heart" "Vita Nova (In the splitting)" from *Vita Nova* by Louise Glück. Copyright © 1999 by Louise Glück. Reprinted by permission of the Ecco Press.

"Heinrich Heine" and "Ocean of Grass" are from *On Love* by Edward Hirsch. Copyright © 1998 by Edward Hirsch. Reprinted by permission of Alfred A. Knopf, Inc.

"Kosmos," "Eclogue at Twilight," "Nude Interrogation," and "Song Thief" are from *Thieves of Paradise,* © 1998 by Yusef Komunyakaa, Wesleyan University Press, by permission of University Press of New England.

"The Two Trees," "In 1967," "The Oldest Living Thing in L.A.," and "Anastasia & Sandman" from *Elegy,* by Larry Levis, © 1997. Reprinted by permission of the University of Pittsburgh Press.

"The Bar at the Andover Inn," "Big Tongue," "Manners," and "Mingus in Shadow" from *After All: Last Poems* by William Matthews. Copyright © 1998 by the Estate of William Matthews. Reprinted by permission of Houghton Mifflin Company. All rights reserved.

Ira Sadoff's "Rapture" is from *Grazing: Poems.* Copyright 1998 by Ira Sadoff. Used with the permission of the poet and the University of Illinois Press.

"Here" and "I Will Love the Twenty-First Century" from *A Blizzard of One* by Mark Strand. Copyright © 1998 by Mark Strand. Reprinted by permission of Alfred A. Knopf, Inc.

Arthur Vogelsang, "Which Way," appeared in *Crazyhorse* (Fall 1997). "Liquids in Quantities" appeared in *Denver Quarterly* (Summer 1995).

"Girlfriend" is from *Tremble* by C. D. Wright. Copyright © 1996 by C. D. Wright. Reprinted by permission of The Ecco Press.

Many of the poems previously appeared in the following magazines and journals.

American Letters and Commentary, American Poetry Review, American Voice, Arshile, Atlanta Review, The Atlantic Monthly, Black Warrior Review, Bloomsbury Review, Boulevard, Brilliant Corners, Carolina Quarterly, Chattahoochee Review, The Colorado Review, Columbia, Connecticut Review, Crazyhorse, Denver Quarterly, DoubleTake, Electronic Poetry Review, Field, Five Fingers Review, Five

continued on page 361

For Larry Levis and William Matthews

Contents

Preface

This anthology is a gathering of poems written since 1995—some (at press time) from books, some from magazines, some previously unpublished. More than a hundred contemporary American poets were solicited, eighty-two of whom responded. In asking for recent work, we hoped to argue against the notion of an anthology as a historical document. By means of this simple guideline, we have fashioned a collection whose virtues include immediacy of effect as well as range. We believe that emphasis on the present moment may serve as a model for readers following American poetry into the twenty-first century.

For almost seventy-five years the Bread Loaf Writers' Conference has played an important role in the development and support of American poets. Many of the anthology's contributors have been connected to the Bread Loaf Writers' Conference, either as faculty or participants, but many have not. While the anthology is meant to showcase a particular moment in American writing, we hope it also reaffirms the conference's commitment to the future of the nation's poetry.

January 1999   M. C. and S. P.

THE NEW

BREAD LOAF

ANTHOLOGY

OF CONTEMPORARY

AMERICAN POETRY

AGHA SHAHID ALI

Ghazal

A language of loss? I have some business in Arabic.
Love letters: calligraphy pitiless in Arabic.

At an exhibit of miniatures, what Kashmiri hairs!
Each paisley inked into a golden tress in Arabic.

This much fuss about a language I don't know? So one day
perfume from a dress may let you digress in Arabic.

Ancestors, you have left us plots in the family graveyard—
Must our epitaphs always coalesce in Arabic?

They say the Koran prophesied a fire of men and stones?
That it will come true, said—Maimonides? In Arabic?

Majnoon, by stopped caravans, rips his collars, cries "Laila!"
Pain translated is O! much more—not less—in Arabic.

Writes Shammas: Memory, no longer confused, now is a homeland—
his two languages a Hebrew caress in Arabic.

When Lorca died, they left the balconies open and saw:
On the sea his *qasidas* stitched seamless in Arabic.

In the Veiled One's harem, an adultress hanged by eunuchs—
So the rank mirrors revealed to Borges in Arabic.

Ah, bisexual Heaven: wide-eyed houris and immortal youths!
To your each desire they say *Yes! O Yes!* in Arabic.

For that excess of sibilance, the last Apocalypse,
so pressing those three forms of *S* in Arabic.

Where there were homes in Deir Yassein, you will see dense forests—
That village was razed. There is no address in Arabic.

I too, O Amichai, saw everything, just like you did—
In Death. In Hebrew. And (Please let me stress) in Arabic.

They ask me to tell them what *Shahid* means: Listen, listen:
It means "The Belovéd" in Persian, "witness" in Arabic.

Ghazal

But first the screened mirror, all I knew of water!
Imagine "the thirstquenching virtue of water."

Who "kept on building castles" "Upon a certain rock"
"Glacial warden over 'dreams come true'" of water?

Of course, I saw Chile in my rearview mirror—
it's disappeared under a curfew of water.

Hagar, in shards, reflects her shattered Ishmael.
Call her the desert Muslim—or Jew—of water.

God, Wordless, beheld the pulled rain but missed the held sun . . .
The Rainbow—that Arrow!—Satan's coup of water.

Don't beckon me, Love, to the island of your words—
You yourself reached it, erasing my view of water.

Her star-cold palanquin goes with the caravan.
Majnoon, now she'll be news—out of the blue—of water.

When the Beast takes off his mask, Love, let it be you
sweetening Tomorrow Doom's taboo of water.

No need to stop the ears to the Sirens' rhetoric;
just mock their rock-theme, O skeleton crew of water.

Are your streets, O Abraham, washed of "the Sons of Stones"?
Sand was all Ishmael once drew of water.

I have signed, O my enemy, your death-warrant.
I won't know in time I am like you of water.

For God's sake don't unveil the Black Stone of K'aaba.
What if Faith too's let love bead a dew of water?

I have even become tears to live in your eyes.
If you weep, Stark Lover, for my breakthrough of water?

Shahid's junk mail has surfaced in a dead letter office.
He's deluxed in the leather *Who's Who of Water.*

Lenox Hill

> She said the sirens sounded like the
> elephants of Mihiragula when his men
> drove them off cliffs in the Pir Panjal mountains.

The Hun so loved the cry, one falling elephant's,
he wished to hear it again. At dawn, my mother
heard, in her hospital-dream of elephants,
sirens wail through Manhattan like elephants
forced off Pir Panjal's rock cliffs in Kashmir:
the soldiers, so ruled, had rushed the elephants.
The greatest of all footprints is the elephant's,
said the Buddha. But not lifted from the universe,
those prints vanished forever into the universe,
though nomads still break news of those elephants
as if it were just yesterday the air spread the dye
("War's annals will fade into night / Ere their story die"),

the punishing khaki whereby the world sees us die
out, mourning you, O massacred elephants!
Months later, in Amherst, she dreamt: she was, with dia-
monds, being stoned to death. I prayed: If she must die,
let it only be some dream. But there were times, Mother,
while you slept, that I prayed, "Saints, let her die."
Not, I swear by you, that I wished you to die
but to save you as you were, young, in song in Kashmir,
and I, one festival, crowned Krishna by you, Kashmir
listening to my flute. You never let gods die.
Thus I swear, here and now, not to forgive the universe
that would let me get used to a universe

without you. She, she alone, was the universe
as she earned, like a galaxy, her right not to die,
defying the Merciful of the Universe,
Master of Disease, "in the circle of her traverse"
of drug-bound time. And where was the god of elephants,
plump with Fate, when tusk to tusk, the universe,
dyed green, became ivory? Then let the universe,
like Paradise, be considered a tomb. Mother,
they asked me, *So how's the writing?* I answered *My mother
is my poem.* What did they expect? For no verse
sufficed except the promise, fading, of Kashmir
and the cries that reached you from the cliffs of Kashmir

(across fifteen centuries) in the hospital. *Kashmir,
she's dying!* How her breathing drowns out the universe
as she sleeps in Amherst. Windows open on Kashmir:
There, the fragile wood-shrines—so far away—of Kashmir!
O Destroyer, let her return there, if just to die.
Save the right she gave its earth to cover her, Kashmir
has no rights. When the windows close on Kashmir,
I see the blizzard-fall of ghost-elephants.
I hold back—she couldn't bear it—one elephant's
story: his return (in a country far from Kashmir)
to the jungle where each year, on the day his mother
died, he touches with his trunk the bones of his mother.

"As you sit here by me, you're just like my mother,"
she tells me. I imagine her: a bride in Kashmir,
she's watching, at the Regal, her first film with Father.
If only I could gather you in my arms, Mother,
I'd save you—now my daughter—from God. The universe
opens its ledger. I write: How helpless was God's mother!
Each page is turned to enter grief's accounts. Mother,
I see a hand. *Tell me it's not God's.* Let it die.
I see it. It's filling with diamonds. Please let it die.
Are you somewhere alive, weeping for me, Mother?
Do you hear what I once held back: in one elephant's
cry, by his mother's bones, the cries of those elephants

that stunned the abyss? Ivory blots out the elephants.
I enter this: *The Belovéd leaves one behind to die.*
For compared to my grief for you, what are those of Kashmir,
and what are (I close the ledger) the griefs of the universe
when I remember you—beyond all accounting—O my mother?

Rooms Are Never Finished

> Many of my favorite things are broken.
> —Mario Buatta

In here it's deliberately dark so one may sigh

in peace. Please come in. How long has it been?
Upstairs—climb slowly—the touch is more certain.
You've been, they say, everywhere. What city's left?
I've brought the world indoors. One wants certainty.
Not in art—well, you've hardly changed—but, why,

in life. But for small invisible hands, no wall
would be lacquered a rain forest's colors. Before,
these walls had just mirrors (I tried on—for size—
kismet's barest air). Remember? You were then
led through all the spare rooms I was to die

in. But look how each room's been refurbished:
This screen in stitches silk-routes a river
down Asia, past laughing Buddhas, China
a lantern burning burning burning for
"God to aggrandise, God to glorify"

in (How one passes through such thick walls!).
Candles float past inked-in laborers
but for whose hands this story would be empty,
rooms where one plots only to die, nothing
Dear! but a bare flame for you to come by

in. *Don't touch the vases!* Long ago
their waists, abandoned by scrolling foliage,
were banded by hands, banded quick with omens:
galloping floods, hooves iron by the river's edge.
O beating night, what could have reined the sky

in? Come to the window: panes plot the earth
apart. In the moon's crush, the cobalt stars
shed light—blue—on Russia: the republics porcelain,
the Urals mezzotint. Why are you weeping,
dear friend? Hush, rare guest. Once a passer-by

in tears, his footsteps dying, was . . . well, I rushed
out and he was gone. Out there it's poison.
Out there one longs for all one's ever bought,
for shades that lighten a scene: When the last leaves
were birds spent wingless on trees, love, the cage to cry

in, was glass-stormed by the North. Now that God
is news, what's left but prayer, and . . . well, if you
love something, why argue? What we own betters
any tale of God's—no? That framed scroll downstairs
and here! this shell drowned men heard God's reply

in. Listen, my friend. But for quick hands, my walls
would be mirrors. A house? A work in progress,
always. But: Could love's season be more than this?
I'll wipe your tears: Turn to me. My world would be
mere mirrors cut to multiply, then multiply

in. But for small hands. Invisible. Quick . . .

DAVID BAKER

Midwest: Ode

in memoriam William Matthews

You could believe a life so plain it means
calmness in the lives of others, who come
to see it, hold it, buy it piece by piece,
as these good people easing from their van
onto the curb where the big-shoed children
of Charm, Ohio, have lined their baskets
of sweet corn, peaches, green beans, and snap-peas.
Each Saturday morning the meeting point
of many worlds is a market in Charm.

You could believe a name so innocent
it is accurate and without one blade
of irony, and green grass everywhere.
Yet, how human a pleasure the silk hairs
when the corn is peeled back, and the moist worm
curls on the point of an ear like a tongue,
how charged the desire of the children who
want to touch it, taste it, turn it over,
until it has twirled away in the dust.

There are black buggies piled high with fruit pies.
There are field things hand-wrought of applewood
and oak, and oiled at the palm of one man.
There are piecework quilts black-striped and maroon
and mute as dusk, and tatting, and snow shawls,
and cozies the colors of prize chickens—
though the corporate farm five miles away
has made its means of poultry production
faster, makes fatter hens, who need no sleep,

so machinery rumbles the nights through.
Still, it is hard to tell who lives with
more placid curiosity than these,
not only the bearded men in mud boots
and city kids tugging on a goat rope,
but really the whole strange market of Charm,
Ohio, where weekly they come, who stare
and smile at each other, to weigh the short
business end of a dollar in their hands.

Ohio Fields After Rain

The slow humped backs of ice ceased
to shadow the savannahs of Ohio millennia
ago, right where we've sailed to a stop.
The shaken woman leaves open her car door
and familiar as relatives we touch hands
in the middle of the wet black road.
To the north new corn enriches by the hour.

South of us—really, just over a fence—
heavy boulders rolled thousands of miles
quit the migration and grew down,
huddled, cropped, scarred by the journey.
"I couldn't," she says, "stop skidding,"
and I know what she means, having
felt the weight of my car planing a scant

millimeter over the highway glaze. Calmly
she slid to one shoulder, I to the other,
and the earth spun onward without us.
What a place we have come to, scooped
hollow of hillsides, cut valleys, drumlins
and plains. And where the rain settles,
the gray beasts growing tame on the shore.

Pulp Fiction

You want more? You want some more of this shit?
so he puts his weight to his elbow jammed
under the jaw of the other one pinned
there, panicked, panting, his back to the bricks.
The others are loud and jeering, and stand
in a jackal circle a spitting-length
away. The cold air is full of bird song.

The sex—sheer sugar—of the flowering trees
turns powder to the sweating skin, and cakes
the sidewalks pale green, and packs the curbs.
Far away a powerful siren cries.
Someone is about to get his ass kicked.
But now the cruel gang spots someone—okay,
it's me—who is writing this whole scene down.

It's so easy to surpass the limits
of the powers of description. *What are*
you *looking at?* There are yellow flowers
sprouting from the downspout above their heads.
The powers of discursion are no less
feeble, frail as the least petal. *Stop it!*
They don't stop it. The one in trouble is

starting to weep and the others to laugh,
as the one with the elbow suddenly
slips a white-handled knife from his pocket.
(Is this the big city? Are there dime bags
dropping from the claws of carrion birds?
Have his bad colors taunted the wrong turf?)
No. No. No. This is just my little town,

and the hostile gang is as easily
eight years old as twenty, out of grade school
since three o'clock. I'm sorry for my mind,
but the spring has spread a violent seed,
and it has taken root in this poem,
as in my heart, in the children beating
each other to a pulp in your city

as well as mine. Is it less barbarous
to turn now toward the beautiful? Once
there was a hillside of white, wild lilies.
The mayapples were spilling there. A first
green froth of spring ferns spread under the pines—,
so the pastoral, unperturbed lilies
stand around our absence in the sunlight.

What have we done to deserve the pollen,
the plant persistence, of our natures? You
want more? The boys beat the daylights out of
the poor boy and I do nothing to help.
And the flowers are fiction—descriptive,
discursive—designed to suggest my mind
in peace or shame. So are the boys, if the

truth be told. So are the sexual trees.
The knife, you understand, is real. The knife is mine.

Romanticism

It is to Emerson I have turned now,
damp February, for he has written
of the moral harmony of nature.
The key to every man is his thought.
But Emerson, half angel, suffers his
dear Ellen's dying only half consoled
that her lungs shall no more be torn nor her

head scalded by her blood, nor her whole life
suffer from the warfare between the force
& delicacy of her soul & the
weakness of her frame . . . March the 29th,
1832, of an evening strange
with dreaming, he scribbles "I visited
Ellen's tomb & opened the coffin."

—Emerson looking in, clutching his key.
Months of hard freeze have ruptured the wild
fields of Ohio, and burdock is standing
as if stunned by persistent cold wind
or leaning over, as from rough breath.
I have brought my little one, bundled and
dear, to the lonely place to let her run—

hoary whiskers, wild fescue, cracks widened
along the ground hard from a winter drought.
I have come out for the first time in weeks
still full of fever, insomnia-fogged,
to track her flags of breath where she's dying
to vanish on the hillsides of bramble
and burr. The seasonal birds—scruff cardinal,

one or two sparrows, something with yellow—
scatter in their small explosions of ice.
Emerson, gentle mourner, would be pleased
by the physical crunch of the ground, damp
from the melt, shaped by the shape of his boot,
that half of him who loved the Dunscore heath
too rocky to cultivate, covered thick

with heather, gnarled hawthorn, the yellow furze
not far from Carlyle's homestead where they strolled,
—that half of him for whom nature was thought.
Kate has found things to deepen her horror
for evenings to come, a deer carcass tunneled
by slugs, drilled, and abandoned, a bundle
of bone shards, hoof and hide, hidden by thick

bramble, or the bramble itself enough
to collapse her dreams, braided like rope, blood-
colored, blood-barbed, tangled as Medusa.
What does she see when she looks at such things?
I do not know what is so wrong with me
that my body has erupted, system
by system, sick unto itself. I do

not know what I have done, nor what she thinks
when she turns toward her ill father. How did
Emerson behold of his Ellen, un-
embalmed face fallen in, of her white hands?
Dreams & beasts are two keys by which we are
to find out the secrets of our own natures.
Half angel, Emerson wrestles all night

with his journal, the awful natural
fact of Ellen's death, which must have been
deeper sacrifice than a sacrament.
Where has she gone now, whose laughter comes down
like light snow on the beautiful hills?
Perhaps it is the world that is the matter . . .
—His other half worried by the wording.

MARVIN BELL

The Book of the Dead Man (#35)

1. About the Dead Man and Childhood

In an evening of icicles, tree branches crackling as they break
      frozen sap, a gull's bark shattering on snow, the furnace
      turned down for the night, the corpse air without exits—
      here the dead man reenters his fever.
The paste held, that was dry and brittle.
The rotting rubber band stuck to the pack of playing cards to keep
      it together.
In the boy's room, the balsa balanced where there had once
      been glue.
Recognition kept its forms in and out of season.
Why not, then, this sweaty night of pursuit?
He has all of himself at his disposal.
He has every musical note, every word, though certain notes of the
      piano have evaporated.
Shall he hear them anyway?
The dead man's boyhood home withholds from its current
      occupants the meaning of desecration, nor shall they be the
      destroyers of the past in their own minds.
You too have seen anew the giant rooms of the little house in which
      you were a child.
You have seen the so-heavy door that now barely resists a light
      hand.
You have walked down the once endless corridors that now end
      abruptly.
Were you so small then that now you are in the way?
You too sat at the impossibly high kitchen table with your feet
      dangling, drawn down by the heavy shoes.

All this and more the dead man remembers the connective
        quality of.
In those days, there was neither here nor now, only there and the
        time it would take to reach it.

2. More About the Dead Man and Childhood

After Adam ate the apple, there was one more, and then one
        more. . . .
After Orpheus looked back, there was another and another. . . .
The dead man discerns betwixt and between, he knows mania and
        depression, he has within him the two that make one, the
        opposites that attract, the summer pain and the winter pain.
He walks both the road of excess and the least path, and lives most
        in the slow-to-ripen spring and extended autumn.
The dead man does not come when called but tries to hit a baseball
        in the dusk.
He does not yet know he wants to ride the horse that took the bit in
        its mouth.
He lives in the attic and the big closet where the radio parts and the
        extra glassware hold their codes.
He is the initiate.
He feigns nothing, he has nothing else in mind, later he will be
        charged with having been a boy.
Even now, in May and September he feels the throbbing tissue of
        that fallow world from which he was forced to be free.
The dead man in adulthood knows the other side, and he winces at
        the fragility of the old songbooks, taped and yellowed, held
        there in time.

The Book of the Dead Man (#61)

1. About the Dead Man and the Late Conjunctions of Fall

The dead man heard a clucking in the trees at maple-sugaring time.
Today he feels a fibrillation in the curling leaves of autumn.

The near-frost lengthens his line of sight, bringing down the moon, while among the spheroid melodies of harvesting, fate detaches the prospects.

The dead man fosters the free flying of the leaves.

He encourages deciduous trees to be done with dying.

There where the Anglo-Saxon and the Latinate meet anew, the dead man bespeaks the continental drift.

There where body and soul conjoin, the dead man rejoins the indivisible nation.

Who but the dead man can fashion a broom from a branch and discern the seasons from wisps of sugar and pollen?

The dead man sandpapers flakes and splinters from the chair where the one oblivious to time sits reading beneath burnt foliage.

He calls to the wild turkey in its infancy to stay still in the brush.

The dead man cedes supremacy neither to the body nor the soul, neither does he stay in one place like a day on the calendar.

The dead man feels like the tree which was tapped for syrup, all in good time.

2. More About the Dead Man and the Late Conjunctions of Fall

The dead man readies himself for the ice skaters whirling overhead, their blades crying *wish* and *wish*.

Which will crack in the brittle days to come, the dead man's ring or the dead man's ring finger?

The dead man does not hasten, nor does he pitch his tent.

The dead man, like others, shall be departing and returning, for such is the grandiloquence of memory in the junctures of separation.

The dead man attaches an epistle to a leaf, he discloses his whereabouts to the harvest moon, he cranks forth leaflet upon leaflet to satisfy the scene.

The dead man's dying leaves, burning, appear as a crimson wash in the autumn dusk.

His is the midnight light of high proceedings beyond the horizon.

The dead man will not twitch lest he frighten the little twigs from their exposed roosts.

When there is no holding on, no letting go, no firm grip, no
     restoration, no hither and yon, no arboreal refuge, then okay
     —say that the dead man in his vigor watches it all.
He holds his tongue lest he sound the alarm.
He hears the fallen extremities swept away by the wind and
     remembers.
The dead man has written an elegy for autumn and a postscript to
     the Apocalypse.

Sounds of the Resurrected Dead Man's Footsteps (#6)

1. Skulls

Oh, said a piece of tree bark in the wind, and the night froze.
One could not have foreseen the stoppage.
I did not foresee it, who had expected a messiah.
No one had yet dared say that he or she was it—target or savior.
In the slippage between time and the turning planet, a buildup of dirty grease
     made movement difficult.
Time slowed down while events accelerated.
The slower the eye moved, the faster events went past.
The raping and pillaging over time became one unending moment.
Nazis, who would always stand for the crimes of culture, clustered in public
     intersections, awaiting deliveries.
The masses would turn in the Jews.
From the officers' quarters could be heard the beautiful Schubert.
And in the camp there was the grieving tenor of the cantor.
The one rose and the other sank.
Today, one can stroll in the footsteps of those who walked single file from
     this life.
Often I stand in the yard at night expecting something.
Something in the breeze one caught a scent of as if a head of hair had passed
     by without a face.
Whatever happens to us from now on, it will come up from the earth.
It will bear the grief of the exterminated, it will lug itself upward.

It will take all of our trucks to carry the bones.
But the profane tattoos have been bled of their blue by the watery loam,
     additives for worms.
Often I stand in the yard with a shovel.

2. Skulls

I am the poet of skulls without why or wherefore.
I didn't ask to be this or that, one way or another, just a young man of words.
Words that grew in sandy soil, words that fit scrub trees and beach grass.
Sentenced to work alone where there is often no one to talk to.
The poetry of skulls demands complicity of the reader, that the reader put
     words in the skull's mouth.
The reader must put water and beer in the mouth, and music in the ears, and
     fan the air for aromas to enter the nostrils.
The reader must take these lost heads to heart.
The reader must see with the eyes of a skull, comb the missing hair of the skull,
     brush the absent teeth, kiss the lips and find the hinge of the tongue.
Yes, like Hamlet, the Jew of Denmark before Shakespeare seduced him.
It is the things of the world which rescue us from the degradations of the
     literati.
A workshirt hanging from a nail may be all the honesty we can handle.
I am beloved of my hat and coat, enamored of my bed, my troth renewed each
     night that my head makes its impression on the pillow.
I am the true paramour of my past, though my wife swoons at the snapshots.
Small syringe the doctor left behind to charm the child.
Colorful *yarmulke* that lifted the High Holy Days.

STEPHEN BERG

In a New Leaf

Three weeks before he died, my father acted as an extra in *A New Leaf*, a movie about an alcoholic, her lover, and a stranger who showed up and would, as it happened, try to save her. Cassavetes and May were making the film in Philly on 13th Street, using a defunct hotel, renamed The Royal, for the battles between the fucked-up couple. Night after night the crew would take their places—at the camera, yelling directions, searching for extras in the crowds lined up six deep around the roped-off set to watch Peter Falk (the stranger) do a scene in which he's passing The Royal on his way somewhere and a whiskey bottle flies out a window and hits the ground at his feet and he looks up, sees someone (the woman, I think) in the window and dashes (there's a scream) into the dark building. It seems the woman and her lover (Cassavetes) are holed-up there, planning a robbery. Falk is tanned, dressed in a custom-cut Navy-blue silk suit and delicate black shoes, Italian style, the kind tap dancers use because they're so flexible, nearly weightless. In and out, in and out he goes, repeating the scene, bottle after bottle arcing from the window, the pieces swept away each time by one of the crew, while none of the fans and gawkers really knows what the story is. It was like watching real life, it doesn't matter whose life, with one big differ- ence: that scene lost all meaning because it was shot so many times. It was be- ginning to get hot the way it does in Philly in early June—thick greasy humid air, hanging on for days so every little thing feels difficult, everything looks like it has sweat and dirt on it. My father had had a massive, fifth heart attack and when we picked him up at his house he was wearing a raincoat, single-breasted with a full button-in camel's-hair liner, and under it a suit, tie and scarf. A gray felt hat and gray doeskin gloves lent the finishing touches. His face was the color of those gloves, it had a dull shine like solder, like those Philly skies before a rain when blossoming puffs of air cool your face but it stays hot, the sun has disappeared, everything is drained of strong color. Well, he walked, shuffling one foot at a time very very slowly, stopping between each step, as if on a tightrope, almost floating, with great caution and weakness and fear, to the car. Settled in the front seat, he barely spoke. We heard the movie was being made, thought it would be fun to watch the production, a rare distraction from all he had gone through. We drove the few blocks to the place, parked, walked over to the people at the ropes circling The Royal, and faded into the crowd. My Dad, for some reason of his own, drifted to another side of the crowd and stood at the back of it. Everything on the street was blue-white under the lights; the mist of humidity in the glare put a fine pearly veil between you and whatever you saw. Once in a while I'd glance around to see how he was. Inch by inch he had slipped from the back of the mob until now he was standing up front pressing against the waist-high rope—all gray: raincoat, glove, hat, face. Except for his Watch-plaid cashmere scarf. He looked like a Mafia Don: implacable mask of a face, a man with secrets and power who refused the world any hint of emotion that might reveal who he was. Was his mind silent as he stood there or did he hear one of those primitive, sourceless, pure, self-defining voices that haunt us, left over from the gods, telling him not to smile, not to speak, not to show anything to the enemy world, telling him to be no one as the line between death and the future evaporated and he edged closer to the playground of the gods by obeying them, by adopting the hero's impassive mask? The fact is he looked like Edward G. Robinson, not Oedipus or Lear immortalized in the revelatory aftermath of cosmic self-discovery. Reticent, masochistic, mildly depressed all his life, he stood there, to me awesome because of his ordeal near death. "He'll never walk out of the hospital," the doctor had said, and here, five months later, he was, as fate would have it, a passerby about to act in a bad movie, about to play one of the gods as they are today. By now Elaine May was pacing the edge of the crowd inside the roped-off area, looking for extras, picking people by their faces to walk past under an arcade twenty or so feet behind Falk during the bottle-throwing scene. She saw my father, nodded a questioning "Yes?" He ducked under the rope, which May lifted for him, and joined a group of eight people, then moved to the outside of the crowd. By now I was standing beside him, listening. All were told to begin walking, briskly, scattered apart, just before Falk reaches the front of the hotel when the bottle hits. Over and over he did it, briskly, until we thought he would drop dead. Over and over I watched his speechless face, betraying nothing, glistening under his hat in the lights, while behind me, off to my right—where the camera was, pointed away from the hotel at Falk and the extras walking by—Falk ran past into the hotel, yelling something, after the bottle crashed, and a woman yelled back at him from the window. Over and over. Finally they got it right and we went home. For months, I waited for the newspaper ads announcing the film so we could all see it. When it finally played, and we went, the scene wasn't even in it. The film was so mediocre it ran less than a week. I tried buying a copy of the scene but they wouldn't sell the footage. Several years since your walk-on part, and it happens anytime: the muggy summer night, the family, gauzy air, you doing what you're told by the director—I'll be teaching, washing dishes, reading, writing, talking with Millie and the kids, a middle-aged man, your son, watching his sick father, but not on the screen in a theater. It's still the street, the live, unknown people, you doing it over and over, over and over the scene being shot, the bottle, the scream, the lights, "Okay—try it again!" coming from behind lights and faceless faces, from the black steel bodies and silent blank lenses of the weapon-like cameras pointed at us.

Legacy

It doesn't even matter who we are, all three of us, sitting in the living room of a house in the city—a sick old dying man, a woman, a younger man—talking over what the sick one wants to leave, and to whom, after he's dead. The man and wife sit in front of a bookcase wall. He's almost dead from a massive coronary. She's half-hysterical. The other man's their son, and he's half-nuts from the sickness and the craziness, from how this moment resurrects an entire family history by condensing it, a primal myth, without imagery from the past, into one room, one time, forever, *forever*, the young man thinks, although he has no memory of other incidents like this, of a mad trio hacking out of their souls sheer loveless misery, so pure it could pose as joy or ecstasy, a singleness of purpose like one of those celebrated Tudor lyrics organized to perfect its argument by coiling it tight around a single image, theme or idea. The drama here is after-death, or whatever term is right for the near-dead writing a will after waiting a lifetime, not consulting his heirs, too ill now to think straight, too terrified to know what he feels about "his loved ones," who should get what?—the car, the tiny row house, the money from a policy or two—all an ambitious businessman, who didn't really make it, has to leave them. The sick man has never admitted he might actually die. The woman has always worried that she would wind up with nothing. She has always felt she had nothing, or less, or not enough. It's impossible to describe the scar on her mind. The air in the room is like old unventilated sweat now. The man, in his faded blue and white striped bathrobe, balances a pad of yellow lined paper on his knee with his right hand, a pencil hung between two fingers like an unlit cigarette. Meanwhile the parents are chattering about the young man (in his late thirties) and what he should get. "He shouldn't be able to sell anything until he's 55," the woman barks. "He'll be a big boy, someday," squeaks the old man, an insane, hostile remark, the young man thinks, knowing he has heard a sentence from his father that will fester permanently. Finally the yellow sheet has writing all over it and the woman is satisfied. The young man, who feels like a weary, abused boy now, hates them both. Three weeks later the man dies. The woman gets what she wants, what there is, although she never forgives the man for—it doesn't matter. All this continues in the mind long after it is over, immortal, as such things are. The identities of the people do not matter, as I've said, because, as the years pass, in the mind, it all becomes the person in whose mind it lives. The only salvation for certain minds is if they believe death destroys everything that was there, in the mind, believe immortality beyond mind doesn't exist—unless one tells in vivid detail the story to someone else, so it becomes part of another mind. But that's mere theory. On the bookshelf, a few inches above those two aging heads—Zola's *Nana*, in a cheap paper binding, several pages still stuck together at erratic spots, six or seven sepia photographic likenesses on slick paper of Nana, scattered throughout, in different naked poses,—a man's head plunged between her breasts; lying on a couch; standing, nipples stiff and pink, semi-profile. They were okay, but as a boy I loved the SEX passages more, where the couple is described fucking or staring at each other undressing or fondling each other's parts or doing strange oral things. Day after day, while I read I jerked off by standing the book on my chest, holding it with my left hand, and, each time just before I'd come, slip the open book down and ejaculate onto the pages, then close the book and put it back on the shelf, hoping my parents would pull out the book someday, try to open those pages, know me.

FRANK BIDART

For the Twentieth Century

Bound, hungry to pluck again from the thousand
technologies of ecstasy

boundlessness, the world that at a drop of water
rises without boundaries,

I push the PLAY button:—

. . . Callas, Laurel & Hardy, Szigeti

you are alive again,—

the slow movement of K.218
once again no longer

bland, merely pretty, nearly
banal, as it is

in all but Szigeti's hands

*

Therefore you and I and Mozart
must thank the Twentieth Century, for

it made you pattern, form
whose infinite

repeatability within matter
defies matter—

Malibran. Henry Irving. The young
Joachim. They are lost, a mountain of

newspaper clippings, become words
not their own words. The art of the performer.

Legacy

When to the desert, the dirt,
comes water

comes money

to get off the shitdirt
land and move to the city

whence you

direct the work of those who now
work the land you still own

My grandparents left home for the American

desert to escape
poverty, or the family who said *You are*

the son who shall become a priest

After Spain became
Franco's, at last

rich enough

to return you
refused to return

The West you made

was never unstoried, never
artless

Excrement of the sky our rage inherits

there was no gift
outright   we were never the land's

LINDA BIERDS

Grand Forks: 1997

An arc of pips across a playboard's field
tightens, then, in the Chinese game of Go,
curls back to weave a noose, a circle closing, closed.

Surrounded, one surrenders. Blind-sided,
collared from behind. Then silence, or so
my friends revealed, the arc across their patchwork fields

not pips, but flood. The dikes collapsed, they said;
the river, daily, swelled. Then *pastures* rose,
as earth's dark water table—brimful—spilled, and closed

behind their backs, the chaff-filled water red
with silt, with coulees, creeks, a russet snow,
all merging from behind. Then through the bay-bright fields

a dorsal silence came, and, turning, filled
the sunken streets, the fallen dikes, the slow,
ice-gripped periphery where frozen cattle closed

across their frozen likenesses. Mirrored,
as when the Northern Lights began their glow
was mirrored, green to green, across the flooded fields—
like haunted arcs of Spring, one circle closing, closed.

The Ponds:
Franz Kafka, June 1, 1924

Always the baths. Although my father in water
was a snared goose—his flappings, then the granular rush
of the foam. No swimmers, we, not really. Still,
from the rough-hewn planks of the changing-hut,
we walked in our nakedness.
I remember his girth. Then that sack of quick kindling

that was my chest. And later, long after,
how pond water, warmed from its rest
near the inner ear, seeped out to my pillow slip. . . .

Just a child, my mother had grasped
her grandfather's toes, asked from his fresh corpse
a gram of forgiveness. Ritual, I think, superstition.
All the toe hairs were scoured to black-tipped nubs—
the chafe, chafe of his thick boots—
nubs and nails and a flesh with the chill

of a brookhouse wall. She told me he bathed
in the languorous river, day after day—in winter
breaking the ice with a net of bricks.
And although he brought the water to him, I am certain,
handful by handful, still
he strokes in my mind just under the ice rim,

piece and then piece, as a boiled shirt
strokes up through the vat: now an arm, now the neck,
now a blister of back.

By open car, I have traveled to the sick-beds
of Vienna, then onward to Kierling.
My larynx, they say, has decayed to the flesh
of an autumn berry. I remember

wind through the car seats, how light was slashed
to some rhythmic flick
by the quick interruption of birch trees.
And Dora, her coat held open between me
and the elements, flapping its musk
of camphor and soot.

There is sunlight today. It casts into great herons
the tapering shadows of nurses. . . .

My throat is treated with injections of alcohol—
and my cousin's spleen with injections of milk!
So death, in the body, forms a flaccid pond. Or the body

in death. It deepens, I think, hour by hour, stretches down
where lightless ligatures tangle and sway.
Death. In the shade of some changing-hut.
Infinite, black-cast, glacial reach.
And I am buoyed by it.

LUCILLE CLIFTON

the times

it is hard to remain human on a day
when birds perch weeping
in the trees and the squirrel eyes
do not look away but the dog ones do
in pity.
another child has killed a child
and i catch myself relieved that they are
white and i might understand except
that i am tired of understanding.
if these
alphabets could speak their own tongue
it would be all symbol surely;
the cat would hunch across the long table
and that would mean time is catching up,
and the spindle fish would run to ground
and that would mean the end is coming
and the grains of dust would gather themselves
along the streets and spell out

these are your children   this is your child

what i think when i ride the train

maybe my father
made these couplers.
his hands were hard
and black and swollen,
the knuckles like lugs

or bolts in a rich man's box.
he broke a bone each year
as if on schedule.
when i read about a wreck,
how the cars buckle
together or hang from the track
in a chain, but never separate,
i think: see,
there's my father.
he was a chipper.
he made the best damn couplers
in the whole white world.

MICHAEL COLLIER

Brave Sparrow

whose home is in the straw
and baling twine threaded
in the slots of a roof vent

who guards a tiny ledge
against the starlings
that cruise the neighborhood

whose heart is smaller
than a heart should be,
whose feathers stiffen

like an arrow fret to quicken
the hydraulics of its wings,
stay there on the metal

ledge, widen your alarming
beak, but do not flee as others have
to the black walnut vaulting

overhead. Do not move outside
the world you've made
from baling twine and straw.

The isolated starling fears
the crows, the crows gang up
to rout a hawk. The hawk

is cold. And cold is what
a larger heart maintains.
The owl at dusk and dawn,

far off, unseen, but audible,
repeats its syncopated intervals,
a song that's not a cry

but a whisper rising from concentric
rings of water spreading out across
the surface of a catchment pond.

It asks, "Who are you? Who
are you?" but no one knows.
Stay where you are, nervous, jittery.

Move your small head a hundred
ways, a hundred times, keep
paying attention to the terrifying

world. And if you see the robins
in their dirty orange vests
patrolling the yard like thugs,

forget about the worm. Starve
yourself, or from the air inhale
the water you may need, digest

the dust. And what the promiscuous
cat and jaybirds do, let them
do it, let them dart and snipe,

let them sound like others.
They sleep when the owl sends
out its encircling question.

Stay where you are, you lit fuse,
you dull spark of saltpeter and sulfur.

Pay-Per-View

Maybe you saw this as I did in a smoke-free
suite of the Allard Hotel in Chicago,
late in the afternoon, an hour away from drinks
then dinner with a friend, after a long day of meetings.

Like me you clicked on the TV, surfed through
weather, CNN, and local news before stopping
at a cooking show where a woman with hair
the color of embalming fluid—a rose-hips red—

held up a pheasant by its legs in one hand
and a chicken in the same fashion with the other.
Both of the birds had been decapitated, plucked,
maybe even oiled, for they shone and glistened.

The pheasant was longer, leaner than the chicken
and, through the sheen, its skin was a whitish-gray
like asphalt dusted with snow. The chicken, robust,
jaundice-colored, hung swollen and fat. The woman placed

each fowl on its own large cutting board. A row of knives
lay waiting, but before she began dressing the birds
I changed channels, once, twice and then rapidly,
turning the screen into a flick book, a cavalcade of images:

the U.S. Congress, a man tying fishing lures, a trial,
a diamond necklace rotating in mid-air, a woman screaming
at a man, a bowling ball smashing silently into pins,
a NASCAR race, and LOTTO numbers, as if they were verses

from Apocrypha, flashed above a blow-up of a check
made out to *John Doe* for *Thirty Million Dollars
and No One Hundredths.* Occasionally the screen filled
with bands of houndstooth or plaid, scrambled colors

behind which figures moved and a steady droning music played,
the kind the Harpies might have made for Sisyphus
each time he reached the hilltop. Beneath the music
and behind the meadowy zippers of color, I heard moaning,

a held-in keening, and staring hard, trying to locate
the sound in the bright reticulating light, I saw a man morph
as if from the inchoate pattern, his head long, Martian green,
arms without hands, his shank and legs as malleable as mercury

and then, as if engrafted to him or giving birth to his form
and deformation, a woman. Zeus made Pandora from clay
and had the four Winds fill her with life. She was not
a real woman but a god's vengeful fantasy of beauty.

And now those winged souls that once escaped
from her exquisite jar—the shadows of our pains, the venom
carriers of our desires—assemble an erotic chaos on the screen.
Delusive hope, which grows the liver back from the shreds

and tatters of the demons' feeding, entered me as perhaps
it enters you—a dryness in the throat, a conviction fed by
a yearning that in time the obscure and pleasure-giving bodies
would emerge clear and free.

The Swimmer

Nothing like him in Bosch or Breughel,
nothing so denatured as to resemble
not a semblance of a human face
but the substance of some form made
and then unmade, or like a lump
of human butter excavated from a bog.

His eyes askew, aligned by a jagged
axis that must have balanced once
across the fulcrum of his nose.
The pupils deep and lost but ever seeing
like water in a well at night.
The head misshapen like a too-ripe

melon, dimpled by the forceps mark
of his accident or whatever extracted him
from normalcy, dipped him
in the searing, crushing waters
of disfigurement and then returned him
to the world to fill it with the childish

worrying sound working its way
from his mouth that's not so much a mouth
as a coin purse cinched tight, sewn
with the fragments of his lips—
the yipping gait of breathlessness
he makes, which makes no sense

without the fluttering exuberance
of his hands that come to rest,
delicately, on my shoulders, as if to say:
"Help tie the drawstring of my suit,
shoulder my towel, fit these sandals
to my feet and lead me to the pool

where you will see how struggling
to be what I am, I become—otter, seal,
dolphin—released from myself, though
not absolved, not ever able to hide
the fin or the fluke, my feet
webbed and unwebbed."

ALFRED CORN

Bloodwork

Somebody's got to do it, even if you
could *define* ho-hum by this job, each sample
analyzed one by one, and best not cheat,
because, though most of them check clean, a few
come from people with a major problem.

Serum tells the truth to those with training—
training she busted it to get, five-figure
school loans and overdrawn accounts of nerve.
Still, Pops was the one who cried at graduation:
"I always hoped you'd have the things I didn't. . . ."

At least *her* blood is healthy, with one eighth
African, one half Choctaw, and the balance,
white. (Genetic math.) But shoot, in this country,
one drop of black blood means that you are black,
so just relax and do your work. Next sample:

Red cells and white, and then invisible
viruses spinning around in the soup of life,
seasoned with their subtle taint. Health, life—
on loan from its opposite, the foreclosure reading:
It's nothing personal; just doing my job.

New York Three Decades On

Jazz cuts through narrative nostalgia—
Louis Armstrong reinventing Storyville
on someone's chrome transistor up the platform
that late August I stepped off the train.
125th Street, East Side—which looked,
on the map, like an easy half-mile to Columbia,
I mean, as the crow flies. I wasn't flying, though,
and here it was: Harlem 1965-style,
still in mourning for Malcolm X,
strung out, almost crazy with America.
Even in that frame-up, people had errands,
in and out of the storefronts, driving off
in gleaming Imperials and battered Mustangs.
Essence on the newsstands, call-and-response
of Haitian and Alabama voices;
but nobody challenged me, no flat-broke
brothers hustled this out-of-it honkey,
it just now dawning on him where he was.

I was in New York, where I'd wanted to be,
an existential French Lit grad student
in Morningside Heights, agog, strolling through
those first unfettered weeks, with every radio
in Fun City blaring Phil Spector's *wall of sound* . . .
My rented room's ancient, scumbled plaster
mimicked the meteoric surface of the moon.
So I tacked up a green bedspread and, to that,
Lautrec's *Aristide Bruant dans son cabaret.*
A neat match for the 1890s
Art Nouveau walnut headboard of the bed
and my landlady's marble-topped dresser,
its fogged mirror tilting forward and down,
a pensive cockroach scoping out the frame . . .
Free at last in *La Bohème.*

Gotham City wasn't gratis, though.
Even that grimy room cost (back then not peanuts,
or not to me) ten bucks a week. So just skip lunch
and, at afternoon tea in Philosophy Hall,
scarf down Oreo after Oreo—sweet dominos
fanned in a half-circle on gold-rimmed china.
Outside the window, a huge bronze *Thinker*,
whose pose I assumed every morning,
staring at the crackled gray enamel of a bathtub
Mrs. Smith was too blind and feeble to scour,
oppressed by the *existential void . . .*

So, how to weigh imponderables, and where
should the singer of inexperience go?—clueless,
friendless, always on the lookout for Mr. Right,
a face without features, imagination's starbright X.

Was that you at the seminar table commenting
on doubt in Montaigne to Professor Frame?
You in the lobby of New York State Theater
strolling the intermission between *Apollo*
and *Western Symphony*? You, slouching
into the Thalia for a matinee of *Breathless*?

I went to JULIUS, slid onto a barstool
and cruised the silvery quadrant that, across
a phalanx of spouted bottles, returned my stare.
Desperate, lonely—where better take that rap
than Metropolis, its solitary angst
the foundation of an urban cult with scriptures
by Baudelaire and Whitman, Rimbaud, the Beats.
My turtleneck, espresso black, dressed the part,
my unfiltered *Gauloises* and buckled Wellingtons
for the first time, by being a misfit, I fit in.

Day long and into midnight during the subway strike,
avenues choked on traffic and exhaust. Strikers won,
and the two-bits fare went the way of Penn Station.
On the night of the Great Blackout, I skipped town
to Jersey with a (distant) marriage prospect
who was bunking at a friend's in East Orange.
We'd connected last May back home—so tell me, Cupid,
can passion be rekindled in a single night?
The Blackout party I missed, but not the fun.
Mr. Right in every way but one: He didn't live in New York.

Next day, returning, the bus slowed and coasted
toward Lincoln Tunnel. Fading trace of last night's tryst,
the grin on my face also registered a city-mouse thrill
that the back-lit horizon of highrise Manhattan
looked like home. It *was* home, and I on my way there,
Aristide astride his new citizenship, habitué
of dark cafés, an existence that preceded
essence, stills from my movie, frame after frame,
smoking philosophy along with Bird
and Miles, starring a sentence in the Selected
Rimbaud: "Love must be reinvented."

A Walrus Tusk from Alaska

Arp might have done a version in white marble,
the model held aloft, in approximate awe:
this tough cross-section oval of tusk,
dense and cool as fossil cranium—

preliminary bloodshed condonable
if Inupiat hunters on King Island may
follow as their fathers did the bark of a husky,
echoes ricocheted from roughed-up eskers

on the glacier, a resonance salt cured
and stained deep green by Arctic seas, whose tilting floor
mirrors the mainland's snowcapped amphitheater.
Which of his elders set Mike Saclamana the task

and taught him to decide, in scrimshaw, what was so?
Netted incisions black as an etching
saw a way to scratch in living infinitives
known since the Miocene to have animated

the Bering Strait: one humpbacked whale, plump,
and bardic; an Orca caught on the ascending arc,
salt droplets flung from a flange of soot-black fin . . .
Farther along the bone conveyor belt a small

ringed seal will never not be swimming, part-time
landlubber, who may feel overshadowed by the donor
walrus ahead. Or by his scribal tusk, which stands
in direct correspondence to the draftsman's burin,

keen enough to score their tapeloop ostinato,
no harp sonata, but instead the humpbacked whale's
yearning bassoon (still audible if you cup
the keepsake to your ear and let it sound the depths).

PETER DAVISON

Falling Water

Wherever it commences perhaps as random
      raindrop tapping on a leaf and tumbling
            into a tea-stained mosscup

it helplessly inquires after
      lower levels whether seeping
            darkly through silt

and marl to enlarge an imprisoned
      aquifer shortcut or taking its chances to trickle
            out through a slit of clay to join its first

brook and amble off into the yielding
      soft-shouldered marsh past fat roots of
            lilies to linger among the slick fronds

of algae paddled by ducks pierced by
      pickerel to hurry itself and
            whisk into the outlet that will boil it

along a streambed grid of gravel toward another
      stairstep of idleness the lax
            lake spritzed with yawning sun

there to seek a breach to tip and hurtle
      into torrent and the great meander
            that will sweep it slow and away out

and empty into the broad salt
        sleep that will cradle it until
                the sun siphons it again
                to knit into more rain.

Little Death

I escaped, spinning off
        to heaven knows what
                location, eluding

control, threatening to
        relinquish: to end up
                bland, inert.

Without intake how should I not
        become my own dull
                monument, lie

immobile, cold as winter dirt, in-
        communicado? Unless I
                exert effort

my presence could harden into
        dead stone. Yet I must and will
                continue. Chest

heaves. Limbs lengthen. Head
        hums with vestiges of
                memory that picks up the scent

of desire. Body starts
        breathing. Listen!
                Bloodstream thumps

once more, tingling. Before
    I can so much as stir,
        my hair
           resumes growing.

On Mount Timpanogos, 1935

Lodged against the mountain's collarbone
    miles above Provo when I was seven,
        my mother, sister, and I

summered fatherless in a board shack
    whose door we hasped at night
        against the knock-knock of bears.

Eating out of a skillet, we lolled
    naked in aspen-green sunlight,
        felt timid only after dark

in the privy. Mine was the once-a-day task
    of retrieving, from a miserly trickle
        that welled from a seam down the slope,

our few gallons of water. Once the spring filled,
    I'd send a pail racketing along a rope,
        race it down a gravelly path

under the overhead clatter of the pulley
    and dunk it;
        then toil back upward

beneath its sloshing weight of water, vaster
    than you could guess, heaving it,
        consecrated, untouchable.

So words lunge upward
    till habit reclaims them
        and they tip into the spillway
        of a lie.

DEBORAH DIGGES

Guillotine Windows

For Larry Levis

Fifty brief summers, fifty northeastern
winters have close to petrified the frames
once carefully recessed and rigged with pulleys, though the ropes have frayed,
the weights like clappers dropped inside the walls.

They're called "eight over twelves," my guillotine windows,
that slam themselves on spring,
and the wooden spoons that prop them up belly like yew bows,
and the empty shampoo bottles *woo*, and the knives, hair brushes,
shoe trees, books, and jewelry boxes,
all will be ruined soon.

Ring the house that wants it to be winter,
a house for wintering, warn the spirits they'll lose a hand,
a tail sailing in and out of the bell tower

above rue festering, the huge moonlight scotch broom,
above my rabid gardens, my complicated gardens.

If the body is a temple, surely one's garden is like a mind,
half-seeded by the wind, ready to slip into its own peculiar madness,

the Russian sage awash over the beech roots strangling my pipes,
and the bellwort rampant, foxglove, violets
banked by my Grecian stones, and blue glass totem toads
and china figs, beheaded angels, and shells I've carried back

from different coasts fashioned like Sapphic cliffs.
Someday they'll think this was a lovers' leap,

the floor of a crossroads wishing well
into which those passing threw what weighed them down—

hair in a locket, keys, rings, bibles and the flowers pressed
in the Psalms, a doll's head, funeral lace

preserved in the historic leaf-rot of a willow,
plum and apple, oak, and two white pines, two sycamores.

I love to imagine someone, say when I'm transplanting
at midnight, finding the remnants of this place.

On my knees in the garden in the dark I can look in the windows
and see fields that will be glaciers,
hillsides on which the headstones dwarf and pitch

above a woods from which my floors came flying
in clouds of animal fur and dust and human hair and ash from a thousand fires
swept from the hearth, saved until spring—tamped down,
drawn up as color into lilacs.

Once I watched a house taken out to sea. From that distance it
looked like the earth bent down to crown
the ocean and the ocean, rising, thus received the crown
of the house that deified the waves a while.

Imagine standing alone there at the threshold,
having an ocean as one's garden for a moment, a garden
of enormous green-blue rollers, sea birds, all four winds, countless clouds!

You can have a good life and not know it.
You can claim that seeing far means seeing into the future,
into the time ahead of you.

But it was all right to have believed in something—
that those you loved, they would outlive you
or simply be here always from time to time,
and you would recognize each other,

take hands and walk through a garden, have a meal together,
talk late into the evening and fall asleep in separate rooms.

See those young selves waving back at shore,
see them running, calling to you as the walls of the house
break up, pulling from the foundation while the roof
slides sideways, gone, and the windows shatter,

and some float in their frames, float shining whole,
carried out, drifting, windows on the sea.

Lilacs

Let's say for that time
I was an instrument forbidding music.
That spring no thief of fire.
I tapped from the source a self sick of love,
and then beyond sickness,
an invalid of my loathing.
Yes, loathing put me to bed each night
and burned my dreams,
in the morning woke me with strong coffee.
And this was loathing's greeting—
Get up. Drink.
All this in spite of the lilacs returning,
their odor the odor of life everlasting,
another year,
another season onward, another spring.
But they bloomed of a sudden pale in unison
like lifeboats rowing into dawn,
the passengers gone mad in their exhaustion in the open,

even the wives, even the mothers
rescued for their children,
their lives, believe me, not their own.
Boats full of lilacs drifting thus,
each grayish bush against my gray house.
But theirs is a short season, a few weeks,
rarely more.
And I was glad to be rid of them,
rid of a thing that could touch in me
what might be called "mercy."
See how one's lips must kiss to make the *m*,
touch tongue to back of teeth and smile.
Pity's swept clean and conscious,
an upstairs room whose floors resound,
but mercy's an asylum,
a house sliding forever out to sea.
As if I were expected to wade out into the yard each night
and swing a lantern!
And just this morning still early into autumn
I noticed how the lilacs had set themselves on fire.
As for me, I have my privacy.
It's mine I might have killed for.
I have my solitude,
the face of the beloved like a room locked in time
and when I look back I am not there.
It's as if the lilacs martyred themselves,
the stories of their journey
embellished or misread
or lacking a true bard, a song associate,
something with starlight in it,
blue lilac starlight
and the sound of dipping oars.
I could sing it for them now,
make it up as I go along,
a detailed, useless lyric among shipwrecking green.
In my heart is the surprise of dusk come early
to ancient shapes like tors,
the cold rising vast, these episodes
of silence at last
like eternity.

Sing with me if you want,
or not, my ferryman's song, my siren's song.
Sing for the dead lilacs.

Winter Barn

A light slant snow dragging the fields, a counter-wind
where the edges of the barn frayed worlds,

blurred outside in. This is what my love could give me
instead of children—the dusk as presence, moth-like,

and with a moth's dust colored flickering stall by stall,
some empty now, certain gone to slaughter, driven north

in open trucks over pot-holed, frozen roads.
Such a hard ride to blood-let, blankness, the stalls' stone

floors hosed out, yet damp, the urine reek not quite
muffled with fresh hay, trough water still giving back lantern

light like ponds at nightfall. Sheep lay steaming, cloud
in cloud. The barn cat slept among last summer's lambs, black

faced, apart, relieved of their mothers. We made our way,
my dogs and I, to say hello to the Yorkshire sow

named Kora, who heaved herself up to greet us,
let the dogs lick her oiled snout smeared with feed,

while I scratched her forehead. Kora of the swineherds,
fallen with Persephone, perhaps in hell a bride's only company.

Prodigal, planetary, Kora's great spined, strict bristled body
wore the black mud of a cold, righteous creation,

burs and mugwort plastered at the gates.
Days her smell stayed with us. The last time we saw her

the plaque bearing her name was gone. Maybe she would be mated.
Sparrows sailed the barn's doomed girth, forsaken,

therefore free. They lit on rafters crossing the west windows
that flared at sunset like a furnace fed on stars.

STUART DISCHELL

Days of Me

When people say they miss me,
I think how much I miss me too,
Me, the old me, the great me,
Lover of three women in one day,
Modest me, the best me, friend
To waiters and bartenders, hearty
Laugher and name rememberer,
Proud me, handsome and hirsute
In soccer shoes and shorts
On the ball fields behind MIT,
Strong me in a weightbelt at the gym,
Mutual sweat dripper in and out
Of the sauna, furtive observer
Of the coeducated and scantily clad,
Speedy me, cyclist of rivers,
Goose and peregrine falcon
Counter, all season venturer,
Chatterer-up of corner cops,
Groundskeepers, mothers with strollers,
Outwitter of panhandlers and bill
Collectors, avoider of levies, excises,
Me in a taxi in the rain,
Pressing my luck all the way home.

That's me at the dice table, baby,
Betting come, little joe, and yo,
Blowing the coals, laying thunder,
My foot on top a fifty dollar chip
Some drunk spilled on the floor,
Dishonest me, evener of scores,
Eager accepter of the extra change,
Hotel towel pilferer, coffee spoon
Lifter, fervent retailer of others'
Humor, blackhearted gossiper,
Poisoner at the well, dweller
In unsavory detail, delighted sayer
Of the vulgar, off course belier
Of the true me, empiric builder
Newly haircutted, stickerer-up
For pals, jam unpriser, medic
To the self-inflicted, attorney
To the self-indicted, petty accountant
And keeper of the double books,
Great divider of the universe
And all its forms of existence
Into its relationship to me,
Fellow trembler to the future,
Thin air gawker, apprehender
Of the frameless door.

A Fugitive Heart

She went to the bridge one weekend morning
Where the artists collected to sell their wares.
You've seen examples, mostly watercolors
Of Chartres, St Paul's, or the Trevi Fountain.
Here and there a clown peers through greasepaint
Or a bouquet of asters has been drawn to scale.
Mostly, though, it's the architectural pictures
That sell their buyers the enduring pleasure,
An evidence of having been somewhere great

Or the good taste to have wanted to be there,
The true north of longing for the fugitive heart.
He was one of the artists, a young man, pleased
With himself, the level of his accomplishment,
And a studio in a sought after district in the city.
He was of a certain type urban centers attract,
Streetsingers whose voices are only passably better
Than the ones that are silent around them on corners,
Whose renditions are not so much heard but witnessed,
As if willingness were the thing that separates
Performers from their audiences. She had not said
She liked his work, but he thought it or did not care.
What mattered to him was how he felt, eyes open
Or shut, he felt good to himself all the same.
Like his presumptive good looks or many silver rings,
Something about him was rough hewn yet buffed,
His long hair a more golden blond than hers,
His blue jeans better fitting. She had been looking
At one of his twilights at sea, bending before
The canvas to catch a closer look at something
That was flotsam or a build-up of paint when she
Caught him through his sunglasses peering down
The line of her blouse, openly and boldly, she thought,
Like a man on deck—not expecting the sun's response.
She colored and frowned. Brightly, he covered
Himself and asked whether she really believed
In the powers of St. Christopher (who hung between
Her breasts like the martyr himself). Off balance,
She began a rambling talk about saints and painters
And dog friends in the country where she had lived
As a girl. She liked the way he focused on her,
Stripping his glasses with an attentive gesture,
Listening and picturing the landscapes she told
The way she might have done them were she the artist.
He was a seasoned veteran of his scene and climate,
Knew that silence and speech were shadow and color
That young women from the country could be inspired
By white tablecloths and glasses of house wine
As he talked of drifting, sacrifice, and the artist's life.
Later at his place, gathering up her underthings

By the light of the city, she stood at the window
Deciding if she would go. She saw herself both
There and here like the tops of the roofs outside
And the reflection of him asleep on the bed.
She saw herself in the here and now, a figure
Amid the figures of cathedrals and clock towers,
Bookshelves and kettles, a geometry of dark and light
Like the brindled ancient streets alterable in a moment.

WAYNE DODD

October Notes

Overnight the leaves have all turned golden and The light
will never be like this again, we think,
as it falls as it spreads as it rises
among the trees, bright radiance
the leaves' undersides
shine with (Tongue that utters us, flame that licks us
and moves on)—their light wave
and flutter.

How it masses in the crowns the maples lift up!
How it washes the low leaves of the Solomon's seal,
of the greenbriar, of the cabbage wort! (See,
it shines full on even the lowliest
of weeds), still standing here, giving thanks.

That pure, unlidded blue . . .

In the dogwood trees the titmice
have come for the berries
in their bright clusters. They pluck
and fly away, pluck
and fly away, the day's brilliance
wrapping birds and fruit
(small, blood-red globes)
in its mantle of sight.

But already it is changing. High up, the wind
is combing the fine, invisible hair
of *What's next?* and evening,
turning its back on us, begins its
daily push of erasers
across the board (All those carefully-drawn words,
with their little valentine centers! figures our hands
traced, sounds our mouths
shaped).
                    Once (it was in Italy),
the light was like this, remember?
Well, not exactly like this.
But like this, perfect. Like this, pure.

It was April, or possibly May.
The light fell straight down
into the center of everything—
roof tiles, olive trees, stone walls,
water—and was part of them.
It made everything real,
solid—even the air that wrapped you
in its pearly silk.

Don't let me forget, you thought. *Don't let me forget*
this day, these colors:
the way stuccoed walls look
in sun, faint blush of rose
in a field of yellow,
like a memory earth holds

of skin, its pale, disappearing hue.

MARK DOTY

Elizabeth Bishop, *Croton*, Watercolor, 9" × 5¾", n.d.

Exiles see exiles everywhere.

And so this leaf's solo,
enisled, its embered coral
barred with freckles of tropic
sable, bits of the lushest darkness
north of Havana. Not *far* north,

though; this little archipelago's
flush chromatics require
sea-light on humid acres
sun-worried to fecundity
and decay. How bright

a homeless one appears,
detached from context,
quickened by singularity!
Castaway not to be rescued,
not needing to go home, really;

this lonesome leaf's a study
never finished, since
we aren't sure what *one*
of anything is. And therefore
must begin the work again—

Try: this elliptical isle's coral
and aglow, beautifully barred
with lesser islands' tropic sable:
Try: this lonesome leaf's islanded,
autobiographical. Or:

Enisled, this ellipse is coral & sable . . .

Fish-R-Us

Clear sac
of coppery eyebrows
suspended in amnion,
not one moving—

A Mars,
composed entirely
of single lips,
each of them gleaming—

this bag of fish
(have they actually
traveled here like *this?*)
bulges while they

acclimate, presumably,
to the new terms
of the big tank
at Fish-R-Us. Soon

they'll swim out
into separate waters,
but for now they're
shoulder to shoulder

in this clear and
burnished orb, each fry
about the size of this line,
too many lines for any

bronzy antique epic,
a million of them,
a billion incipient citizens
of a goldfish Beijing,

a Sao Paolo,
a Mexico City.
They seem to have sense
not to move but hang

fire, suspended, held
at just a bit of distance
(a bit is all there is), all
facing outward, eyes

(they can't even blink)
turned toward the skin
of the sac they're in,
this swollen polyethylene.

And though nothing's
actually rippling but their gills,
it's still like looking up
into falling snow,

if all the flakes
were a dull, breathing gold,
as if they were
streaming toward—

not us, exactly,
but what they'll
be ... Perhaps
they're small enough

—live sparks, for sale
at a nickel apiece—
that one can actually
see them transpiring:

they want to swim
forward, want to
eat, they want what
anyone wants

to take place. Who's
going to feed or cherish
or even see them all?
They pulse in their golden ball.

Sea Grape Valentine

Loose leaf:
golden
fire-streams

branching into bayous
of darker flame,
breaking apart

near the rim
to finer, finer veins:
unnavigable Amazonia

in the shape of a heart
—a real heart, dear,
not the idealized kind,

and thus all throb
and trouble, and fallen
as if to remind us

we're fire at the core,
various heats,
though everything

mottles,
at this latitude:
fruit and flower

and once-pink
porch columns,
even the puddle

between the bakery
and Kingdom Hall
giving up thunderhead

and rainbow, even
the concrete pier
a slow study

in corrosion's arts:
nothing unchecked
or unstippled,

(old pink taxi
rusting in the sun)
nothing simple or im-

pervious to decay:
why not
this fallen valentine,

candybox token
veined in hot gold,
its tropic wax

embalmed and blazing?

RITA DOVE

Against Flight

Everyone wants to go up—but no one can imagine
what it's like when the earth smoothes out, begins

to curve into its own implacable symbol.
Once you've adjusted to chilled footsoles,

what to do with your hands? Can so much wind
be comfortable? No sense

looking around when you can see
everywhere: There'll be no more clouds

worth reshaping into daydreams, no more
daybreaks to make you feel larger than life;

no eagle envy or fidgeting for a better view
from the eighteenth row in the theater . . .

no more theatre, for that matter, and no
concerts, no opera or ballet. There'll be

no distractions except birds,
who never look you straight in the face,

and at the lower altitudes,
monarch butterflies—brilliant genetic engines

churning toward resurrection in a foreign land.
Who needs it? Each evening finds you

whipped to fringes, obliged to lie down
in a world of strangers, beyond perdition or pity—

bare to the stars, buoyant in the sweet sink of earth.

Evening Primrose

> Poetically speaking, growing up is mediocrity.
> —Ned Rorem

Neither rosy nor prim
not cousin to the cowslip
nor the extravagant fuchsia,
I doubt anyone has ever
picked one for show
though the woods must be fringed
with their lemony effusions.

Sun blathers its baronial
endorsement, but they refuse
to join the ranks. Summer
brings them in armfuls,
yet, when the day is large,
you won't see them fluttering
the length of the road.

They'll wait until the world's
tucked in and the sky's
one ceaseless shimmer—then
lift their saturated eyelids
and blaze, blaze
all night long
for no one.

Lullaby

(after Lorca's *Cancion Tonta*)

> Mother, I want to rest in your lap again
> as I did as a child.

Put your head here. How it floats,
heavy as your whole body was once.

> If I fall asleep, I will be stiff
> when I awake.

No stiffer than I.

> But I want to lie down and do nothing
> forever.

When I was angry with your father, I would take to my bed
like those fainting Victorian ladies.

> I'm not angry at anyone.
> Mostly I'm bored.

Boredom is useful for embroidery,
and a day of rest never hurt anyone.

> Mother, I want the birthday supper of my childhood,
> dripping with sauce.

Then you must lie down while I fix it!
Here, a pillow for your back.

> I can't. The schoolbus is coming.
> She'll be waiting at the corner.

Already? So soon!

Sic Itur ad Astra

Thus is the way to the stars.
—Virgil

Bed, where are you flying to?
I went to sleep
nearly an hour ago,
and now I'm on a porch
open to the stars!

Close my eyes
and sink back to
day's tiny dismissals;
open wide and I'm
barefoot, nightshirt
fluttering white as a sail.

What will they say
when they find me
missing—just
the shape of my dreaming
creasing the sheets?
Come here, bed.

I need you! I don't know my way.
At least leave my pillow
behind to remind me
what affliction I've fled—
my poor, crushed pillow

with its garden of smells!

Vacation

I love the hour before takeoff,
that stretch of no time, no home
but the gray vinyl seats linked like
unfolding paper dolls. Soon we shall
be summoned to the gate, soon enough
there'll be the clumsy procedure of row numbers
and perforated stubs—but for now
I can look at these ragtag nuclear families
with their cooing and bickering
or the heeled bachelorette trying
to ignore a baby's wail and the baby's
exhausted mother waiting to be called up early
while the athlete, one monstrous hand
asleep on his duffel bag, listens,
perched like a seal trained for the plunge.
Even the lone executive
who has wandered this far into summer
with his lasered itinerary, briefcase
knocking his knees—even he
has worked for the pleasure of bearing
no more than a scrap of himself
into this hall. He'll dine out, she'll sleep late,
they'll let the sun burn them happy all morning
—a little hope, a little whimsy
before the loudspeaker blurts
and we leap up to become
Flight 828, now boarding at gate 17.

CORNELIUS EADY

Hope

When I see the seven pairs of crutches
Before the grotto at Lourdes,
Each of different style and height,
I wonder if this is simply an announcement
Of belief, or proof from
Seven humans who shed
What ailed them.

What do I see
As the line snakes and curves
In, under and out?
Merely history, the long reach
Across oceans. Here, the moment
The faith reached Asia,
There, where its feet
Touched the jungle.

And the strange gauntlet the faithful
Must endure or ignore
To touch the moment Bernadette touched:
The 3-D portraits of the cross,
The holy names of the hotels
As if to imply God is the town's
Silent partner.

O, poor electric tourist,
Who can only notice the drive-thru
McDonald's later
Instead of the hope that
The body be stung. O, weary eyes,
Which can only perceive
Kneeling, water, rock.

Like Bernadette, wash your face
Says the multilingual sign at the spigots,
And pray that God will cleanse your heart
And I watch as they light their candles,
Each with their own desire,
And then trudge back up the long road
Towards the other truths of the world.

Hummingbird

It is almost impossible
To imagine the scale
Of your small life,
A pin of feathers
Among the blossoms.
As difficult to conceive
Of your bright hunger

As it is, I hear, for you
To awake each morning,
Pulling yourself back from
Some great distance,
Gambling you've saved
Just enough fuel
To shock your heart.

Yellow-throated hot rod,
How unsettling to think
That the only time death
Might be fast enough
To catch you with its spoon
Is when you move
As quick as me.

Speed

I have seen the swallows spin
Above the bell tower,

Quick feathers gathering air.
If an arrow could think

These are the handsome moves
It would choose for itself.

In Florence, the swallow
Is a swirl of pigment,

A blurred hunger under
Dappled light.

I am big and clunky,
I am dressed incorrectly,

And I have yet to think
At the speed of the world.

NANCY EIMERS

Arlington Street

Some lost trumpet blast from Revelations tucked inside the brain
of an aphasiac.
He laughs
as if his tongue were a siren,
as if his teeth were jackhammers.
I've felt the dumptruck of his larynx
churn inside me.
I only know the laugh the way I know the boards in the fence
the laugh comes leaping over every morning, every afternoon,
behind its fence a face
no one has ever seen.
He rambles on that crooked bicycle
of a laugh teetering around a corner, falling off the edge of the joke.
That laugh
of metal stairsteps ending midair, halfway up a burning building,
no way down.
Some days he merely growls
the lower notes of an emery board,
as if the trees and houses on this street
were empty. Mereness. Gold and silver numbers
nailed to shingles,
broken porch swings,
hollow trees.
Some days he makes no sound. As if his mouth were gone.
As if he were the bygone hoot of a derailed commuter train.
As if his mouth were trying to haul the rest of him away.

Crossroads Mall

If I close my eyes, I can picture how it looks in the dark—

rustic benches, Sunglass Hut, Gazebo of the Nape of the Neck
and Bend of the Knee,
petshop window of kittens draped softly over and under each other
sleeping as deeply as bedroom slippers . . .

this is the living mall, the one with the carousel,
where in the daytime horses ride but not up and down,
they just ride around and around,
happiness put out to pasture.
The faces of the riders are not the faces of children any more,
this one looks embarrassed, that one looks strained.
But at night in bed the spookiness

comes back and restores them to themselves,
and they sleep.

At Abercrombie and Fitch the mannequin on skis
has Little Orphan Annie eyes.
At the Limited, there are rows of torsos,
sweater girls without their heads,
the nipples hard.

On the other side of town is the ghost mall:
the Department of Public Safety, a movie house
busy on weekends, dead on oceanic weekday afternoons,
stores and stores of emptiness
and at its epicenter, statues: three,
women in Grecian drapery, each one as rapt as somebody who isn't there,
each head untenanted, resounding like an empty dare.
Sometimes, after a movie, I walk around them, in circles,
stand in the path of their forsaken eyes
to sober up
from all that dark.

But the mall of the living, the ruin
built out of someone's recovered memory
of a castle,
parking lot of forgetting all around it:
I could walk through, up and back, criss and cross, with my eyes closed,
the crossroads of my days and nights marked out for me
like the lines on my palm.
I ride the escalator down
to see my mother riding up, opposite me.
Her face turned away from me, it is
the underside of a leaf.

I hear my sister's voice behind the curtain
of the tabernacle next to mine.
Then in my abode I clothe my soul in haste
with a pair of Guess jeans and a v-neck tunic sweater
but when I look in the mirror it is too late, I am drowning in it
and my sister has departed from me,

shirts and pants and dresses shed like skins
and tossed on the little bench and floating across the dead seas
up a stream to a floodplain littered with straight pins.
Wherever she has taken her body
it must be lighter than it was
in the instant ago of our former life.
Into the aether:
into the upper regions of the mall
where Christmas lights are strung. Maybe she is one of the lights,

a child cradled in the arms of Santa
looks up at tearily: the face of her mother
snuffed by Santa's beard.

Sometimes I come here just to be a lost mariner
but I am never lost:
there are the snowflakes frozen to the porthole of a jewelry store,
here is the treasure chest open to a single pearl
laid on a velvet slab,
there is the plashing of faces in the aisles
and the row of lockers stuffed with the coats and hats of the drowned.

My mother has picked up one of the kittens
and walks away with it in the crook of her arm,
my sister is trying out the rowing machine
but she isn't getting anywhere
and so the only way I will ever find them is
if everyone else holds still and shuts their eyes
and we disappear
and it is night, and the moon rows over
the gentle waters of the parking lot.

Lunar Eclipse

for my brother and sister, visiting me in Cornwall

Tonight as the merest ghost of us
passes over the moon and washes its face
a dirty orange, we have to try and spot the instant of eclipse,
though some change moves at the speed of flowers, not of something
counted into the hand, so maybe all we'll see
is all we ever see, what's happened
and is done with us,
bygones be bygones,
hands washed, period, end of the line,
a copper moon, then a dun moon, then a pumpkin moon,
fed up and sickly moons whose parent moon is still a mystery,
we the puzzled look on its face,
dead seas blind to our own faces,
deaf to what stone circles want to ask
an ancient smile drawn with a stick in the dust,
our breaths cartoon clouds wisping Earth,
where yellow streetlights are the dotted lines
that hold streets true to their course all night,
our voices one voice, high and low tones in the dark,
waking Marcus the pony at the fence, feet shuffling
to walk the long way back to sleep,
along the lane, beyond the glow of Carbis Bay, over the stars,
around Knill's monument and up the tors
where it will finally be black
whether our eyes are open or closed.

ROLAND FLINT

Tributaries

Ten straight days of rain roiled from clouds,
with temperatures in the fifties (so you
close windows, and retrieve the winter pj's)
can almost blot how plump and April green
is the world of your county now, Montgomery
in Maryland, everything ready to bloom, but
here is rain and rain and rain to lose you
in one long sentence by Gabriel Garcia Marquez,
with no way out till the sky has said all
it has of cats and dogs, pitch-forks and hammer-
heads, frogs and fish, moths and monkeys,
quims and bums, corn silk and willow leaf,
jets and pets and lily pads, dodges, chevies,
steering wheels and rumble seats, the tin-tin,
the sluice and runnel of all you love, wetly
rinsing your ears, until: the old woman dies,
buried in the sump of her grave, the colonel
ascends only to lose in the rank sweat of an
allusion, some of the heirs meet and marry
in the rain, the state falls, the last dictator
fingers girls, dreams of sun or snow all
turned to rain pouring into the next county or
country, the next day, week, month, year,
drowning the sewers, but not the rats,
until, all verbs, rivers and prayers at flood
stage, it empties into the sea, on which,
just now, the sun begins to shine.

Wake

In the gunny dusk of a dream
the old man looks too small
for his best blue suit—as he
lies in state, or as he boards
the train to bear him away.
"Wait," says the dreamer,
still adream or awake,
like a voice reaching idly
after his father, who glances
with fitful resentment
but doesn't wait.

It could be the passenger car
of a country train, its steps
painted black, its skinny sweep
of hand-rail brass, the rest
dull green. Or else he lies
where all his get were got,
where the old man and mother
lay, struggled, and slept for
fifty-five years. Is he propped
there or getting aboard?—both
are in the dream—

And other choices. But propped
up there or boarding, the dream
smells gumbo: of depot, of potato
warehouse or subway, of turnip,
dry-rot, sweat. And the malign
and abused old man does not
look up from the bed where he
lies, or down from the steps
but turns away to mount the
train, his fixed face all
sallow-creased and gray.

The bed has grown or the old man,
though fatter in old age, grows
smaller in death's reprise.
Its fake brass frame of hollow
tubes may be the handrail on
the train, but its springs
are deeply silent, formal,
all turned to catafalque.
Stilled too the old man's
ripping voice, even its late
susurring lisp is gone.

But broken and softened by dying,
sunken down into this repose of
death's fat baby, the face still
speaks its power, balefully, of
his father. And whether glaring
away from the dreamer, or refusing
all solace from the bed, propped
or climbing, he lies where he lies
or mounts where he mounts, alone,
in the gunny dusk of the dream.

CAROL FROST

Burdock

In the April sun that doesn't yet smell, brown and red birds declaring hunger,
I appear from the inner world—a hell of beetles and voles—appointed to
     multiply.
If tender, I'm streamy with orange dye, used to the gardener's scritching hoe,
     rock-
rooted. Buried, lopped up, drowned, how can I be hurt, when I resurrect? I
     resurrect
at the sun's behest, my leaf liquors concentrating into bitter-meated flowers
and stiffening into stalks. When my eggs burr the coats of animals, who can
     neither mate
with me nor eat me, they take the future into the cold fields. I'm here in this
     late
morning, to tell you there is satisfaction, even when I die; there are reasons
and consequences. I am compact of laws, emerging continually from the inner
     world.

Flicker

    "Beauty is for amateurs"

Chisel-billed, eye cerulean, with a crimson nuchal patch,
flicker lay on the ground, still warm, and went on aging:
intricate, stricken watch, pear in a dessicating wind.

I brought it home and began with the box of watercolors
to wash the eye with milk for the clouds and sky it fell from,
then dragged my partly dried brush over the rough paper surface

for true textures on the wings, imagining old orchards, umber and sienna,
where I'd seen the undulating flight of loose flocks. I studied
the yellow undertail, then daubed with the colored water

along the gray and dun stripes. As for my pulse, I felt for temperament—
for gravestone, for shadow—to affect the utter silence after a long, long day
of call, *whurdle, peah,* drum, and *wicka.* Then I blotted and scraped the throat.

I saw dusk falling like a comment on each detail
that led to it and gradually was lost and leaving.
A hint of song must be caught, a clarity of neither light nor memory,

and it must be in the physical form of the flicker
and the orchard where the wind makes a soft racket—song that breaks the
        learned heart.

I stared and stared by lamplight, stroking the white,
thinking sour-gum, dogwood, poison ivy berry, river mist, imagining the free
        side of the hills
when a bead of liquid formed in the flicker's beak and pooled on my desk.

My evasions went up in smoke. With colors, tones, casements,
and stars with exact names, who could but feign the moments
once lived that will never be lived again?

Who has a home in this good world and doesn't yearn?
I do. It's mine. I do.

Waking

It was dusk, the light hesitating
and a murmur in the wind, when the deer, exhausted,
turned to look at me, an arrow in its side.

Though I pity dreamers, taking a thread
and weaving it upon the loom of Self—the secret,
gaudy, wonderful new cloth—, I will tell the end of the story.

His shoulder was torn, the joint held by one sinew,
which I severed with the blade of the arrow,
so when he ran there were no impediments.

The black dogs that followed were swifter,
their barking ancient, despicable.

As he fell, his chest turned to breast plate,
his one powerful arm covered with pagan signs.

Nearly stupid in my waiting for what would happen next,
each breath propelling me and him toward dust,
I woke, the sheets soaked, heart fluttering—:

When death comes into the sleeping room as through a tiny hole,
like a rent in the Covenant, it hurts.

TESS GALLAGHER

Laughter and Stars

I didn't make present
those days he didn't complain
but I knew he was sick, felt
sick, and a look would pass between us,
a doomed look that nonetheless
carried streamers of light like a comet
scratching light across the tablet of the night sky.
We looked into each other
and like the comfort a small branch is to a bird
on a long migration, we took comfort in
the two-way knowing of that look.

I didn't make present enough
his beautiful will as he went to his room
with the fireplace and heaped the fire up
to match the inner burning of his body's candle,
the cells igniting so fast by then
it kept him awake, pacing him wall to wall
in the cage of his body's luster like a panther
of the will, supple and searching its parameters.
He fed the fire; he wrote
                    poems.

No, I couldn't make present
the tender way he took my body in the night
into his arms, holding his one radiance to me
like a wet match upon which one
dry spot remained and he turned just so and struck himself
against me and there was a blazing up, the way the night
ignites with more than lips and parted legs
when two souls
in their firefly selves
come together asking
to be buried in the no-song-left-but-this

                                        dark.

Had I been able to give these things
I might have described his innocent laughter
with a friend and me the night before his death, laughter
at the clumsiness of the body, his body,
with the oxygen tank attached, making sure the tube
was in his mouth. His wanting to go out onto
the deck of the house to see the stars again. The wheelchair
catching on the rug, the oxygen tank
trying to jolt loose, but somehow everything jangling along
out the sliding glass doors, and the sky huge
with a madman's moon, huge as a man's heart on its last
breath-beat so we had to shield ourselves
and turn away to find the

                            stars.

Such a plaintive, farewell hissing
they made, like diamonds imbedded
in the blue-black breast of forever. But then
it was the night before my love's last morning,
and we were together, one body to another, laughter
and stars, laughter and stars.
Then he got up, stood up with everything still attached and we
helped him hack open a bright crevasse in the night, to hurl
his heart-beat like the red living fist it was
one more time
out across the sleeping thresholds
of the living.

Owl-Spirit Dwelling

Especially what matters, this being America
so our absences from the loved place
make it harbor-like while we rummage in the elsewhere.
Without us it ebbs and flows, tidal
but recording too what we would do
and what was done, caressing
that unaccountable corridor leading to the moment after
the bird has flown. To fashion such articulate

waiting is to trace an interior something like a runway
where nothing impedes our taking off, yet
we are sword-hilt sheathed by intention whether at lift-off or
touching down, and we *do* touch
down, do soar. For these are airways bright
with haunting, as when cloud-shadow supposes
along a far ridge, then smudges into tree line until
our looking outward is a hooding above

as from below, an owl's lids, the eye abundant
yet human-sized, capable of simultaneous focus, near
and far, the rooms incredibly light-gathering
and light-concentrating, particularly comblike where
in darkness interlaced with branches
flight is a smooth, soundless muscle our mind causes,
its body opened finally like a bowl speckled
with rainwater. As if the forest had moved in, we too
are speckled, pinged by a multitudinous

sense of homecoming. Like an owl captured in the silo
of its thoughtless concentration, we must turn,
raise or lower the entire head
to take in our surround which yields through
a nictitating membrane over all, translucent and protective
as in a struggle with prey or when
with tremors we hear a voice say: 'Nobody comes here now
but me.' Shaftlike then with remove, a wise sweetness
punctuates, as if a well had been made to stand above earth
and still hold water deeply for dipping into, the sound

of overspill and bucket-clang, gull-flicker 'out there' too
and the light, clothesline playful. And because we are there
when most far off, something of the sea
roars inchoate so we are enfolded
in thought become memory, all-purpose, yet also historic
as in a succession of rooms in a Chekhov story where
the grandfather killed himself in the bedroom and in the dining-room
a man had been flogged to death. Somewhere the languor
of the handsome man 'spoilt by too much love' leads to

a ballroom of elderly ladies dressed like young ones. Domelike
that knowledge at the top of sun-drenched stairs that 'the hour
cometh.' One room then especially and only
for dying. The owl-soul which perches there able to hear
'the footfalls of a beetle in the grass at a distance of
well over 100 yards,' its placement asymmetrical as if
it were a second nest, the first having been destroyed or
disturbed. A place of incubation. An echo

of alcoves throughout, admitting continually that step
to the side in order to inhabit or to cherish, though a wing would
call this more habitat than nest—the sounds
to be made here soft and far-carrying, slightly tremulous:
three short notes, a pause, then one longer, concluding note,
until we have drifted down through something, a place
which repeats two distances, until the moon, even that
goes down with it and the word 'solace,' only that.

Urgent Story

When the oracle said, 'If you keep pigeons
you will never lose home,' I kept pigeons.
They flicked their red eyes over me,
a deft trampling
of that humanly proud distance
by which remaining aloof
is its own fullness. I administered
crumbs, broke sky with them like breaking

the lemon-light of the soul's amnesia
for what it wants but will neither take
nor truly let go. How it revived me,
to release them! And at that moment of flight
to disavow the imprint, to tear
their compasses out by the roots of
some green meadow they might fly over
on the way to an immaculate freedom, meadow

in which a woman has taken off
her blouse, then taken off the man's flannel shirt
so their sky-drenched arc
of one, then the other above
each other's eyelids is a branding of daylight,
the interior of its black ambush
in which two joys lame the earth a while
with heat and cloudwork under wing-beats.

Then she was quiet with him. And he
with her. The world hummed
with crickets, with bees nudging the lupins.
It is like that when the earth counts
its riches—noisy with desire
even when desire has strengthened our bodies
and moved us into the soak of harmony.

Her nipples in sunlight have crossed his palm
wind-sweet with savor and the rest
is so knelt before
that when they stand upright
the flight-cloud of my tamed birds shapes an arm
too short for praise. Oracle, my dovecot
is an over and over nearer to myself
when its black eyes are empty.
But by nightfall I am dark
before dark if one bird is missing.

Dove that I lost from not caring enough,
Dove left open by love in a meadow,
Dove commanding me not to know
where it sank into the almost-night—for you
I will learn to play the concertina,
to write poems full of hateful jasmine and
longing, to keep the dead alive, to sicken
at the least separation.
Dove, for whose sake
I will never reach home.

FORREST GANDER

Downstroke

From where you stand, how could you fix intention?
I tendered him as my eyes, the sculptor famous
At twenty six, although I poisoned him.

                                        How could I stifle
What I would do before it happened?
His eyelashes, island mosquitoes
Gathering at my throat. My birthday,
I spat out the stone he tongued between my lips:

                                        tiny frog
In an amber nugget. And the iris's weird
Pattern in his eyes, eros constellating

                              in my mouth, his fingers
Painted red and with crescendo.

                    Striations radiated through his forearms. To me,
His sculptures mean nothing. It was
Himself doing the meaning. Veins flaring in his neck
Like wax trails on a candle. Mornings at my mirror,

                                        he combed the hair
Out of his dandruff
While I watched from the bed. Shirt stuck to his back.
He had me practice walking naked
Gripping the lightest chisel
With the muscles of my sex.

                    I needed both hands
To lift his hammer. His swollen knuckles
Completely original, my sensations
Nothing I had known. And then

                    he withdrew so abruptly

There was no time to recover
The yolk of myself
For his method of knowing something
                              was to draw its form
Out of it. Leaving a shell, he broke me,
My body tapped
And tapped into Carrera marble
Until I dimmed like an underluminous galaxy
As the stone warmed and shone and breathed.

Travelers

On the grooved highway at sixty-five, a hum rises

Except intimacy

There is nada   That

Was a scissortail, the man says

In the backseat the boy blows

A coke bottle

But stops when they pass

The mowing machines

Spiked lobelia, crown vetch, trumpet vine

Under the blades of the Ditch-witch tremble

What is the true jelly of an animal

Asks the boy, tonguing his tooth

On its last string

The woman turns her face smiling

The skyline jumps over the moon

The man drives with his finger

Inside her

Eleven years of marriage slough off

Theories unfit to live on

They hold sway the long diagonals

Foretelling connected desires

Only dust was sent duration

They know

That they are naked

LOUISE GLÜCK

Vita Nova

You saved me, you should remember me.

The spring of the year; young men buying tickets for the ferry boats.
Laughter, because the air is full of apple blossoms.

When I woke up, I realized I was capable of the same feeling.

I remember sounds like that from my childhood,
laughter for no cause, simply because the world is beautiful,
something like that.

Lugano. Tables under the apple trees.
Deckhands raising and lowering the colored flags.
And by the lake's edge, a young man throws his hat into the water;
perhaps his sweetheart has accepted him.

Crucial
sounds or gestures like
a track laid down before the larger themes

and then unused, buried.

Islands in the distance. My mother
holding out a plate of little cakes—

as far as I remember, changed
in no detail, the moment
vivid, intact, having never been
exposed to light, so that I woke elated, at my age
hungry for life, utterly confident—

By the tables, patches of new grass, the pale green
pieced into the dark existing ground.

Surely spring has been returned to me, this time
not as a lover but a messenger of death, yet
it is still spring, it is still meant tenderly.

The Burning Heart

... No sadness
is greater than in misery to rehearse
memories of joy ...

Ask her if she regrets anything.

I was
promised to another—
I lived with someone.
You forget these things when you're touched.

Ask her how he touched her.

His gaze touched me
before his hands touched me.

Ask her how he touched her.

I didn't ask for anything;
everything was given.

Ask her what she remembers.

We were hauled into the underworld.

I thought
we were not responsible
any more than we were responsible
for being alive. I was
a young girl, rarely subject to censure:
then a pariah. Did I change that much
from one day to the next?
If I didn't change, wasn't my action
in the character of that young girl?

Ask her what she remembers.

I noticed nothing. I noticed
I was trembling.

Ask her if the fire hurts.

I remember
we were together.
And gradually I understood
that though neither of us ever moved
we were not together but profoundly separate.

Ask her if the fire hurts.

You expect to live forever with your husband
in fire more durable than the world.
I suppose this wish was granted,
where we are now being both
fire and eternity.

Do you regret your life?

Even before I was touched, I belonged to you;
you had only to look at me.

Formaggio

The world
was whole because
it shattered. When it shattered,
then we knew what it was.

It never healed itself.
But in the deep fissures, smaller worlds appeared:
it was a good thing that human beings made them;
human beings know what they need,
better than any god.

On Huron Avenue they became
a block of stores; they became
Fishmonger, Formaggio. Whatever
they were or sold, they were
alike in their function: they were
visions of safety. Like
a resting place. The salespeople
were like parents; they appeared
to live there. On the whole,
kinder than parents.

Tributaries
feeding into a large river: I had
many lives. In the provisional world,
I stood where the fruit was,
flats of cherries, clementines,
under Hallie's flowers.

I had many lives. Feeding
into a river, the river
feeding into a great ocean. If the self
becomes invisible has it disappeared?

I thrived. I lived
not completely alone, alone
but not completely, strangers
surging around me.

That's what the sea is:
we exist in secret.

I had lives before this, stems
of a spray of flowers: they became
one thing, held by a ribbon at the center, a ribbon
visible under the hand. Above the hand,
the branching future, stems
ending in flowers. And the gripped fist—
that would be the self in the present.

Vita Nova

In the splitting up dream
we were fighting over who would keep
the dog,
Blizzard. You tell me
what that name means. He was
a cross between
something big and fluffy
and a dachshund. Does this have to be
the male and female
genitalia? Poor Blizzard,
why was he a dog? He barely touched
the hummus in his dogfood dish.
Then there was something else,
a sound. Like
gravel being moved. Or sand?
The sands of time? Then it was
Erica with her maracas,
like the sands of time
personified. Who will

explain this to
the dog? Blizzard,
Daddy needs you; Daddy's heart is empty,
not because he's leaving Mommy but because
the kind of love he wants Mommy
doesn't have, Mommy's
too ironic—Mommy wouldn't do
the rhumba in the driveway. Or
is this wrong. Supposing
I'm the dog, as in
my child-self, unconsolable because
completely pre-verbal? With
anorexia! O Blizzard,
be a brave dog—this is
all material; you'll wake up
in a different world,
you will eat again, you will grow up into a poet!
Life is very weird, no matter how it ends,
very filled with dreams. Never
will I forget your face, your frantic human eyes
swollen with tears.
I thought my life was over and my heart was broken.
Then I moved to Cambridge.

LINDA GREGERSON

Eyes Like Leeks

It had almost nothing to do with sex.
                    The boy
            in his corset and farthingale, his head-

voice and his smooth-for-the-duration chin
                    was not
            and never had been simply in our pay. Or

was it some lost logic the regional accent
                    restores?
            A young Welsh actor may play a reluctant

laborer playing Thisby botching
                    similes
            and stop our hearts with wonder. My young friend

—he's seven—touched his mother's face last night
                    and said *It's*
            wet and, making the connection he has had

to learn by rote, *You're sad.*
                    It's never
            not like this for him. *As if,*

the adolescents mouth wherever California spills
                    its luminous
            vernacular. *As if,* until

the gesture holds, or passes. Let's just
                    say
          we'll live here for a while. O

habitus. O wall. O moon. For my young
                    friend
          it's never not some labored

simulacrum, every tone of voice, each
                    give, each
          take is wrested from an unrelenting social

dark. There's so much dark to go around (how
                    odd
          to be this and no other and, like all

the others, marked for death), it's a wonder
                    we pass
          for locals at all. Take Thisby for instance:

minutes ago she was fretting for lack of a beard
                    and now
          she weeps for a lover slain by a minute's

misreading. Reader, it's
                    sharp
          as the lion's tooth. Who takes

the weeping away now takes delight as well,
                    which feels
          for all the world like honest

work. They've never worked with mind before,
                    the rich
          man says. But moonlight says, *With flesh.*

Noah's Wife

is doing her usual for comic relief.
               She doesn't
             see why she should get on the boat, etc.,

etc., while life as we know it hangs by a thread.
               Even God's
             had one or two great deadpan lines:

Who told you (this was back at the start—
               the teeth
             of the tautology had just snapped shut) *Who*

told you you were naked? The world
               was so new
             that death hadn't been till this minute

required. *What makes you think* (the
               ground
             withers under their feet) *we were told?*

The woman's disobedience is good for
               plot,
             as also for restoring plot to human

scale: three hundred cubits by fifty
               by what?
             What's that in inches exactly? Whereas

an obstinate wife is common coin.
               In
             the beginning was nothing and then a flaw

in the nothing, a sort of mistake which amplified, the
               nothing
             mistranscribed (it takes such discipline

to keep the prospect clean) and now the lion
                    whelps
                the beetle rolls its ball of dung, and Noah

with no more than a primitive double-
                    entry audit
                is supposed to make it right.

We find the Creator in an awkward bind.
                    Washed back
                to oblivion? Think again. The housewife

at her laundry tub has got a better grip.
                    Which may
                be why we've tried to find her laughable,

she's such an unhappy reminder of what
                    understanding
                costs. Ask the boy who cannot, though

God knows he's tried, he swears
                    each bar
                of melting soap will be his last, who cannot

turn the water off when once he's turned it on.
                    His hands
                are raw. His body seems like filth to him.

Who told you (the pharmacopoeia has
                    changed
                the malady's still the same) *Who told you*

you were food for worms?
                    What
                makes you think (the furrow, the fruit)

I had to be told?

MARILYN HACKER

The Boy

Is it the boy in me who's looking out
the window, while someone across the street
mends a pillow-case, clouds shift, the guttterspout
pours rain, someone else lights a cigarette?

(Because he flinched, because he didn't whirl
around, face them, because he didn't hurl
the challenge back—*"Fascists"*—not *"Faggots"*—*"Swine!"*
he briefly wonders—if he were a girl . . .)
He writes a line. He crosses out a line.

I'll never be a man, but there's a boy
crossing out words: the rain, the linen-mender,
are all the homework he will do today.
The absence and the privilege of gender

confound in him, soprano, clumsy, frail.
Not neuter—neutral human, and unmarked,
the younger brother in the fairy-tale
except, boys shouted *"Jew!"* across the park

at him when he was coming home from school.
The book that he just read, about the war,
the partisans, is less a terrible
and thrilling story, more a warning, more

a code, and he must puzzle out the code.
He has short hair, a red sweatshirt. They know
something about him—that he should be proud
of? That's shameful if it shows?

That got you killed in 1942.
In his story, do the partisans
have sons? Have grandparents? Is he a Jew
more than he is a boy, who'll be a man

someday? Someone who'll never be a man
looks out the window at the rain he thought
might stop. He reads the sentence he began.
He writes down something that he crosses out.

Invocation

This is for Elsa, also known as Liz,
an ample-bodied gospel singer, five
discrete malignancies in one full breast.
This is for auburn Jacqueline, who is
celebrating fifty years alive,
one since she finished chemotherapy,
with fireworks on the fifteenth of July.
This is for June, whose words are lean and mean
as she is, elucidating our protest.
This is for Lucille, who shines a wide
beam for us with her dark cadences.
This is for long-limbed Maxine, astride
a horse like conscience. This is for Aline
who taught her lover to caress the scar.
This is for Eve, who thought of AZT
as hopeful poisons pumped into a vein.
This is for Nanette in the Midwest.
This is for Alicia, shaking back dark hair,
dancing one-breasted with the Sabbath bride.
This is for Judy on a mountainside,
plunging her gloved hands in a glistening hive.
Hilda, Patricia, Gaylord, Emilienne,
Tania, Eunice: this is for everyone
who marks the distance on a calendar
from what's less likely each year to "recur."
Our saved-for-now lives are life sentences
—which we prefer to the alternative.

DANIEL HALL

The Birds of the Holy Land

Our guesthouse is cruelly refrigerated, the guide's
smile frankly insincere, God's in his heaven....
But drawn by losses, or the promise of emptiness
to be filled one square at a time—well, we're here.

Was there ever an air so clean, so scrubbed
by the diamond-grit of its own past falling, lo,
these many millennia? Badlands, maybe? Death Valley?
One piece of sacred ground after another.

So give us not the vagabond with its nimbus
of rarity, but the humdrum indigene
in full view, well-lit, wing-bar and gorget
unmistakable. Call us to prayer. Stop up our mouths,

for our desires are prolific, and we cannot
cease uttering them. When our bus swerves in
with a sneeze of brakes and we shuffle off for a look,
let the speck set on the topmost twig of a cedar

put us in mind of something, anything, everything
else, let it all come to seem the same, wisdom
our only reward—along with the X's
strewn through the still-new-scented book.

Neoclassical

Round the point flotillas of swans come trailing
sunlit V's and W's, otherworldly,
but a little corny. When they arrived here
no one remembers.

Nor can we remember the explanation
why the swans are in the ascendant, surging
even as our own population trickles
out to the suburbs.

Garbo Lobster's fleet has been sold; Monsanto,
windows broken, whistles an absent air; New
Yorkers long since bought up the nicer houses;
God, it's depressing. . . .

Village life is moribund, swans or no swans,
ever since the agora folded up and
drifted down Route 1 to the A&P (that
meeting of waters).

There the blue-haired villagers wander endless
aisles of wontons, jicama, squid-ink pasta,
lemongrass—a vision of purgatory
clear to myopics.

Yesterday a family of tourists watched as
swans ripped loaves of bread into soggy tatters,
hissing, stabbing. . . . Finally the little girl said,
Can't we go home now?

One, still hungry, paddled in closer, striking
poses learned through aeons of evolution,
tensely splayed, like someone who cannot bear to
touch his own body.

Likewise our millennial rage for order.
That these birds are immigrants makes the yearning
even keener: we should just round them up and
—What am I saying?

Yes, go home, the village is saying, softly,
firmly, in its passive-aggressive way, there's
nothing left but realtors, antiques, a newsstand.
On your way out, though,

scan the racks of three-for-a-dollar postcards.
What's with all the classical architecture?
Columns, spaces—beauty and truth, I guess? what's
made and what happens?

Evening finds us high in our rooftop aeries
facing westward, scanning the late edition:
Heaven's *vide papier* has been scribbled over
over and over.

Why this vague anxiety? Ah, it isn't
Lyme disease or equine encephalitis
that we fear, but wind from the wing of boredom
passing above us.

Right on cue, as bold as you please, a loner
cleaves the sky from sunset to moon rise. Funny,
how that *who-ah, who-ah* of twanging wingtips
deepens the silence.

Elsewhere, tuned a half-tone apart, the bellbuoys
pass the time in chitchat, retailing no news,
good news: one more lunatic, mundane round of
rising and falling.

DANIEL HALPERN

Desperados

We were desperate. No, we were beyond desperation.
We were beside ourselves. At wit's end.
We said we could slip outside, that was it.
Get in the car and just keep on driving. Never look back.
No second thoughts. No chance of posing as salt.

But they'd find us, you said. *They'd bring us back
and it would begin again.* We could start a new life.
We could begin again, trying the something new.
The road ahead again untrod, winding beyond the next curve
with speed and assurance. Did I say we were desperate?

The lightning took over and revealed the night.
The landscape looked altered—rocks and trees
no longer where they had been hours before.
We hadn't made a move, but we were desperate.
Desperate still—Oh, desperate beyond description.

But they'd find us, you said. *They'd bring us back.*
We said we could slip outside, that was it.
Never look back. No second thoughts.
We were desperate. At wit's end. Beside ourselves.
The landscape looked altered, beyond description.

We could begin again. Something new.
The landscape looked altered. Never look back.
Did I say desperate to try something new?
A new life? The road ahead untrod, winding beyond.
We hadn't made a move—just keep on driving.

Her Body

1. The Fingers

They are small enough to find and care for a tiny stone.
      To lift it with wobbly concentration from the ground,
            from the family of stones, up past the pursed mouth—

for this we are thankful—to a place level with her eyes
      to take a close look, a look into the nature of stone.
            Like everything, it is for the first time: first stone,

chilly cube of ice, soft rise of warm flesh, hard
      surface of table leg, first and lasting scent of grass
            rubbed between the tiny pincer fingers. And there is

the smallest finger poking the air, pointing toward the first heat
      of the single sun, pointing toward the friendly angels
            who sent her, letting them know contact's made.

2. The Eyes

We believe their color makes some kind of difference,
the cast of it played off the color of hair and face.

But it makes no difference, blue or brown,
hazel, green, or gray, pale sky or sand.

When sleep-burdened they'll turn up into her,
close back down upon her sizeable will.

But when she's ready for the yet-to-come—
oh, they widen, grow a deep cool sheen

to catch the available light and shine
with the intensity of the newly arrived.

If they find you they'll hold on relentlessly
without guile, the gaze no less than interrogatory,

fixed, immediate, bringing to bear what there's been
to date. Call her name and perhaps they'll turn to you,

or they might be engaged, looking deeply into the nature
of other things—the affect of wall, the texture of rug,

into something very small that's fallen to the floor
and needs to be isolated and controlled. Maybe

an afternoon reflection, an insect moving *slowly*,
maybe just looking with loyalty into the eyes of another.

3. The Toes

Who went to market?
Who stayed home?
This one goes,
this one doesn't.
This one eats

the flesh
of grass-eating mammals,
this one does not.
In the 17th century
Basho—delicate master

of the vagaries of who
went where—
wrote to one he loved
not of market
and not of meat,

but something brief,
abbreviated,
like five unburdened toes
fluttering like cilia
in the joy of a drafty room,

we call *soul*, like air, both resident
and owner of the body's estate.
But *her* soul, only partially

unpackaged, sings
through the slate that guards it,
contacts those of us waiting here

with a splay of its soft,
scrutinizing fingers.
Her soul is a sapling thing,

something green, dew-damp
but resolute, entering this world
with an angel's thumb pressed

to her unformed body at the very last,
a template affixed to her body
when they decided it was time

to let her go, for her to come to us
and their good work was done.
An angel's thumbprint, a signature, her soul.

You go,
I stay.
Two autumns.

4. *The Soul*

Who knows how they get here,
beyond the obvious.
Who packaged the code

that provided the slate for her eyes,
and what about the workmanship
that went into the fingers

allowing such intricate movement
just months from the other side?—
Who placed with such exactness

the minute nails on each
of the ten unpainted toes?
And what remains

beyond eye and ear, the thing
most deeply rooted in her body—
the thing that endlessly blossoms

but doesn't age, in time
shows greater vitality? The thing
unlike the body that so quickly

reaches its highest moment only
to begin, with little hesitation,
the long roll back, slowing all the way

until movement is administered
by devices other than those devised
by divine design. The ageless thing

MICHAEL S. HARPER

How to Forgive the Father Who Screams at His Son

for Patrice Cuchulain Harper on his Birthday 3/8/98

Fear, and more than fear, how delicate the wings
one needs for flight; it isn't want but *need*;

the ancients reminded us about the wax,
Motown the fare, dancing with no tact for money;

to live in this world you must have time & money,
the hard currency of effects (this is not job-talk);

Jonathan could not stand a raised voice:
don't holler at me, you make me nervous

was his refrain; I heard my siblings
chortle in their tongues in sleep

caressing one another in nightmare:
I learned their speech.

You have a hero's name, two names,
whose increments salute the void

and I will not permit
a fall from grace.

Of course you must find it for yourself,
that space for aerial delights

the fragrance of women who ascend,
they are the complements of the world.

I saw you born near noon in roses,
I saw your perfect teeth

so I know the warrior in this domain,
and elsewhere those attributes that reign:

this is a whisper that you hear at rest
when you sojourned at inner flight upon my breast.

Matchbook: The Spinnaker (Sausalito)

in memory of Bill Evans

Adrift in your own spittle
(eyebrows on vibrato knuckles)

we are across the bay
from reality;

but reality hits in waves
and Tatum weaves

into the picture:
Pittsburgh, Bill Basie

filling in
until the man arrived.

There will be no talk
of mechanics

the smack direction
enough for any master's

fingers, and the wrists
are flexible

as any girl;
the speed limits

on the bridge
are foggy

and out of gear:
T-birds, Mercedes

roll off Tiburon;
Mill Valley

is the papaya
of Vietnam;

French music
in your appreciation

is orchestrated
around Dien Bien Phu

because of the craft
of the French:

Pres and Bud
only alive

for awhile
because of it:

Paradise

in memory of Roger Rath

At Saratoga you were in whites
at the races, even the bucks
dancing a rhythm of money
if you were Scott Fitzgerald
but you were only on the make;
nothing short of an epic
would satisfy you,
and you were taking a day off
from the mansion at Yaddo;

I remember apparition
is what you most resembled,
and that R. V. Cassill
was a mentor
and you might be looking
for *Pretty Leslie*
or Profumo's girl
for subject matter;

you spent time here
according to the archivist
who wrote a history
of the college;
85 with a bad heart
and seldom in his cups
he mentioned when he retired,
that he came back part time,
and you are not recorded
in the history of the college,
which he had written;

he did mention you on campus
with a rifle—that if you taught
it was probably out of season,
and that you broke hearts
as the Egyptians did
in mummification;

the river is almost frozen;
I have asked for you;
the man who replaced you
edits the campus magazine
which is more than local;

there are painters and sculptors
passing through,
courtesy at the grand union,
French on local radio,
the border a half hour away;

Gihon is not in the dictionary;
you can hunt in the Bible
or gloss Milton
to find the tributaries
and transcendence;

they say you were drunk
as you went off the road nearby;
I hope you were:
Keats, who loved the word *azure*,
gave us the road map
for your condition:
bliss, ecstasy, bliss
as his letters say.

JEFFREY HARRISON

Arrangement

in memory of Priscilla Connell (1926–1997)

The flowers that thrive on the margins,
by the tracks and roadsides as we pass
on our way somewhere else,
planted by no one and often unnoticed,
their beauty gratuitous, prodigal,
have nothing to do with us,
have nothing to do with decoration
but with survival.

        You survived
seven years after the diagnosis
and always noticed them, even when
you grew too weak to go out among them
in the early hours with your Nikon,
looking for things that others
might not see otherwise: the spider
that sews a lightning bolt into its web,
the monarch probing a milkweed's globe.

Now at the end of summer we drive home,
umbels of Queen Anne's lace and yellow tassels
of goldenrod swaying in the wake of our passing
and yours. Loosestrife in profusion
spreads its purple fabric through the marshes
spiked with dead trees. An occasional mullein
stands like a spear thrust into the earth as a marker,
its hilt flecked with one or two small blooms . . .

. . . their presence alongside us so faithful
we can't help having the delusion
that they are there because we need them,
even though you wouldn't have believed it.
You didn't want a funeral or flowers,
but these I have gathered without breaking
a single stem, and I think you would allow me
to place them on your grave.

Family Dog

A succession of Newfoundlands
of diminishing nobility
and with names like English maids—
Flossie, Rosie, Nelly—
gave way, long after I'd left,
to this hyperactive black lab
who (like me?) never grew up,
always the exuberant puppy
to almost everyone's annoyance,
and whose name—Jess—is so much
like my own that when I'm home
and hear my father call the dog
or say his name in irritation
when he's gotten in the garbage
or chewed up someone's shoe,
I'm forced to relive an unpleasant
split second I lived many times
as a teenager, when my father
and I were chronic enemies—
a quick shock through my heart
and the thought, *Oh God, what
have I done now?* Followed now
by the realization, *It's only the dog,*
a sigh of relief, a quiet laugh . . .
I'm almost always fooled,
as if the pitch of my father's voice

triggered some switch
in my nervous system, my body
still wired for sound
decades later, bringing back,
before I have time to think,
the fear, the rancor,
things I would rather forget,
the way a dog forgets
and always comes back, comes home
when his name is called,
knowing his master loves him.

My Grandfather's Necktie

I found it in the back
of my grandmother's top drawer,
coiled and brightly banded
like a tropical snake
hiding among the soft rocks
of rolled-up socks—
but one whose pattern
(red gold blue copper green)
said: harmless, even
marvelous, like something
out of a fable . . .
a fable about a snake
that carries messages
between the underworld
and this world, to and from
a dead husband
and his living wife—
as, in a sense, the tie
had done for seven years,
reminding my grandmother
of my grandfather each time
she opened the drawer.
But now she too had died

and we were going through
her things, deciding who
got what, and what
to throw away—
that's when I found it
in her drawer,
that snake-like tie I kept
to remember them both by.
When I put it on
it's as if I'm winding the skin
of that fabulous snake
around my neck,
a family amulet
tying them to me—
though as time goes on
I wear it more rarely
because its sleek silk
has begun to fray,
and each time I untie it
I hear its fabric
tear a little more.
Soon it will be a relic
I keep in a drawer
near his Swiss Army knife,
the one he let me use
one evening long ago
to cut my steak,
handing it to me
with a mischievous smile
and the casual remark,
"Just yesterday I used it
to skin a snake."

BRENDA HILLMAN

range   condition

A Geology

What we love, can't see.

If Italy looks like a boot to most people, California
          looks like the skin of a person about to sit
          down, a geology.

Consider the Coast Range. We can achieve
          the same results by pushing a pile of wet
          papers from the left and finally
          they were just in love with each other.

Consider the faultline; with only two sides of it,
          how come you never thought of one of them.

A place we love, can't see.   A condition
          so used   to becoming . . .

(Those who have straddled reference know a map
          will stand for wholeness)

When you were trying to quit the drug and broke
          in half you said . . .

And you had to trust it (that is, needing it)

Landforms enable us to scare. Where
            Berkeley is, once a shallow sea with
            landforms to the west, called Cascadia.
            No kidding. I read this.

A geology breaks in half to grow. A person whose drug like
            a locust jumps across someone's foot, singing—;
            we disagree with D, who hates similes.

locust   disagree

The Transverse Ranges holding Los Angeles spit out
          a desert on their hazard side, a power
          transformed from a period of thrall into
          an ordinary period of lying here.

There are six major faults, there are skipped
          verbs, there are more little
          thoughts in California. The piece of coast
          slides on the arrow; down is
          reverse. Subduction means the crust

goes underneath the continent, which is
          rather light. It was my friend. I needed it.
          The break in the rock shows forward; the flash
          hurts. Granite is composed of quartz, hornblende
          and other former fire. When a drug

is trying to quit it has to stretch. Narrow comes
          from the same place as glamor.

A scarp hangs over the edge as it does from
          Monterey to Santa Barbara. When we
          were trying to quit it had to shout.
          (The rest of our party had gone up ahead.)
          Exaggeration has no effect upon silence.

It took my breath, I gave it willingly, I told
          it to, and the breath listened—

Consider the place of I-80 towards outcroppings.
          When you've gotten to Auburn, a whole
          dog-shaped ground has broken through,

the rock struggling with features, its bachelor joy, caused
          by the power that has kissed you.

silence   re-used

What happened, happened a lot. Not to glamorize
        what can't be helped. A bunch of fiery
        islands floated over and sutured themselves to us

a hundred million years ago. I liked

to hold one. Just, really, light it. Put my
        mouth on it.

It's appropriate to discuss features when we speak of California,

daylight's treatment of a sudden

movement in rock. It pretended not to mind. You
        passed him on the path. Miocene lava
        smiled as it ordered the darker

color to sit down.

When he was trying to quit he based his reasoning
        on the way mountains slip. California's
        glaciers never reach the sea. The drug

was trapped in you, and fit. The Klamath mountains love
        the veins of excellent stress, see figure 12.
        Between the time two mountains slip, nothing.
        Between two points of resolution, nothing
        less. A little more
        almost and the slip happened; it happened
        a lot just 30 million years ago.

I saw between the flames four types of instruments:
        with one they touched my mouth,
        with another you touched
        her feet. Rocks of the oldest

time are barely represented. This is the voice
from the cave, Oleiria. He was coming
to fuck me but my face had been removed.

excellent   fault

The fault went under artichokes in 1982. She talked
       to the permanent fire about it;

what pushes up from under isn't
       named. Or is that "What makes you do this
       to yourself."—What makes you . . . A language
       caught up under, like a continent.
       She was inhaling though they told her not to.

In the Gabilan Range, small volcanoes erupted
       softly, then this throw-rug-over-the-carpet
       in-a-bowling-alley type of effect. A California

is composed of moving toward, away, or past; a
       skin is not separate; a poem is

composed of all readings of it. Elements
       redeem themselves plenty, alchemists say so.
       I gave my breath quite easily, then. Sorry it's

ashes, sorry it's smoke all the way down. Gravity
       has to practice. The disciple of angles
       smashed planet after planet, rubbing the cave
       of chalk onto his cue, and put them
       into corners like Aquinas's five
       proofs for the existence of God. Nice
       touch on that boy, nice touch on those
       who sleep till noon, sleep the sleep
       of the uninsured till noon and wake with maps
       of Sacramento on their hands.

What made the Sierra lift from the right. Telluric Poptart.
       Geologists refer to the range as
       trapdoorlike. It made him cry, he gave it
       willingly, the bartender brought him

free drinks and sent him out into the pale
wrong proud civilian night—

A geology can't fix itself. Nor can description.
Horses run upside down in
the undermath. A power has twinned itself
in that place. We follow it until we are
its favorite, and then we live. Does the drug
recover? The Pacific Plate

began this recent movement 20 million years ago. Fresno
was underwater; the small creatures
barely noticed.

She smelled it till it stopped looking pretty; let's call a spoon
a spoon. We dig right down into ourselves
for the rocks of the middle kingdom. Gold

folded into the Motherlode often twinned
with quartz. They seemed to like each other.
Addicts stay on the porch together, lighting them,

and elsewhere, lighthouse cliffs recall the tremors
that brought them there. Cascadia . . . I *whered*
the wheel and the continent moved over

but I still wanted it.

Los Angeles cheap bedding. You'd allow her
to go first and then you'd go, pull the youngest
blanket over her—bang. If that's
how you like it, fine. Like warm sandstone.

We're living at the dawn of creation as far as
California is concerned. The skin
goes first. Most beaches are losing sand,
it drifts south to Mexico. He sold it, she mixed it, we

proud   civilian

bought the pfft in 198X, trying to endure
        the glassfront curve in the unaccountable
        ghostman's pleasure. Get down

off that ladder, you. Ceiling stars. Little fiery

islands were light as they ordered Nevada
        to move over. The white thing took
        her breath, she let it slide, it recognized
        what to do; after it started no
        change, seeing you was methodone
        for seeing you.

The number of faults in middle California
        is staggering—that is, we stagger
        over them till it's
        difficult to follow our own. Each tremor
        is the nephew of a laugh—
        sandstone, shale, chert from the Triassic
        near I-Forgetville. He lined
        them up, they made white sense,

stretchmarks on her body like
        public transportation, very coastal,
        very Sierra traintracks that click click
        down the sides of thighs, stretchmarks
        where the soul has grown too quickly
        from inside—

But in a way, not really. A geology

has its appetites. New islands are forming
        to get the gist of it. Much of the coast
        moved on its own to get free. Sometimes
        he'd just pass it to you, the prince of stains,—
        the universe cried through him. The sea

was glassing itself over Half Moon Bay. Should have
      dropped again suddenly, in the service
      of some burnt out Eden.

It's appropriate to discuss what can't be
      helped. Phyllites, schists, cherts,
      marbles. An angel in the annunciation,
      little subzero Mary kneeling
      before you in the bathroom while you were
      burning your skin off.

You went east and you went south. They
      took out their little fear schedules. The Pacific
      Plate on the left moving north while
      the right stands still if you
      look down on it. There's no way

to say progress had been made. I never did

not think about lighting them, not one day,
      as if a requiem could help how chords
      fell out the bottom, Cascadia breathed, I tried
      program, H tried program after program,
      D tried specific harvests
      of bubbles. 12 step ashes. Extra metal

on the stove. The rest of our party
      had gone on ahead. Don't name it. The lithosphere
      likes to float on the aesthenosphere, the soft
      mobile voice of the unseen. *I slide*

below you sweet and high. It wants

to hear you. It wants to touch you. It wants
      to be happy and it wants to die.

burnt   bubbles

Phyllites, shales, cherts, marbles. Press #
        when you are finished. No one knows why
        the arc of minor islands sewed themselves
        to us in that way. When I put it

to my mouth I had no ability to stop it.
        The sea ate the colors a hundred million years ago.

A geology is not a strategy. When an addict tries to leave,
        the desire to make himself over shifts from
        what it felt like to have been a subject;

L.A. will dwell beside San Francisco eventually.

Tempting to pun on the word *fault*. All right,
        say *plot*. All right, *happens*. The tendency
        to fault relieves the strain. New islands
        were forming to get the gist of it. We wanted
        the extraordinary stranger in our veins.

Whether it's better not to have been held by something.
        The oldest limestone, prevalent between Big Sur
        and Calaveras, is not "better than," say,
        any other kind. The suffering wasn't luckier,
        it wasn't a question of asking.

In the instead hour, the minutes of not recovering
        from the difference of what we loved;
        sameness is also true: stone like a spider

sucking the carapace the same color as itself.

In the expiation of nature, we are required to
        experience the dramatic narrative of matter.

The rocks under California are reigning in their little world.

This was set down in strata so you could know
        what it felt like to have been earth.

EDWARD HIRSCH

Heinrich Heine

I come to you as a whole-hearted man.
I have had myself carried here today
on what we may call my mattress-grave
where I have been entombed for years
(forgive me if I don't stand up this time)
to speculate about the nature of love.

As a cripple talking about physical love,
a subject I've been giving up for years,
I know that my situation (this time
he's gone too far!) is comical and grave.
But don't I still appear to be a man?
Hath not a Jew eyes, etc., at least today?

I am an addict of the human comedy
and I admit every pleasure, especially love,
is like the marriage of the French and Germans
or the eternal quarrel between Space and Time.
We are all creeping madly toward the grave
or leaping forward across the years

(Me, I haven't been able to leap in years)
and bowing under the fiendish blows of Time.
All that can distract us—gentlemen, ladies—
is the splendid warfare between men and women.
I don't hesitate to call the struggle "love."
Look at me: my feverish body is a grave,

I've been living so long on a mattress-grave
that I scarcely even resemble a man,
but what keeps me going is the quest for love.
I may be a dog who has had his day
(admittedly a day that has lasted for years)
but I'm also a formidable intellect of our time

and I'm telling you nothing can redeem Time
or the evident oblivions of the grave
or the crippling paralysis of the years
except the usual enchantments of love.
That's why the night hungers for the day
and the gods—heaven help us—envy the human.

For man and woman, the days pass into years
and the body is a grave filled with time.
We are drowning. All that rescues us is love.

The Magic Mirror

I was standing in front of *The Magic Mirror*
        by Jackson Pollock in the Menil in late September.
                I was looking at a woman looking in the mirror—

abstracted, but with a feathered headdress.
        She was made of oil, granular filler, and glass
                fragments brushstroked across the canvas

in 1941, the year my parents turned fourteen
        and started "dating." The War was on,
                and black stormclouds loomed on the horizon.

I have imagined it all in slow-motion—
        their two bodies coming together as one
                body exploding in rage into seeds and rain.

I was standing in front of *The Magic Mirror*.
      I was looking at a woman looking in the mirror.
            I was walking through the skin of the mirror

into the watery burial grounds of childhood.
      I felt the strokes—black, purple, yellow, red—
            raining down upon me, somehow freed

from the canvas—thick-skinned, light-filled—
      and suddenly I was summoning all the wounded
            animals inside me, totems of childhood,

and letting them go one by one—the mockingbird
      of grief, the nasty crow, the long-beaked
            hawk floating past a picture window flooded

with rain, heading for the Northwest Coast.
      Oh let the wind release me from the past
            wing by wing, bird by bird, ghost by ghost.

I was standing in front of *The Magic Mirror*.
      I was looking at a woman looking in the mirror.
            I was walking through the skin of the mirror

into the unexpected country of childhood.
      I watched my body dispersed and reunited
            somewhere else, transformed, transfigured.

Ocean of Grass

The ground was holy, but the wind was harsh
and unbroken prairie stretched for hundreds of miles
so that all she could see was an ocean of grass.

Some days she got so lonely she went outside
and nestled among the sheep, for company.
The ground was holy, but the wind was harsh

and prairie fires swept across the plains,
lighting up the country like a vast tinderbox
until all she could see was an ocean of flames.

She went three years without viewing a tree.
When her husband finally took her on a timber run
she called the ground holy and the wind harsh

and got down on her knees and wept inconsolably,
and lived in a sod hut for thirty more years
until the world dissolved in an ocean of grass.

Think of her sometimes when you pace the earth,
our mother, where she was laid to rest.
The ground was holy, but the wind was harsh
for those who drowned in an ocean of grass.

Portrait of a Writer

Keys on a battered typewriter,
        letters waiting absentmindedly
                to come together in words that will
                        save the night from a grave stillness.

Pages and pages of low-grade
        white paper, some of it blank,
                some festooned with mistakes and
                        sentenced to death in a wicker basket.

How many books has he pro-
        posed to this room? How many
                selves has he discarded while
                        the dog slept restlessly at his feet

and the moon burrowed a hole
              in the clouds? He has stared
                     at scars rivered into the desk
                            and wondered about the stranger

he has become to himself and
              others. What exile is this?
                     And who are these solitaries glow-
                            ering from photographs in the hallway,

always dropping their suitcases
              and wandering off into the un-
                     suspecting fate that awaits them?
                            They are a tribe of failures on the move ...

He is tired of this broken-
              hearted tradition of losses,
                     Lord, tired of these breaches
                            and ruptures, these promissory notes

to the dead hand of the past.
              He is tired of memories advancing
                     into the future, fanatical dust,
                            and a dispossession without grace.

This sleeplessness has lasted
              forty years in the desert.
                     He knows its delirious exile
                            and in the midst of night

he wrestles with absence
              like a mysterious stranger,
                     he strives against darkness
                            until daybreak when he can sleep.

RICHARD JACKSON

Filling in the Graves at a Cherokee Site

for John Anderson

Night walks through our days and no one notices.
We like to think of the intricate beauty of a swallow's flight,
but it is only a desperate, open mouthed search for insects.
There are three truths you have taught me here: that
our shadows will desert us for other, better objects;
that Time steps away from the clock like the song of a blind bird;
and that our maps are the empty husks of desire. So, what can
we say, then, to the greed of men that has given us
these broken pieces of sky? You might as well try
to shake the wind until it crumbles. You can
almost scrape yourself on the nails of light hammered
through the trees where some stupid men have peeled
back the eyelids of the graves, their mocking words
strewn about like the rusted cans that flake in my hands.
Each of their thousand bottles left here is filled with dark.

You have this way of taking the smoke from the sage,
cupping it into your heart and smudging the whole
universe that gathers around you. Standing among all these
open eyes, I am afraid I will dissolve like the prey
the falcon leans towards. I am here with a woman for whom
even the stars shiver and I can tell you the light around her
tastes so sweet I could believe in your world that flies
above this one. I don't know how many of my words for her
have been siphoned into these lives. We are stepping
over the mussel shells of history.

                    Now the blue
herons are trying to gather the souls that hover
just above the water. Their calls fall around us
like a blanket. And who here is not buried in another
person's heart? Everything we breathe is a gift
from the past. This late in the season even the spider
webs have disappeared. A few stars are setting
into nests below the horizon. A few words like these are
never going to shovel the terrible past into place.
We can smell the overwhelming must of these graves,
the broken wings of these souls, but we will never smell
what they dreamt. Maybe it is all right. We are filling
our lives with whatever love they've left.

                    Now the trees are going
to let their dreams fly out like bats, like herons,
like bees, like anything that lives and dies, the vapor
trail caught for a moment in the light before it disappears,
the moon starting to open its eyes with something like hope.

Reincarnation of a Lovebird

What's wrong with money is what's wrong with love;

it spurns those who need it most for someone
already rolling in it.
                    —William Matthews

Already it is snowing, the branches spattering out of darkness
in a way I imagine the nerve endings of that grasshopper did
on my sill last summer while the nightingale finished it.
Already old fears condense on the panes
with you a thousand miles or words away, my friend
recently buried, the light in my room blaring all night
the way it's done in prisons, trying to keep too much emotion
from scurrying out of the corners. There's a blind spot in
the middle of your eye, the guilt you feel for loving so fully
in the face of death, or dying in spite of love's power.
These verbs are searchlights for memories gone over the wall.

It's all we can do to embrace the distance between us
while night limps across these rooftops, while we preside
over the heart's fire sale. Outside the streetlights hook
a reluctant sky. Memory won't save everything.
That nightingale disappeared into the pyracantha bush
to flute a song we call imitation but may only be
another lie. Charlie Mingus' bass would die
into an arrangement, then reincarnate itself as a form of
love. It's time to decide if this is an elegy or a love
poem lurking behind one of the smoked glass windshields
that go up or down the street every few minutes. What we
should have said to each other waits like an insect
all winter for a false spring. The language of stars no longer brings
consolation or love. The Egyptians invented the phrase, "eat,
drink and be merry," you know the rest, but kept a skeleton
hung at dinner parties in case you tried to forget. Sometimes,
my love, the heart taps its way along sidewalks
like a blind man and muggers are gleeful on the corners.
What we need are more emergency vehicles for the soul.
We need to knock at the door of the heart's timekeeper.
The tracks I'll leave later when I go out into the purity of
snow will destroy it. The scientist's light on the atom alters
what was there. Every glass we raise we eventually have to lower.

MARK JARMAN

Fox Night

What have I done to merit that regard?
Seeing the fox, I thought of diction like that:
Merit that regard, as if the wild demanded
A formal recognition of its grace
When passing through our world. What *had* I done,
So that I thought the world, at least my family,
Should know a fox was looking back at me?
V of head and ears tilted, lean waist
Humped with a serpent's frozen listening,
It poised like the green snake on the back road
My girls and I had found one summer day,
Back when we found such things on summer days.
The snake had let us study, then urge it on
To belly-waddle sideways, s- and elbowing,
Clumsy only because we made it hurry,
Into the roadside vetch and vinca blossoms.
It had endured us with the noble patience
Of relics, like an ancient copper bracelet
Uncoiled. And yet it flicked its tongue out, testing.
But with the fox, its red fur drenched in shadows,
Only the tail-tip gathering enough streetlight
To show its whipped-up, egg-white whiteness, I
Was by myself, come out to stow some trash,
The TV muttering in the den behind me.
The fox had come to eat the fall persimmons,
The harvest of the tree in our front yard,
Acknowledged me, and turned away, of course,
And crossed the road back through a screen of oaks,
A wall that halved the sky, with chinks of starlight.

There was no one to instruct, no one to show
That happiness, though speechless, could be shared.
And so I made a comment to myself
In language that, if I'd repeated it,
Might have made my daughters look at one another
And wonder at the nature of the world.

George Herbert

Who is wise enough today to be George Herbert,
    Who though he lost his temper could remain
Tractable to a loving, patient voice?
    Washing his parishioners' feet, as the collar chafed
And softened. Writing his fastidious verses,
    Like the coffin-shaped stones of his century,
Decked with skulls and propped in churchyard corners.
    Death, a puddle of dust, drew under his door,
Like talcum powder, clinging to his shoes.
    And love, whose board he hammered with his fist,
Drew him in and offered him its meat,
    That ambiguous unambiguous word. George Herbert
Was wise enough to sit and clean his plate.

The World

The world works for us and we call it grace.
It works against us and, if we are brave,
We call it nothing and we keep our faith,
And only to ourselves we call it fate.
What makes the world work? No one seems to know.
The clouds arrange the weather, the sea goes
Deep, a black stillness seethes at the earth's core,
And somebody invents the telephone.
If we are smart, we know where we fit in.
If we are lucky, we know what to bid.

If we are good, we know a charming fib
Can do more good than harm. So we tell it.
The world was meant to operate like this.
The working of the world was ever thus.

The working of the world was ever thus.
The empty air surrounds us with its love.
A fire in the skull ignites the sun.
The skin of water opens at a touch.
And earth erupts, earth curves away, earth yields.
Someone imagines strife and someone peace.
Someone inserts the god in the machine
And someone picks him out like a poppy seed.
In every new construction of desire,
The old dissatisfactions rule the eyes.
The new moon eats the old and, slice by slice,
Rebuilds a face of luminous delight,
In which we see ourselves, at last, make sense.
It is the mirror in everything that shines.

It is the mirror in everything that shines
And makes the soul the color of the sky
And clarifies and gradually blinds
And shows the spider its enormous bride.
And we show our reluctant gratitude,
Searching the paths and runways for a spoor
Of cosmic personality, one clue,
Even the fossil light of burned-out proof.
It is enough and not enough to sketch
The human mask inside the swarming nest
And hold the face, a template, to the egg
And stamp its features on the blank of death.
Although we break rock open to find life,
We cannot stare the strangeness from the leaf.

We cannot stare the strangeness from the leaf,
And so we spin all difference on a wheel
And blur it into likeness. So we seize
The firefly and teach it human need
And mine its phosphor for cold light and call
Across the world as if it were a lawn,
Blinking awake at summer dusk. We talk
Ceaselessly to things that can't respond
Or won't respond. What are we talking for?
We're talking to coax hope and love from zero.
We're talking so the brain of the geode
Will listen like a garden heliotrope
And open its quartz flowers. We are talking
Because speech is a sun, a kind of making.

Because speech is a sun, a kind of making,
And muteness we have always found estranging,
Because even our silences are phrasing
And language is the tongue we curl for naming,
Because we want the earth to be like heaven
And heaven to be everywhere we're headed,
Because we hope our formulae, like hexes,
Will stop and speed up time at our behesting,
There is no help for us, and that's our glory.
A furious refusal to acknowledge,
Except in words, the smallness of our portion,
Pumps heart, lights brain, and conjures up a soul
From next to nothing. We know all flesh is grass.
And when the world works, we still call it grace.

BRIGIT PEGEEN KELLY

The Garden of the Trumpet Tree

Someone stuck an apple in the stone head's open mouth. A grave insult. But I did not take it out. Maybe a boy did, running through the gardens at night, his pockets full of fruit. Or maybe it was a ghost bored with its lot. It does not matter. Today I stood for the first time before the bodiless head and the strange flowering tree it guards. I tried not to laugh. I tried not to laugh. The head on its post stood no taller than I. The head that had bullied me for so long, the great stone head that only darkness had been able to silence, bagging it each night with a soft cloth sack the way the heads of those to be hanged are bagged, made no sound. I tried not to think: This is your just dessert: Pillar of pride, pilloried. I touched with both hands the eyes of the head the way a blind person might. They were huge and swollen like the eyes of the deaf composer, or the eyes of the mad poet whose wife so rarely possessed the pleasure of his company because he spent his days in paradise. I touched with one finger the warm fruit. Against the pale cast of the stone the apple shone uncommonly bright, and behind it the thousand and thousand blossoms of the trumpet tree shone uncommonly bright. The fruit and the blossoms were the same scarlet color and I could see for the first time in the yellow morning light the curious tree for what it was. Not a tree in flower, as I had so long thought, but a flowerless tree coupled with a blossoming trumpet vine. The vine had grown snakelike up and around the trunk, had grown so large it had half-strangled the small tree, crawling over every branch and shoot, until the vine and the tree were almost indistinguishable, green flesh and charred wood, flowers and rot, a new creation, a trumpet tree, tree out of time, the smoldering center of some medieval dream. The flowers swam forward in the light, each scarlet bloom so intricate and unlikely—downswung, fluted, narrower than the narrowest piping, forked with yellow silk—it looked as if it had been sewn by hand, the whole improbable tree looked as if it had been worked with impossible patience by a woman's pale hands. Bees stumbled in and out, shaking the flowers. From nowhere a hummingbird appeared, iridescent, green, flipping its shining tail, creature more fish than bird, more insect than fish, spinning and sipping. To nowhere it returned.

The garden stood perfectly still. And for a moment in that garden it seemed as if sound and silence were the same thing, for a moment it seemed as if the thousand and thousand tiny trumpets were blowing a thousand and thousand shining notes, blown glass notes, the liquid substance of the air itself, glass and fire, the morning flushed to perfect fullness. I stood for a long time. I breathed in the strange perfume of those scentless flowers. I thought of how the crow would come in an hour or two and plant his dusty feet on the carved head and pluck the fruit apart piece by sweetened piece. I looked at the blossoming tree. I looked at the stone head. I touched the warm fruit. And I took the apple out. There was no sound. It was like closing the eyes of the dead.

The Orchard

I saw the dog in a dream. Huge white
Boney creature. Big as a horse. At first
I thought it was a horse. It was feeding
On apples. As a horse might. Though not
With a horse's patience. For it was starving.
Its hipbones were empty bowls. The horse
Wolfed down the apples. Without breathing.
Without looking up. The way a dog wolfs
Down meat. And then it growled. And I saw
That the horse *was* a dog. But the apples
Were still apples. Windfall from the orchard
Above the lake. Pitiful place. The few trees
There grow black and yellow. And the thin grasses
Stagger down to the abandoned north field,
Which floods in winter and then freezes—
Blue ground, marbled with red and white,
Like a slab of meat—and when the far deer
Cross over it, and the birds cross over it,
It is as if the memories held within
The meat were rising from it. Or it is like
Flies crawling. . . . I saw the dog in a dream.
And then, days later, just before dawn,
I climbed to the orchard. And there he was.
The same dog. Chewing on a dead doe.

And it was troubling. I thought I might
Still be dreaming—as was the case
When for many months I could not sleep
And I lost the power to tell the figures
In my dreams from those we call real.
I thought the scene might have been staged
For me. By my mind. Or by someone
Who could read my mind. Someone
Who was having a good laugh
At my expense. Or testing me
In some way I could not understand.
Beneath the black and yellow trees,
The dog's skin seemed abnormally white.
And the blood on his broad muzzle shone
Like wet paint. I closed my eyes. Not because
The ghostly creature was now biting
At the neck of the doe, the way
Those dark creatures who drink blood
And live forever do—since the river
Of blood flows forever, the streams
Of an eternal city, forever running,
Forever carrying their musky loads
Of blooming and expiring words
And figures, a thousand thousand
Yellow lights forever flickering off
And on in the black liquid, gold,
Sweet liquid, fallen—I closed my eyes.
Not out of distaste. But to see if the dog
Would disappear, the way the mist
Had thinned and vanished as I climbed
The hill. But the dog was still there
When I opened them. Staring straight at me.
He lifted his large paw. Placed it
On the doe's chest, and started to rip
At her belly. There was the sound
Of cloth tearing. And what did I do?
I picked up an apple. I wanted to see

If the dog—when the apple struck his side
And he fell—would rise in a second form,
And then a third. As dream figures do.
Dog. To horse. To man. Or I wanted to see
If the apple would pass through the dog
As through a ghost. And if the dog
Like the best of ghosts would turn
And instruct me in my confusion.
Or I wanted to bring the scene down
To size. The way the bright lights
That clank on at the end of the play
Show the mad king to be nothing
But a skinny man holding a costume
Of cloth and paste. I wanted the dog
To be just a stray, gnawing on a bone.
Or maybe I wanted none of these things.
Maybe I wanted what the hunter
Wanted when he struck the doe. Maybe
I wanted a piece of the dog's feasting,
The way the hunter wanted a piece
Of the doe's improbable swiftness.
The gun fires. The smell of burnt powder
Sprays up. A knotted string of birds
Unspools across the white sky. And deep
In running blood a man thrusts his hands.
I wanted something. But I did not throw
The apple. It was a small fruit. The size
Of a child's hand. Black and yellow. Riddled
With worms and misshapen. I put my teeth
To it. I took a bite. Chill flesh. Rank.
The dog kept feeding. I was not bothered
By the blood. The last of the red leaves
Scudded about me. And a few drops fell
From the dark sky. There is blood
Everywhere. The trees shed it. The sky.
There is no end. And isn't it pretty?
We say. Isn't it pretty? Amn't I?
Isn't the starving dog? Isn't the doe?

Even half-eaten? She gave her body
To the dog. The fallen body looked
So heavy. It looked like it weighed
Ten thousand pounds. More than the lake
Or the frozen field. The doe dreamed
Of her death and it came to pass.
She courted the hunter and he shot her.
And she fell. And then the man stood
Over her. A white shadow. Laughing.
And then the dog stood over her. A black
Shadow. Laughing. And the dog came close.
The way a lover might. Had the doe
Been human. And he put his mouth to her.
As a lover might. Had he been human.
And her chastened flesh was a chalice.
And she was peaceful. And there was bliss
In this. And some horror. Around her
The thorns shone black and yellow.
And the fallen fruit lay black and yellow.
And black and yellow are the colors
Of the orchard's hive when it masses
And the queen in a fiery constellation
Is carried to new quarters. The wind
Stirred in the orchard. The dog bit
Into the doe's chest. And the apple
In my hand, against my lips, small,
Misshapen, the size of a child's fist,
Full of worms, turned suddenly warm
And soft. And it was as if, on that hill,
While the dog fed and the lake lay
Frozen, I was holding in my hand,
Against my lips, not a piece of fruit,
Not a piece of bitter, half-eaten fruit,
But the still warm and almost beating
Heart of some holy being—just lifted
From the dead body. And the heart
Was heavy. And wet. And it smelled
As it would smell forever. Of myrrh.
And burning blood. And gold.

GALWAY KINNELL

How Could She Not

for Jane Kenyon (1947–1995)

It is a day after many days of storms.
Having been washed and washed, the air glitters;
small heaped cumuli are blowing across the sky;
a shower, its parallel streaks visible
against the firs, douses the crocuses.
We knew it would happen one day this week.
Now, when I hear that she has died,
from the open door I look across at New Hampshire:
There, too, the sun is bright and clouds
make their shadowy ways along the horizon,
and it occurs to me: How could it not have been today?
In another room, Kiri Te Kanawa is singing
the *Laudate Dominum* of Mozart, faintly,
as if far in the past, as if just barely hearable
above the rattle of an ancient mowing machine
which is drawing its cutter bar's little
reciprocating triangles through the timothy
to stalks being made to lie down in the sunshine.

Did she wake, in the dark of early this morning,
almost used up by a year of pain and despair
remitted now and then by hope
that had an inner-taste of lead? Did she glimpse,
in first light, the world as she loved it
and see that, now, it would not be wrong for her to die
and that she could leave her beloved in a day like paradise?
Did her hold loosen a little, near sunrise?

Having these last days spoken her whole heart
to him, who spoke his whole heart to her,
might she not have felt that now, in the silence,
he would not feel any word was missing?
When full daylight came, how could she not
have slipped into a spell, with him next to her,
his arms still holding her, as they had done,
it may have seemed, all her life?
How could her cheek not press a moment to his cheek,
which presses itself to hers from now on?
How could she not rise and go, with sunlight
at the window, beloved arms around her, and the sound,
fading, deepening, hard to say, of a single-engine
plane in the distance no one else hears?

Why Regret?

Didn't you like the way the ants help
the peony globes open by eating off the glue?
Weren't you cheered to see the ironworkers
sitting on an I-beam dangling from a cable,
in a row, like starlings, eating lunch, maybe
baloney on white with fluorescent mustard?
Wasn't it a revelation to swim all the way
from the estuary, to the river, the kill,
the pirle, the run, the brook, the beck,
the sike gone dry, to the shock of a spring?
Didn't you almost shiver to hear the book lice
rustling their sexual dissonance inside the old
Webster's New International, perhaps having
just eaten out of it izle, xyster, and thalassacon?
What did you imagine lay in store anyway
at the end of a world where the sub-substance is
muck, birdlime, slime, mucus, gleet, ooze?
What could the joke have been that night when even
at the tables out of earshot the people were laughing?

Don't worry about becoming emaciated—think of the wren
and how little flesh is needed to make a song.
Didn't it seem somehow familiar when the nymph
split open and the mayfly struggled free
and flew and perched and then its own back
split open and the imago, the true adult,
slowly somersaulted out backwards and
took flight toward the swarm, mouth parts vestigial,
alimentary canal unfit to digest food,
a day or hour left to find the desired one?
Or when Casanova threw the linguine in squid ink
out the window, telling his startled companion,
"The perfected lover does not eat"?
As a child didn't you find it calming to think
of the pinworms as some kind of tiny batons
giving the cadence to the squeezes and releases
around the downward march of debris?
Didn't you once glimpse what seemed your own
inner blazonry in the monarchs, veering
and gliding, in desire, in the middle air?
Weren't you reassured at the thought that these
hinged beings might navigate their way to Mexico
by the flair of the dead bodies of ancestors
who fell in this same migration a year ago?
Isn't it worth missing whatever joy
you might have dreamed, to wake in the night and find
you and your beloved are holding hands in your sleep?

YUSEF KOMUNYAKAA

Eclogue at Twilight

The three wrestle in the grass
five or ten minutes, shaking blooms
& winged seeds to the ground.
The lioness lays a heavy paw on the jackal's chest,
almost motherly. His mate
backs off a few yards. Eyeball
to eyeball, they face each other
before she bites into his belly
& tugs out the ropy entrails
like loops of wet gauze.
Time stops. She'd moved
through the tall yellow sage
as they copulated,
stood only a few feet
away, enveloped in the scent
that drew them together.
When they first saw her
there, they couldn't stop.
Is this how panic & cunning
seethe into the bloodstream?
Without the power to forgive,
locked in ritual, the fight
began before they uncoupled.
A vulture, out of the frame,
draws an unbroken spiral
against the plains & sky.
Black quills scribble
slow as the swing of a hypnotist's
gold chain. For a moment, it seems
she's snuggling up to the jackal.

Maybe the wild aroma of sex
plagues the yellow grass.
A drizzle adds its music
to the background,
& a chorus of young girls
chants from across the hills.
For a man who stumbles
on this scene, with Hegel
& awe in his head, he can't
say if his mouth is opened
by the same cry & song.

Kosmos

Walt, you shanghaied me to this
oak, as every blood-tipped leaf
soliloquized "Strange Fruit"
like the octoroon in New Orleans

who showed you how passion
ignited dogwood, how it rose
from inside the singing sap.
You heard primordial notes

murmur up from the Mississippi,
a clank of chains among the green
ithyphallic totems, betting your heart
could run vistas with Crazy Horse

& runaway slaves. Sunset dock
to whorehouse, temple to hovel,
your lines traversed America's
white space, driven by a train whistle.

❧

Believing you could be three places
at once, you held the gatekeeper's daughter,
lured by the hard eyes of his son,
on a voyage in your head

to a face cut into Mount Rushmore.
You knew the curse in sperm
& egg, but had faith in the soil,
that it would work itself out

in generations, springs piercing bedrock.
Love pushed through jailhouses, into bedrooms
of presidents & horse thieves,
oil sucked into machines in sweatshops

& factories. I followed from my hometown
where bedding an oak is bread on the table;
where your books, as if flesh, were locked
in a glass case behind the check-out desk.

❧

Wind-jostled foliage—a scherzo,
a bellydancer adorned in bells.
A mulatto moon halved into yesterday
& tomorrow, some balustrade

full-bloomed. But you taught home
was wherever my feet took me,
birdsong over stockyards or Orient,
fused by handshake & blood.

Seed & testament, naked
among fire-nudged thistle,
from the Rockies to below
sea level, to the steamy bayous,

I traipsed your footpath.
Falsehoods big as stumbling blocks
in the mind, lay across the road,
beside a watery swoon.

≉

I'm back with the old folk
who speak your glossolalia of pure
sense unfolding one hundred years.
Unlocked chemistry, we're tied to sex,

spectral flower twisted out of
filigreed language & taboo
stubborn as crabgrass. You slept
nude under god-hewn eyes & ears.

Laughter in trees near a canebrake,
I know that song. Old hippie,
before Selma & People's Park,
your democratic nights a vortex

of waterlilies. The skin's cage
opened, but you were locked inside
your exotic Ethiopia. Everything
sprung back like birds after a shot.

Nude Interrogation

Did you kill anyone over there? Angelica shifts her gaze from the Janis Joplin
poster to the Jimi Hendrix, lifting the pale muslin blouse over her head. The
blacklight deepens the blues when the needle drops into the first groove of "All
Along the Watchtower." I don't want to look at the floor. *Did you kill anyone?*
Did you dig a hole, crawl inside, and wait for your target? Her miniskirt drops
into a rainbow at her feet. Sandalwood incense hangs a slow comet of per-
fume over the room. I shake my head. She unhooks her bra and flings it
against a bookcase made of plywood and cinderblocks. *Did you use an M-16,*

a handgrenade, a bayonet, or your own two strong hands, both thumbs pressed against that little bird in the throat? She stands with her left thumb hooked into the elastic of her sky-blue panties. When she flicks off the blacklight, snowy hills rush up to the windows. *Did you kill anyone over there? Are you right-handed or left-handed? Did you drop your gun afterwards? Did you kneel beside the corpse and turn it over?* She's nude against the falling snow. *Yes.* The record spins like a bull's-eye on the far wall of Xanadu. *Yes,* I say. *I was scared of the silence. The night was too big. And afterwards, I couldn't stop looking up at the sky.*

The Song Thief

Up there
in that diorama of morning
light through springtime branches,
how many feathered lifetimes
sifted down through green
leaves, how many wars sprung up
& ended before the cowbird figured out
laws of gravity in Cloudcuckooland,
before the songbird's egg
was nudged from its nest?
Maybe a flock followed a herd
of heifers across a pasture,
pecking wildflower seed
from fresh dung
when the first urge of switcheroo
flashed in their dirt-colored heads.
What nature of creature comforts
taught the unsung cells this art,
this shell game of odds
& percentages in the serpent's leafy
Babylon? Only the cowbird's mating song
fills the air until their young
are ravenous as five
of the seven deadly sins
woven into one.

LI-YOUNG LEE

The Hammock

When I lay my head in my mother's lap
I think how day hides the stars,
the way I lay hidden once, waiting
inside my mother's laughter. And I remember
how she carried me on her back
between home and the kindergarten,
once each morning and once each afternoon.
I don't know what my mother's thinking.

When my son lays his head in my lap, I worry
his lips, swollen with his father's kisses,
won't keep his father's worries from becoming
his. I think, *Dear God*, and remember
there are stars we haven't heard from yet
they have so far to arrive. *Amen*,
I think, and I feel almost comforted.
I've no idea what my child is thinking.

Between two unknowns, I live my life.
And what's it like? Between my mother's hopes,
older than me by coming before me,
and my child's wishes, older than me
by outliving me, what's it like?
Is it a door, and good-bye on either side?
Is it a window, and eternity on either side?
Yes, Yes, and a little singing between two great rests.

The Lily

As for the lily, who knows what we face
isn't the laughter of one who went

while the time was green for going, or a voice
one room ahead of our own dreaming, and we die

in the perfect wake of each day's spending
back—or is it forward? Who can tell? Anyway,

away, as prow and the surrendered foam
go on forgetting, our very looking the light

feasting on the light. As for hunger,
each must cross to a body as yet unnamed.

Who needs a heart unless it's one we share
with a many-windowed sea? A heart,

and not the dark it moves through, not the waves
it births, but, visited by blood, unoccupied,

is the very wheel installing day, the well
from which paired hands set out, happy
to undress a terrible and abundant yes.

PHILLIS LEVIN

Cumulus

They, too, labor,
And if we envy them we should remember
How brief their stay in the ether is.

Unfolding without reason, like forgiveness,
Or summoning
Themselves at the wind's bidding, they flee.

We do not know where they go, we go
As carelessly, as helplessly, finally
Too full of time.

But we are true
To ourselves so rarely, while they are always
Open to darkness, squandering light.

A floating prison, a dream-balloon,
The setting sun's
Chameleon, or the sliding screen of the moon—

When nothing else contains us we turn to them,
And all we ever gather appears
Less tangible.

Part

Of something, separate, not
Whole; a role, something to play
While one is separate or parting;

Also a piece, a section, as in
Part of me is here, part of me
Is missing; an essential portion,

Something falling to someone
In division; a particular voice
Or instrument (also the score

For it), or line of music;
The line where the hair
Is parted. A verb: to break

Or suffer the breaking of,
Become detached,
Broken; to go from, leave,

Take from, sever, as in
Lord, part me from him,
I cannot bear to ever

A Portrait

It was getting dark, and all the while
Something in you was coming forward,
The way a mountain appears to loom
At the end of day. We were talking

About myriad things as dusk dissolved
The table between us, where a bottle
Of wine floated in summer's aura.
Then the light changed, your profile

Sharpened, and suddenly I saw
A side of you that could kill.
Calmly I sat, watching something
That all along had been hiding

In the background, under your shyness,
Under your stillness. Your shoulders,
Broad enough to hold years of silence,
Bore no weapon, but surely your hands

Had carried one, reluctantly, securely.
And your arms folded before me
Posed an enormous question
Forbidding any answer.

PHILIP LEVINE

"He Would Never Use One Word Where None Would Do"

If you said, "Nice day," he would look up
at the three clouds riding overhead,
nod at each, and go back to doing what-
ever he was doing or not doing.
If you asked for a smoke or a light,
he'd hand you whatever he found
in his pockets: a jack knife, a hankie—
usually unsoiled—a dollar bill,
a subway token. Once he gave me
half the sandwich he was eating
at the little outdoor restaurant
on Laguardia Place. I remember
a single sparrow was perched on the back
of his chair, and when he held out
a piece of bread on his open palm,
the bird snatched it up and went back to
its place without even a thank you,
one hard eye staring at my bad eye
as though I were next. That was in May
of '97, spring had come late,
but the sun warmed both of us for hours
while silence prevailed, if you can call
the blaring of taxi horns and the trucks
fighting for parking and the kids on skates
streaming past silence. My friend Frankie
was such a comfort to me that year,
the year of the crisis. He would turn
up his great dark head just going gray
until his eyes met mine, and that was all
I needed to go on talking nonsense

as he sat patiently waiting me out,
the bird staring over his shoulder.
"Silence is silver," my Zaydee had said,
getting it wrong and right, just as he said,
"Water is thicker than blood," thinking
this made him a real American.
Frankie was already American
being half German, half Indian.
Fact is silence is the perfect water:
unlike rain it falls from no clouds
to wash our minds, to ease our tired eyes,
to give heart to the thin blades of grass
fighting through the concrete for even air
dirtied by our endless stream of words.

If You Are Here

Two women walk side by side at dawn
along the canal bank. July, '96.
The sun has cleared the eastern mountains.
The tall woman's your sister, the other

your second wife. They have a common bond
you thought was you, but it's your children,
the one saved, the one lost. Your sister stops
to peer down into the running waters

as though she'd caught a hint of something
moving beneath the surface. Since you died
she has these moments when a dark shape
like a shadowed cloud under water

suggests a presence she can't explain.
Your widow stands waiting in silence:
she's seen this before, she's even known
something similar, usually at night

when she is sure she hears a car stop
in the drive and throws on her old robe
to go to the door to welcome . . . Who?
Or what? Let's go back to the dawn walk.

A cool wind is blowing down the valley
suggesting rain, so rare in summer.
The two women, who have been kneeling,
rise as one until your sister loses

her balance a moment and reaches out
to take the offered hand of your wife
to steady herself. In the swift water
another cloud shape darkens into being,

but now they both turn their gaze upward
toward the sky turning pale blue at last,
the familiar blue that separates them
from nothing, that simply rises higher

toward another perfect blue, also
unstained, cool, and utterly silent.
If you are anywhere you are here
with these two. If death were not death

you could be the dark cloud under water
absorbing everything like blood in milk,
you would tear in their throats like a sob,
you would be you, writing these final words.

Keats in California

The wisteria has come and gone, the plum trees
have burned like candles in the cup of earth,
the almond has shed its pure blossoms
in a soft ring around the trunk. Iris,
rose, tulip, hillsides of poppy and lupin,

gorse, wild mustard, California is blazing
in the foolish winds of April. I have been
reading Keats—the poems, the letters, the life—
for the first time in my 69th year, and I
have been watching television after dinner
as though it could bring me some obscure,
distant sign of hope. This morning I rose
late to the soft light off the eucalyptus
and the overbearing odor of orange blossoms.
The trees will give another year. They are giving.
The few, petty clouds will blow away
before noon, and we will have sunshine
without fault, china blue skies, and the bees
gathering to splatter their little honey dots
on my windshield. If I drive to the foothills
I can see fields of wildflowers on fire until
I have to look away from so much life.
I could ask myself, Have I made a Soul
today, have I sucked at the teat of the Heart
flooded with the experience of a world like ours?
Have I become a man one more time? At twenty
it made sense. I put down *The Collected Poems*,
left the reserve room of the Wayne library
to wander the streets of Detroit under a gray
soiled sky. It was spring there too, and the bells
rang at noon. The out-patients from Harper
waited timidly under the great stone cross
of the Presbyterian church for the trolley
on Woodward Avenue, their pinched faces flushed
with terror. The black tower tilted in the wind
as though it too were coming down. It made sense.
Before dark I'll feel the lassitude enter
first my arms and legs and spread like water
toward the deep organs. I'll lie on my bed
hearing the quail bark as they scurry from
cover to cover in their restless searching
after sustenance. This place can break your heart.

Pasadena Elegy

We met for the final time in the L.A. airport.
He'd flown down from Berkeley with a friend;
I'd driven alone from Fresno in a borrowed car.
Why was I so small, he wanted to know.
He'd told the friend I was huge and powerful.
Then he had his first drink, a martini,
before ten A.M. followed immediately
by another, and we hadn't yet left the airport.
"Empson taught me how to manage my drinking.
You fill a carafe each morning, and
when that's gone you're done." "How large a carafe?"
I asked. "One liter and no more!" A brilliance
I loved was killing itself methodically
before my eyes. I could see death in the lines
slashing his mouth, in the way he flung one arm
out as he spoke, the trembling cigarette held away
from his body. Three hours later I heard him read
the great new work to a huge, silent audience
breathing uneasily in the dark. 1959. Spring came
early to California, the streets were littered
with violet garbage from the jacarandas. We drove
after drinks to Forest Lawn where a man white-washed
a ghostly version of Michelangelo's David. In Pasadena
a cop shoved a gun into the tanned belly of a kid
who'd stepped from a car, his hands above his head,
his pale eyes enormous. The day darkened
into dusk and then night. The friend slept
on the hotel bed while he paced. "The mind dies
in these misunderstandings," he said, "these places.
The mind freezes." He sent me for a second bottle,
but by this time everything was closed, and I
got lost and wandered the side streets
looking for the Green Hotel, which existed although
the only person out that late told me
it had been torn down years before. She was old
—not as old as I am now—, a Mexican domestic
I spoke to in Spanish while we stood side by side

eyeing each other, waiting for the light
to change on the empty boulevard as the sky
slowly burned from black to gray. The woman
trudged ahead of me, head down, purposeful,
an athletic bag slung over one shoulder, the other
dipping into the dawn wind as the air parted to get
her back to work, and I followed with nothing
planned for the merciless day waiting ahead.

The Unknowable

Practicing his horn on the Williamsburg Bridge
hour after hour, "woodshedding" the musicians
called it, but his woodshed was the world.

The enormous tone he borrowed from Hawkins
that could fill a club to overflowing
blown into tatters by the sea winds.

Taught him humility, which he carries
with him at all times, not an amulet
against the powers of animals that mean

him no good or the lures of the marketplace.
No, a quality of the gaze downward
on the streets of Brooklyn or Manhattan.

Hold his hand and you'll see it, hold his eyes
in yours and you'll hear the winds singing
through the cables of the bridge that was his home,

singing through his breath—no rarer than your own—
through his became the music of the world
thirty years ago. Today I ask myself

how he knew the time had come to become
the voice of the air and no more, how he
decided the time had come for silence,

for the world to speak any way it could?
He doesn't answer. No doubt he finds
the question pompous. He plays for money.

The years pass, and like the rest of us
he ages, his hair and beard whiten, the great
shoulders narrow. He is merely a man—

after all—a man who stared for years
into the breathy, unknowable voice
of silence and captured the music.

LARRY LEVIS

Anastasia & Sandman

The brow of a horse in that moment when
The horse is drinking water so deeply from a trough
It seems to inhale the water, is holy.

I refuse to explain.

When the horse had gone the water in the trough,
All through the empty summer,

Went on reflecting clouds & stars.

The horse cropping grass in a field,
And the fly buzzing around its eyes, are more real
Than the mist in one corner of the field.

Or the angel hidden in the mist, for that matter.

Members of the Committee on the Ineffable,
Let me illustrate this with a story, & ask you all
To rest your heads on the table, cushioned,
If you wish, in your hands, &, if you want,
Comforted by a small carton of milk
To drink from, as you once did, long ago,
When there was only a curriculum of beach grass,
When the University of Flies was only a distant humming.

In Romania, after the war, Stalin confiscated
The horses that had been used to work the fields.
"You won't need horses now," Stalin said, cupping
His hand to his ear, "Can't you hear the tractors
Coming in the distance? I hear them already."

The crowd in the Callea Victoria listened closely
But no one heard anything. In the distance
There was only the faint glow of a few clouds.
And the horses were led into boxcars & emerged
As the dimly remembered meals of flesh
That fed the starving Poles
During that famine, & part of the next one—
In which even words grew thin & transparent
Like the pale wings of ants that flew
Out of the oldest houses, & slowly
What had been real in words began to be replaced
By what was not real, by the not exactly real.
"Well, not exactly, but . . ." became the preferred
Administrative phrasing so that the man
Standing with his hat in his hands would not guess
That the phrasing of a few words had already swept
The earth from beneath his feet. "That horse I had,
He was more real than any angel,
The housefly, when I had a house, was real too,"
Is what the man thought.
Yet it wasn't more than a few months
Before the man began to wonder, talking
To himself out loud before the others,
"Was the horse real? Was the house real?"
An angel flew in and out of the high window
In the factory where the man worked, his hands
Numb with cold. He hated the window & the light
Entering the window & he hated the angel.
Because the angel could not be carved into meat
Or dumped into the ossuary & become part
Of the landfill at the edge of town,
It therefore could not acquire a soul,
And resembled in significance nothing more
Than a light summer dress when the body has gone.

The man survived because, after a while,
He shut up about it.

Stalin had a deep understanding of the *kulaks*,
Their sense of marginalization & belief in the land;

That is why he killed them all.

Members of the Committee on Solitude, consider
Our own impoverishment & the progress of that famine,
In which, now, it is becoming impossible
To feel anything when we contemplate the burial,
Alive in a two-hour period, of hundreds of people.
Who were not clichés, who did not know they would be
The illegible blank of the past that lives in each
Of us, even in some guy watering his lawn

On a summer night. Consider

The death of Stalin & the slow, uninterrupted
Evolution of the horse, a species no one,
Not even Stalin, could extinguish, almost as if
What could not be altered was something
Noble in the look of its face, something

Incapable of treachery.

Then imagine, in your planning proposals,
The exact moment in the future when an angel
Might alight & crawl like a fly into the ear of a horse,
And then, eventually, into the brain of a horse,
And imagine further that the angel in the brain
Of this horse is, for the horse cropping grass
In the field, largely irrelevant, a mist in the corner
Of the field, something that disappears,
The horse thinks, when weight is passed through it,
Something that will not even carry the weight
Of its own father
On its back, the horse decides, & so demonstrates
This by swishing at a fly with its tail, by continuing
To graze as the dusk comes on & almost until it is night.

Old contrivers, daydreamers, walking chemistry sets,
Exhausted chimneysweeps of the spaces
Between words, where the Holy Ghost tastes just
Like the dust it is made of,
Let's tear up our lecture notes & throw them out
The window.
Let's do it right now before wisdom descends upon us
Like a spiderweb over a burned-out theater marquee,
Because what's the use?
I keep going to meetings where no one's there,
And contributing to the discussion;
And besides, behind the angel hissing in its mist
Is a gate that leads only into another field,
Another outcropping of stones & withered grass, where
A horse named Sandman & a horse named Anastasia
Used to stand at the fence & watch the traffic pass.
Where there were outdoor concerts once, in summer,
Under the missing & innumerable stars.

In 1967

Some called it the Summer of Love; & although the clustered,
Motionless leaves that overhung the streets looked the same
As ever, the same as they did every summer, in 1967,
Anybody with three dollars could have a vision.
And who wouldn't want to know what it felt like to be
A cedar waxwing landing with a flutter of gray wings
In a spruce tree, & then disappearing into it,
For only three dollars? And now I know; its flight is ecstasy.
No matter how I look at it, I also now know that
The short life of a cedar waxwing is more pure pleasure
Than anyone alive can still be sane, & bear.
And remember, a cedar waxwing doesn't mean a thing,
Qua cedar or *qua* waxwing, nor could it have earned
That kind of pleasure by working to become a better
Cedar waxwing. They're all the same.

Show me a bad cedar waxwing, for example, & I mean
A really morally corrupted cedar waxwing, & you'll commend
The cage they have reserved for you, resembling heaven.

Some people spent their lives then, having visions.
But in my case, the morning after I dropped mescaline
I had to spray Johnson grass in a vineyard of Thompson Seedless
My father owned—& so, still feeling the holiness of all things
Living, holding the spray gun in one hand & driving with the other,
The tractor pulling the spray rig & its sputtering motor—
Row after row, I sprayed each weed I found
That looked enough like Johnson grass, a thing alive that's good
For nothing at all, with a mixture of malathion & diesel fuel,
And said to each tall weed, as I coated it with a lethal mist,
Dominus vobiscum, &, sometimes, *mea culpa*, until
It seemed boring to apologize to weeds, & insincere as well.
For in a day or so, no more than that, the weeds would turn
Disgusting hues of yellowish orange & wither away. I still felt
The bird's flight in my body when I thought about it, the wing ache,
Lifting heaven, locating itself somewhere just above my slumped
Shoulders, & part of me taking wing. I'd feel it at odd moments
After that on those long days I spent shoveling vines, driving trucks
And tractors, helping swamp fruit out of one orchard
Or another, but as the summer went on, I felt it less & less.
As the summer went on, some were drafted, some enlisted
In a generation that would not stop falling, a generation
Of leaves sticking to body bags, & when they turned them
Over, they floated back to us on television, even then,
In the Summer of Love, in 1967,
When riot police waited beyond the doors of perception,
And the best thing one could do was get arrested.

The Oldest Living Things in L.A.

At Wilshire & Santa Monica I saw an opossum
Trying to cross the street. It was late, the street
Was brightly lit, the opossum would take
A few steps forward, then back away from the breath
Of moving traffic. People coming out of the bars
Would approach, as if to help it somehow.
It would lift its black lips & show them
The reddened gums, the long rows of incisors,
Teeth that went all the way back beyond
The flames of Troy & Carthage, beyond sheep
Grazing rock-strewn hills, fragments of ruins
In the grass at San Vitale. It would back away
Delicately & smoothly, stepping carefully
As it always had. It could mangle someone's hand
In twenty seconds. Mangle it for good. It could
Sever it completely from the wrist in forty.
There was nothing to be done for it. Someone
Or other probably called the LAPD, who then
Called Animal Control, who woke a driver, who
Then dressed in mailed gloves, the kind of thing
Small knights once wore into battle, who gathered
Together his pole with a noose on the end,
A light steel net to snare it with, someone who hoped
The thing would have vanished by the time he got there.

The Two Trees

My name in Latin is light to carry & victorious.
I'd read late in the library, then
Walk out past the stacks, rows, aisles

Of books, where the memoirs of battles slowly gave way
To case histories of molestation & abuse.

The black windows looked out onto the black lawn.

Friends, in the middle of this life, I was embraced
By failure. It clung to me & did not let go.
When I ran, brother limitation raced

Beside me like a shadow. Have you never
Felt like this, everyone you know,

Turning, the more they talked, into . . .

Acquaintances? So many strong opinions!

And when I tried to speak—
Someone always interrupting. My head ached.
And I would walk home in the blackness of winter.

I still had two friends, but they were trees.
One was a box elder, the other a horse chestnut.

I used to stop on my way home & talk to each

Of them. The three of us lived in Utah then, though
We never learned why, me, *acer negundo*, & the other
One, whose name I can never remember.

"Everything I have done has come to nothing.
It is not even worth mocking," I would tell them,
And then I would look up into their limbs & see
How they were covered in ice. "You do not even
Have a car any*more*," one of them would answer.

All their limbs glistening above me,
No light was as cold or clear.

I got over it, but I was never the same,

Hearing the snow change to rain & the wind swirl,
And the gull's cry, that it could not fly out of.

In time, in a few months, I could walk beneath
Both trees without bothering to look up
Anymore, neither at the one

Whose leaves & trunk were being slowly colonized by
Birds again, nor at the other, sleepier, more slender

One, that seemed frail, but was really

Oblivious to everything. Simply oblivious to it,
With the pale leaves climbing one side of it,
An obscure sheen in them,

And the other side, for some reason, black, bare,
The same, almost irresistible, carved indifference

In the shape of its limbs

As if someone's cries for help
Had been muffled by them once, concealed there,

Her white flesh just underneath the slowly peeling bark

—while the joggers swerved around me & I stared—

Still tempting me to step in, find her,

And possess her completely.

THOMAS LUX

From Gradeschool Window
Watching Local Bookie Arrested

They led him from his candy store in cuffs, the cops
whose sons played ball with his, for whose teams
his numbers' money bought caps and suits.
In *his* suit once, at the cleaners: two grand,
in a roll, wrapped in rubberbands.
My father and my father's friends bet a buck
or half every day on their lucky digits.
Once, hitting it meant a washing machine,
a dryer, and an orange rug, which made my mother happy,
some. They hauled him out,
to a bigger town nearby—over a mountain,
across a river. He did his time,
90 days, and when released
(it was his third offence)
he never took a bet again
until some decades later
in the black black belly of tumors
when the Dr. told him: The 8 horse, Quicksand,
(out of Leadmine, sired by Tub of Dust)
in the 4th at Aqueduct,
going off at 33-1, don't
bet on him, don't bet on that dead horse.

The Man into Whose Yard You Should Not Hit Your Ball

each day mowed
and mowed his lawn, his dry quarter acre,
the machine slicing a wisp
from each blade's tip. Dust-storms rose
around the roar: 6 P.M., every day,
spring, summer, fall. If he could mow
the snow he would.
On one side, his neighbors the cows
turned their backs to him
and did what they do to the grass.
Where he worked, I don't know
but it sets his jaw to: tight.
His wife a cipher, shoebox tissue,
a shattered apron. As if
into her head he drove a wedge of shale.
Years later his daughter goes to jail.
Mow, mow, mow his lawn
gently down a decade's summers.
On his other side lived mine and me,
across a narrow pasture, often fallow;
a field of flyballs, the best part of childhood
and baseball, but one could not cross his line
and if it did,
as one did in 1956
and another in 1958
it came back coleslaw—his lawnmower
ate it up, happy
to cut something, no matter
what the manual said
about foreign objects,
stones, or sticks.

Marine Snow at Mid-Depths and Down

As you descend, slowly, falling faster past
you, this snow,
ghostly, some flakes bio-
luminescent (you plunge
and this lit snow doesn't land
at your feet but keeps falling below
you): single-cell plant chains, shreds
of zooplankton's mucus foodtraps, dust motes,
fishy fecal pellets, radioactive fallout, soot,
sandgrains, pollen . . . And inside
these jagged falling islands
live more micro-lives
which feed creatures
on the way down
and all the way down. And you, a human,
in your sinking isolation
booth, you go down, too,
through this food-snow,
these shards, blown-off
bits of planet,
its flora
and flesh, you
slip straight down, unreeled,
until the bottom's oozy silt, the sucking
baby-soft muck
welcomes you
to the deep sea's bed,
a million anvils per square inch
pressing on your skull.
How silent here, how much life,
no place deeper on earth,
nor with more width.

Plague Victims Catapulted over Walls into Besieged City

Early germ
warfare. The dead
hurled this way turn like wheels
in the sky. Look: there goes
Larry the Shoemaker, barefoot, over the wall,
and Mary Sausage Stuffer, see how she flies,
and the Hatter twins, both at once, soar
over the parapet, little Tommy's elbow bent
as if in a salute,
and his sister, Mathilde, she follows him,
arms outstretched, through the air,
just as she did
on earth.

CAMPBELL MCGRATH

A Dove

If May is the month of the mockingbird, September is the season of the dove.
On the roof they have gathered to drink from warm puddles of yesterday's
rainwater, preening and cooing in the shade, while their brothers the pigeons
line the telephone wires in radiant sunshine, waiting for their daily feed to spill
forth from Mr. Johnson's sack of seed and cracked corn. Sunday morning, 10
a.m. High African clouds in the west, alamanda spilled in yellow spikes and
coils across the fence. In the back yard: a neighbor's cat. At the sound of the
opening window it flees, startled, then hesitates at the top of the wall to glance
back—at what?—and as my eye tracks its gaze I catch a sudden motion in the
overgrown grass, frantic circling too big for a lizard, too desperate, and even as
I notice it and begin to speak, even as I call out *Hey, come see something strange
in the yard* I realize, in that instant, what it must be—a bird, mauled, its weary
struggle for survival—and wish I could unsay it, wish I could avert the gaze of
my conscience because already I foresee the morning slipping away—a box, a
warm towel, a bowl of water, and the calls to the Humane Society, and the drive
to Fort Lauderdale to tender its fragile body to the Wild Animal Hospital, a
shaded compound of blackbirds and parrots, box turtles and one-eared rab-
bits—and now Sam has come over to watch with me and I cannot will away the
obvious, and he dashes out the back door to investigate, and now the day has
been taken from us, seized, wrenched away, a day of rest I would covet even
against that ring of blood and spilled feathers, the slender broken bones in the
lawn, and now we are drawn into the circle of its small life, obligated by our
witness, impossible to deny or retract, committed long before the dull slow
course of a thought can be born into language, before the image is set into
words, as Sam's words come to me now across the hot summer grass: *Dad, it's
alive. A kind of bird. It's hurt. A dove.*

El Balserito

Because my Spanish is chips-and-salsa simple, and I am desirous of improving upon it, and delighted whenever I can puzzle out on my own some new word or phrase, I am listening in on the conversation of the two Cuban men next to me at the counter of the plumbing supply store in Little Haiti, and when I hear the word *balserito* I recognize this to be a diminutive of *balsero*, "the rafter," that symbol of the Cuban-American experience, those cast ashore on scrapwood rafts emblematic of an entire community's exile, and when the one man goes out to his truck and comes back with a little plastic dashboard toy of Goofy and another Disney character floating in an inner tube, and the other man, laughing and smiling at the joke asks, *Quien es el otro?*, pointing at the smaller figure, I know that this is Max, Goofy's son, because we have just taken Sam to see "A Goofy Movie," a story of father-son bonding in the cartoon universe, a universe in many ways more familiar to me than this one, though of course I say nothing to the men, not wanting to admit I have been eavesdropping, or betray my linguistic insufficiency, the degree to which I am an outsider here, in Miami, a place unlike any other I have known, a city we have fixed upon like Rust Belt refugees eager to buy a little piece of the sunshine, to mortgage a corner of the American Dream, where already Sam has begun to master the local customs, youngest and most flexible, first to make landfall, betraying the generational nature of acculturation the way the poems of my students at the state university do, caught between past and present worlds, transplanted parents looking back to Havana while the children are native grown, rooted to the soil, though the roots of *las palmas* are notoriously shallow, hence their propensity to topple in a hurricane, tropical storm, even the steady winter tradewind bearing its flotilla of makeshift sails across the Straits of Florida, so many this season that some mornings, jogging along the boardwalk in the shadow of the luxury hotels, I have come upon three rafts washed up in a single mile of beach, ragged planks and styrofoam and chicken-wire, filthy and abandoned but curiously empowered, endowed with a violent, residual energy, like shotgun casings in a field of corn stubble or the ruptured jelly of turtle eggs among mangroves, chrysalides discarded as the cost of the journey, shells of arrival, shells of departure.

Las Vegas

1

My first time in town, passing through with Charlie, long before the Babylonian captivity of that neon oasis, before the Hard Rock and the Liberace Museum, the space needle Kong-a-coaster, white tigers and mute centurions, before the hyper-textualization of our dreams when we were yet content with mere demesnes of poppy-colored bulbs and a cheap room at the Prince Albert and the big cowboy waving howdy and a long night roaming the sports books cadging tequila sunrises from zombie-tranced keno girls amid the zero hour jangle of the slots. Blissful oblivion. Noise and nothingness. That was all, but we loved it, loved it completely, and when we tired of dropping slugs we did what we always did in the places we loved: memorialized them through the consummation of our consumerist selves, which is to say, we bought some souvenirs.

Bolo ties and Elvis ashtrays, scorpions in lucite, lucky dice frozen on boxcars and snake-eyes.

Junk, of course, pure junk, holy junk from the sacred trove, and we loved it wholly, unironically, with the purity of disciples, not as kitsch but as artifacts of something splendid and inexplicable, as we loved the textured velvet of the city itself, loved the golden sheen of the pawn shops as we loved the old women shoveling tokens into handbags and the hotel maids speaking Spanish at the bus stop and the way the wind scoured the avenues as if to render all this to Sphinxian obliquity. In the morning we saddled up at the breakfast buffet, moved on to LA, that crazy, long-forgotten scene.

This was when—1981, 1982?

I have a photo of it pinned to the bulletin board: Charlie in his Schlitz beer cowboy hat beneath the globe that proclaims World's Largest Souvenir Store haloed by clouds streaked with luminous fire,

Viking longboats put to the torch by sunset,

vessels cast flaming westward for Valhalla.

Fifteen years later I'm best man at my brother's wedding at the Silver Bells chapel on the Strip, and before the exchange of vows I hug him and hand the rings to Elvis, presiding, young and sneering, one of his less grotesque earthly manifestations, who says to the bride—my new sister-in-law—"Do you promise to love him tender, to care for his hound dog, never to step on his blue suede shoes?" Etc. At the end he sings "Viva Las Vegas" as a recessional while Sam gets up and dances in the aisle and it's all much too familiar to me from hallucinations I once was prey to concerning internment in a netherworld of go-go girls and sepulchral lights derived from the dance sequences of the very worst Elvis movies.

Clambake. Blue Hawaii. Live A Little, Love A Little.

Like a black-light painting of fluorescent gnomes, daylight drains the mystery from the city, but at night it fills back up again, a magician's trick with a glass of water. For three days we chose to see it as half-full, a fun trip for the family in its way, even with the "World of Concrete" convention in residence among us, which may or may not explain why the pall of cigarette smoke and bells and whistles induced a form of nausea that persisted even as we paraded with Sam through the pure synthetic cash-and-carry family joy rides therein assembled, a sunny new gloss for the city of sin, a facade as misplaced as anything I can imagine, circus posters pasted across the entrance to the gas chamber, penitents come to gorge at the altar of their enslavement.

Our last morning we drove out to visit the Hoover Dam, stopping for pancakes in Boulder City before descending into the vault of that

titanic concrete angel wing

to watch vast turbines spun by weight of falling water, valves and relays riven with the electric intake and outrush, systole, diastole—

standing there and watching it, mesmerized, alive and breathing—

the many-chambered heart of a thing beyond our knowing.

Manitoba

Ten miles in we came upon the locusts, road striped and banded with them, fields plagued and shadowed with their mass, fulsome, darker than cloud-dapple, slick as shampoo beneath the wheels. In the next town we stopped to scrape them from the radiator with our pocket knives. Grasshoppers, their bodies crushed and mangled, scaled and armatured, primordial, pharoanic, an ancient horde of implacable charioteers, black ooze caking the headlights to blindness, mindless yellow legs still kicking. Not much in that town: sidewalks grown with goldenrod, grain elevator on the old railroad siding. Not much besides wheat and gasoline, the ragged beauty of the heat-painted prairie, wind with the texture of coiled rope, the solitude of the plains unrolling beyond limit of comprehension. It was time to hit the road. Charlie grabbed a rootbeer; I topped-up the oil. We hosed out the dead and drove on.

HEATHER McHUGH

Etymological Dirge

'Twas grace that taught my heart to fear.

Calm comes from burning.
Tall comes from fast.
Comely doesn't come from come.
Person comes from mask.

The kin of charity is whore,
the root of charity is dear.
Incentive has its source in song
and winning in the sufferer.

Afford yourself what you can carry out.
A coward and a coda share a word.
We get our ugliness from fear.
We get our danger from the lord.

The Father of the Predicaments

He came at night to each of us asleep
And trained us in the virtues we most lacked.

Me he admonished to return his stare
Correctly, without fear. Unless I could,

Unblinking, more and more incline
Toward a deep unblinkingness of his,

He would not let me rest. Outside,
In the dark of the world, at the foot

Of the library steps, there lurked
A Mercury of rust, its cab half-lit.

(Two worldly forms were huddled there, and they
Knew what they meant. I had no business

With the things they knew. Nor did I feel myself
Drawn back through Circulation into Reference,

Till suddenly its freezing blue
was everywhere—the ICU of mind,

Its monitor abuzz
With is's etymologies.)

A Salt: Three Variations on Five Senses

> a worn knobbed stick between his legs
> to keep off dogs
> —W. C. Williams

1

a sip, a whiff,
a glimpse of the single
unsung note (a dangle
between doubles, bare
as earshot's sheer
ephemerality).
a wing across
a fingertip

2

a gulp from the gutter, a snort from the shovel:
eyeloads gobbled and the shelves of self
all helped to heaps
of heaving overtones:
a muddy mind, immodest, and
five himalayas of massage

3

in light of all of this,
best just, to taste, take in (inhale)
detecting's cast: the wave-point brings
to mind an eye: to ear a shell: to hand
a ring. a sailed-in fact. a tact in things.

JAMES MCMICHAEL

Above the Red Deep-Water Clays

      Capacity is both how
much of a thing there is and how
much it can do. From a solid
magnetized and very hot core, the earth

suffers itself to be turned outside.
Closest to its heart are the deepest submarine
trenches and sinks. Its lava finds

clefts there in the old uplifted crust,
the ocean floor a scramble. Wrapping at depth huge

shield volcanoes, the North Atlantic

down- and upwells, its denser layers making
room behind them through the blue-green shortest
wavelengths of light. Inside the cubic
yards it levies, league by league, respiring,
budgeting its heat, it hides

its samenesses of composition through and through.
For the normal water level, an ideal

solitary wave is surplus. Any wave's
speed is what it is
only if reversing it would render it still.

Surfaces are almost without feature
at Sea Disturbance number one.
When the wind stretches them, their wrinkling gives it
more to hold onto. Three is

multiplying whitecaps.
Spray blows in well-marked streaks at six.
In the foam-spewed rolling swell that takes a
higher number, small and medium
ships may be lost to view for a long time.

Waves are additive. Doming

up on the tidal bulge into a storm's
barometric low,

the distances between them widen
as from the Iceland-Faroes massif
leeward for another
three hundred miles southeast
they build unblocked. Little

enough for them the first outlying gabbro
islets and stacks. These are not yet *The British
Countryside in Pictures*, not yet the shoals
off Arran in the Firth of Clyde.

Posited

That as all parts of it
agree in their low resistance to flow,

so can it be agreed to call it water.
To say of water that it floods both
forward and back through places
difficult to place demands that the ensouled

themselves make places for their parts of speech,
the predicates arrayed in
front of or behind the stated subject—

water, in the case at hand. Water

attains to its names because it shows as one thing
speech is about.

It shows as water.
To say no
more than that about however broad a sea is

plural already,
it says there must be something

else somewhere,
some second thing at least, or why say
how the thing shows? Before it can be taken

as a thing, as sea,
there have to have been readied for it other
possible-if-then-denied pronouncements—land,
the sky. Possible that
somewhere in the midst of waters there could

be such things as might be walked on,

hornblende and
felsite, quartzite, remnant
raised beach platforms, shales,
a cliff-foot scree.

Until given back accountably as
extant and encountered,
nothing counts. Nothing counts until
by reason it is brought to stand still.
Country. That it stands over

against one stands to reason. Not without
reason is it said of country that it
counters one's feet. To count as

groundwork for a claim about the ground,

reason must equate with country.
To be claimed as that, as country,
sand blown inland from the dunes must
equal its having landed grain by grain.

All grains have their whereabouts.
From emplacements in their clumps of

marram grass and sedges, some will be
aloft again and lime-rich
grain by grain will land.

Country is its mix of goings-on.
For these to tally, befores from
afters must at every turn divide.
Before it turns,
a cartwheel has its place to start from. It

stands there in place. In place an
axle's width away, another

parallel wheel is standing.
Not for long.
After each wheel in concert leaves its
first place for a second,

it leaves again at once a third and more. No more nor

fewer are its places on the strand than it has
time for in its turning.
Imprinted
one at a time,
these places are the lines the cart

makes longer at each landward place.
Not late for what goes

on there as its heft at each next place bears
down onto the loams and breaks them,
the seaweed-laden

cart is in time. Time is the cart's

enclosure. There for the taking, time is
around the cart,
which takes it from inside. Around
stones in the dry-stone dyke are

times out of mind,
those times the stones' embeddings let them go.
The hill-grazings
also are in time, and the three cows.
The blacklands are in time with their

ridged and dressed short rows of barley.
As it does around

bursts that for the places burst upon
abandon where they were before,
time holds around

the moving and the resting things.

WILLIAM MATTHEWS

The Bar at The Andover Inn, 1995

The bride, groom (my son), and their friends gathered
somewhere else to siphon the wedding's last
drops from their tired elders. Over a glass
of Chardonnay I ignored my tattered,
companionable glooms (This took some will:
I've ended three marriages by divorce
as a man shoots his broken-legged horse),
and wished my two sons and their families
something I couldn't have, or keep, myself.
The rueful pluck we take with us to bars
or church, the morbid fellowship of woe—
I've had my fill of it. I wouldn't mope
through my son's happiness or further fear
my own. Well, what instead? Well, something else.

Big Tongue

The spit-sheathed shut-in, sometimes
civil, lolls on its leash in its cave
between meals, blunt little *feinschmecker*.
He seems both sullen and proud, not
an unusual combination. Well, that little
blind boy knows his way around the mouth.
An aspirate here, a glottal stop there—
he's a blur. He works to make sensible
noise at least as hard as an organist,
and so giddily pleased by his own

skill that for the sheer bravura
of it he flicks a shard of chicken
salad free from a molar *en route*
to the startling but exact finish
of a serpentine and pleasing sentence.
God knows the brain deserves most
of the credit for the sentence, but then
wasn't it God who insisted from the first
that whatever "it" means, it isn't fair?
Theology can be stored in a couplet:

The reason God won't answer you
is God has better things to do.

I mention only briefly, *mia diletta*,
lest I embarrass you by lingering,
how avidly this tongue nuzzled your nub,
how slowly (glib is his day job) he urged
your pleased clamor. Think then how he might feel—
the spokesman, the truffle pig, Mr. Muscle—
to sense along the length of his savor
a hard node, like a knot in a tree, and thus
to know another attack's begun. First one
side of the bilateral tongue will stiffen

and swell to two or three times normal size
(it's like having a small shoe in your mouth),
and then, as it subsides, after three or four
hours, the other side grows grandiose.
(Your salivary glands are like grapes
on steroids. Your speech is feral—only vowels,
and those from no language you recognize.)
Pride goeth before a bloat. Start to puff yourself up
and next thing you know you'll be on TV,
in the Macy's Parade. *Vae, puto deus fio*

("Damn, I think I'm becoming a god," said
the emperor Vespasian on his deathbed).

But let's bring this descant back down to earth:
names ground us, and this humiliation's called
angiodema, short (?!) for *angioneurotic*
edema, often "an expression of allergy,"
as Webster's Third has it. What's the humbled
tongue, sore from strenuous burgeon and wane,
allergic to? Whatever it is, it may well be
systemic, and the "attack" a kind of defense,
a purge, a violent recapture of balance,
like a migraine or an epileptic seizure.

"Who needs this?" I might cry out. The answer
might be: I do. So why am I exchanging vows
with my allergies? Although I hate it when my
competence is sick, I hereby refuse
to make mine allegorical, though not before,
you'll note, I had my fun with that possibility—
for where's "the bribe of pleasure" (as Dr. Freud,
that gloomy *mensch*, called it) in being sick
if I can't loll in limelight for a while?
Where next? My dressing room, to wipe off the drama

and stare at the mirror,
met by ordinary fear.

Manners

"Sweetypants," Martha Mitchell (wife of John
Mitchell, soon to be Nixon's Attorney General)
cried, "fetch me a glass of bubbin,
won't you?" Out of office, Nixon
had been warehoused in Leonard Garment's
New York law firm and had begun to clamber

his way back toward Washington.
The scent of his enemies' blood rose
hotly from the drinks that night.
Why was I there? A college class-
mate's mother had suggested he invite a few
friends; she called us "starving scholars."

It's hard to do good and not advertise
yourself, and not to need the needy
even if they don't need you. I'd grown used
to be accused of being somewhere else.
I plied my nose, that shrewd scout, into book
after book at home, and clattered downstairs

for dinner not late but tardy. I dwelt
as much as I could at that remove
from the needs of others we call "the self,"
that desert isle, that Alcatraz from which
none has escaped. I made a happy lifer.
There is no frigate like a book.

"Outside of a dog, a book is a man's
best friend," said Groucho Marx. "Inside of a dog,
it's too dark to read." So what if my friend's
mother was a fool. So what if Martha
Mitchell would later rat on her rat
of a husband when Nixon's paranoid

domain collapsed under its own venal
weight and it took Nixon all his gloomy
charisma to load his riven heart
onto a helicopter and yaw upward
from the White House lawn. He might have turned
to Pat and asked, like a child on a first

flight, "Are we getting smaller yet?"
I was too young to know how much I was,
simply by being born, a hostage
to history. My hostess's chill,
insulting grace I fended off with the same
bland good manners I used to stay upstairs

in my head until time had come for food.
A well-fed scholar, I sought out and brought
back a tall bubbin for the nice lady.
Yes, there's a cure for youth, but it's fatal.
And a cure for grace: you say what you mean,
but of course you have to know what that is.

Mingus in Shadow

What you see in his face in the last
photograph, when ALS had whittled
his body to fit a wheelchair, is how much
stark work it took to fend death off, and fail.
The famous rage got eaten cell by cell.

His eyes are drawn to slits against the glare
of the blanched landscape. The day he died,
the story goes, a swash of dead whales
washed up on a Baja beach. Great nature grieved
for him, the story means, but it was great

nature that skewed his cells and siphoned
his force and melted his fat like tallow
and beached him in a wheelchair under
a sombrero. It was human nature,
tiny nature, to take the photograph,

to fuss with the aperture and speed, to let
in the right blare of light just long enough
to etch pale Mingus to the negative.
In the small, memorial world of that
negative, he's all the light there is.

W. S. MERWIN

227 Waverly Place

When I have left I imagine they will
repair the window onto the fire escape
that looks north up the avenue clear
to Columbus Circle long I have known
the lights of that valley at every hour
through that unwashed pane and have watched with no
conclusion its river flowing toward me
straight from the featureless distance coming
closer darkening swelling growing distinct
speeding up as it passed below me toward
the tunnel all that time through all that time
taking itself through its sound which became
part of my own before long the unrolling
rumble the iron solos and the sirens
all subsiding in the small hours to voices
echoing from the sidewalks a rustling
in the rushes along banks and the loose
glass vibrated like a remembering bee
as the north wind slipped under the winter sill
at the small table by the window until
my right arm ached and stiffened and I pushed
the chair back against the bed and got up
and went out into the other room that was
filled with the east sky and the day replayed
from the windows and roofs of the Village
the room where friends came and we sat talking
and where we ate and lived together while
the blue paint flurried down from the ceiling
and we listened late with lights out to music
hearing the intercom from the hospital

across the avenue through the Mozart
Dr Kaplan wanted on the tenth floor
while reflected lights flowed backward on the walls

Another River

The friends have gone home far up the valley
of that river into whose estuary
the man from England sailed in his own age
in time to catch sight of the late forests
furring in black the remotest edges
of the majestic water always it
appeared to me that he arrived just as
an evening was beginning and toward the end
of summer when the converging surface
lay as a single vast mirror gazing
upward into the pearl light that was
already stained with the first saffron
of sunset on which the high wavering trails
of migrant birds flowed southward as though there were
no end to them the wind had dropped and the tide
and the current for a moment seemed to hang
still in balance and the creaking and knocking
of wood stopped all at once and the known voices
died away and the smells and rocking
and starvation of the voyage had become
a sleep behind them as they lay becalmed
on the reflection of their Half Moon
while the sky blazed and then the time lifted them
up the dark passage they had no name for

Night Turn

In late summer after the day's heat is over
I walk out after dark into the still garden
wet leaves fragrance of ginger and kamani
the feel of the path underfoot still recalling
a flow of water that found its way long ago
toads are rustling under the lemon trees
looking back I can see through the branches
the light in the kitchen where we were standing
a moment ago in our life together

Sheep Passing

Mayflies hover through the long evening
of their light and in the winding lane
the stream of sheep runs among shadows calling
the old throats gargling again uphill
along known places once more and from the bells
borne by their predecessors the notes
dull as wood clonk to the flutter of all
the small hooves over the worn stone
with the voices of the lambs rising through them
over and over telling and asking
their one question into the day they have
none will know midsummer the walls of the lane
are older than anyone can understand
and the lane must have been a path a long time
before the first stones were raised beside it
and must have been a trail from the river
up through the trees for an age before that
one hoof one paw one foot before another
the way they went is all that is still there

What Is a Garden

All day working happily down near the stream bed
    the light passing into the remote opalescence
it returns to as the year wakes toward winter
    a season of rain in a year already rich
in rain with masked light emerging on all sides
    in the new leaves of the palms quietly waving
time of mud and slipping and of overhearing
    the water under the sloped ground going on whispering
as it travels time of rain thundering at night
    and of rocks rolling and echoing in the torrent
and of looking up after noon through the high branches
    to see fine rain drifting across the sunlight
over the valley that was abused and at last left
    to fill with thickets of rampant aliens
bringing habits but no stories under the mango trees
    already vast as clouds there I keep discovering
beneath the tangle the ancient shaping of water
    to which the light of an hour comes back as to a secret
and there I planted young palms in places I had not pondered
    until then I imagined their roots setting out in the dark
knowing without knowledge I kept trying to see them standing
    in that bend of the valley in the light that would come

CAROL MUSKE

Oblique Muscle
(Meditation on a Famous Blindness)

When I consider how my light is spent . . .

I close my eyes, I see a man I know who's
an eye surgeon. A coke addict: as he's been for years,
    steady in his gem-clear obsession.

Through decades of other people's pointless excess &
abstention he works on, dogged. At dawn he scrapes
    pure pharmaceutical grains

from the ice-blue sugar block delivered to him
as topical anesthetic. He inhales, holding a glass
    slide—or perforates a vein.

In my mind's eye, he looks a little bit like Freud,
bearded, a brain-miner, clicking infra-red hatch-marks
    onto the lidless translucent ball

filled with fluid—peering toward the pale optic disk.
He wears huge magnifying lenses and his tools
    are prisms, steep knives of light.

The eye, exposed in its smart cuff, murky as a flashed bulb,
has seen through its thinking images. Now how sparingly
    the blade renders it object, a reduction

to the literal: *how light is spent!* Behind the aqueous humor
is the vitreous humor and the sheaths of rectus muscle which
    he lasers through, sectioning tissue, stapling

back the veined curtains covering the room where Mother's nipple,
blood-grapes, disconnected wires, amber scales of fish,
        red-lit lampshade, green neon EATS

all disorient for the moment—like bees without the seizure of
hive-vision, one readable pulse like context, or sex. Impossibly high,
        he wields the light-scalpel. Choiring voices echo

in his skull through the earphones. To see or hear but not just through
the senses, he is *reading,* Off-key, but on-key. Like my friend who reads only
        the first important scene in a novel. Page twenty-seven

of *The Red and the Black,* where Julien is sitting on the rafter
above the screeching sawmill, reading deeply and his cruel peasant father
        knocks the book out of his hands into the great blade.

Before Julien can cry out, the father strikes him, drops him from his perch
fifteen feet above the gears, then catches him in his huge left hand. Saves our
        reader.
        That's all, that's what he knows about *The Red and the Black*—

how the reader is blindsided, how the reader is perched above human action &
discourse, then saved by the grasp of rapacity. The father is a shrewd bully,
        he injures, then saves his son. So the son will always respect him.

That's what my surgeon knows about how we see the soul—and it is enough:
that lit ballet of images leaping among printed symbols. It's enough, then. He
        cuts—
        Think of how your light is spent. *Blink.* It's enough.

Our Kitty

She is swinging in a contraption above the heads
of the audience,
            reflected in the glass lamps on the tables.

She sits in one of those fin-de-siècle gilded sleighs
hung from the ceiling
            by braids of sparkling hemp.

Here come all the poet-accountants pushing in
to talk about cate-
            gories of experience. Wine, sex.

The ceiling is hammered tin, alight and jumping
with her shadow
            cast upward by the table-lamps.

As she swings, she rubs herself, adjusts herself
in the seat so she
            can be seen through the see-through bottom.

Pink cheeks has Kitty. A pop-open camisole. Mother
is striking her
            name from the family bible. But

She has to eat, does Kitty. She is so petite & incautious
that all the poet-
            accountants are taking copious notes.

They can use her: she may be the littlest
Whore of imagination.
            She might even be how they imagine

The twentieth-century's end: just like the end
of the last century,
            the dream of body parts floating

Above cigar smoke. In other words, *more war.*
Kitty inspires all
of them to think about triage.

The end of the twentieth century. Artist or banker—
who should be saved?
The artist in his same old tourniquet? The banker

With a dented skull? Try to guess. The poet-
accountants have
already guessed. They know the price of

this ending. They've seen the banker and his surgeons,
the poet bleeding
all over the sterile gauze. Who wants to be

John Keats? Well, the poems, yes—but not the death.
Now they hear Kitty
coughing. I'm Keats, she gasps.

I'm John Fucking Keats returned in Kitty's body.
Forlorn she cries *forlorn*
but they refuse to listen to her

As she swings, pale and beautiful, glittering, above them,
holding out her
living hand, warm, capable—as ever, untaken.

MARILYN NELSON

Live Jazz, Franklin Park Zoo

Kubie sobbed when a nearby jazz band stopped playing.
—Christian Science Monitor, 8/27/96

A tree grew. Oh, remembering gorillas!
O Orpheus singt! Oh, Africa in the ear!
The recluse, Vip, came out. Gigi sat still
and wide-eyed, black face pressed against the bars.

Kubie lay on his back, as he usually does,
vacantly staring. Then he turned over, hairy chin
on one huge leather palm; with his other hand
he scratched his head, contemplatively picked his nose.

The zebras' ears twirled. Behind their fancy fences,
the silenced animals listened to something new.
Suddenly their calls, even the lion's roar,

shrank in their hearts, as they knew something more.
And where there had been, at most, a nest of boughs
to receive it, music built a cathedral in their senses.

The Perceiving Self

Ft. Smith, Kansas, ca. 1874

The first except birds
who spoke to us, his voice high
and lilting as a meadowlark's,
with an undertone of windsong,
many-petaled as the meadow,
the music shaped and colored
by brown lips, white teeth, pink tongue.
Walking slowly, he talked to us,
touched our stamens
pleasured us with pollen.
Then squealed, a field mouse taken
without wingbeat,
with no shadow.
His yellow feet crushed past, running,
his bare legs bruised, he trampled, his spew
burned, his scalding urine.

The icedrift of silence.
Smoke from a torched deadman, barking laughter
from the cottonwoods at the creek.

Washboard Wizard

Highland, Kansas, 1888

All of us take our clothes to Carver.
He's a wizard with a washboard,
a genie of elbow-grease and suds.
We'll take you over there next week:
By that time you'll be needing him.
He's a colored boy, a few years older
than we are, real smart. But he stays
in his place. They say
he was offered a scholarship
to the college. I don't know
what happened, but they say
that's why he's here in town.
Lives alone, in a little shack
filled with books
over in dingetown.
They say he reads them.
Dried plants, rocks, jars of colors.
A bubbling cauldron of laundry.
Pictures of flowers and landscapes.
They say he painted them.
They say
he was turned away when he got here,
because he's a nigger. I don't know about
all that. But he's the best
washwoman in town.

WILLIAM OLSEN

Face

for John Woods, in memory

To make, or merely *to shine, to appear,*
to peer from the eyewater in an eyewink—
but that's the verb of it—the dying noun
and all its old light revealed a hunter's woods.
The hands of his wristwatch spun and spun
like a little train with faces at every window.
The knife-edge hands of that face press the future
back past midnight but time's face just can't end,
so anonymous and we who are his lost thoughts
must seem almost over before we cross the floor.
An elder down to a few scant friends, trying to smile,
my old friend who'll die afraid for every leaf
never farther from his songs, his lives,
in this inhuman effortless place that came
out of our skull with the catheters and the drip,
the wounded world inside him fed by tubes.
This hospital of a world happens to be
a hospital—veins tethered to a metal tree.
This is a woods wherein the face will pale
to some appalling verbal funeral,
but no death mask, nothing that stuporous,
nothing will be impossible, nobody knows
anything for sure the light will speak,
light of some pain pill from a twilight of pills,
light bared and sometimes barred and strapped,
gnawed and drooled in little braids of lace.
One day the faces of clouds could disperse, and they do.
An ageless confusion will stare from us,
small vast stratagems outridden unto the last,

out of our element even in the face of our loves—
there is no world except we face it down—
enfeebled by inscrutable refusals, notch
by notch diminished, less and less disguised—
boredom and its hyperactive cousin, dread
making the face a never-ending landslide,
face with a name strapped to a calcined wrist,
name posting the rented room no more.
The used car salesman reads a face better,
the *souk* shopkeeper, the executioner, and
the luck-stricken can't tell happy from sad . . .
Time to slow down, the cadences will say,
for life as well as death to last forever,
bitterness to serenely drag its talons
down a face that is no more a face,
inside the blood that is no more, the past
so timely, staring out at us, open to the last—
time to turn inside out, from seed to leaf.
His skin seems to have come from inside him,
like breath upon a window:
out of his veins all sorrow was to drain,
his face was to gleam like a corner store
gliding under its streetlight for the night,
with aisles of unassailable mopped light,
fruit still in cans, and all needs honestly met.
But now look at it,
its eyes see two or three friends and everything else
but themselves, by all the sickly life inside
are held. Eyes wide . . . inside the blood
but less in the dark than blood, inside so long
inside is no inside: and saying so
is bloodless: we look down, all we see
is our shoes, their tongues bound, not one rusted tear
falls from the metal eyelets.
And yet, if not just yet, I am drinking this face,
this wooden bowl cut from rain and fire and grass
sight must take to its lips, and gently tip
his kind look merely rain and flesh and grass—
his look looks up, its handsomeness intact,
touched, shaken, shrugging off little dead regrets.

On Plans to Decimate the Entire British Herd

Every day to stand in the piss and shit of self
which pools and pools to the bottom of things—
the very hoofprints are drowned mouths sucked up—
or to stare down a green slope to the sea,
lowering the automotive engine of the head,
the head looking and listening.
A calf has a face that looks to have risen
shining from the soaked grass.
The mother this calf has been nuzzling against
like a boat against a dock
moves off to a coffin trough
and she drinks from her face.
Not one has a prophecy,
my heart going out to all this tripe and gristle,
the spinal cords soon scattered to used-up spools.
Their faces do not mean to alarm me from my delusions,
their faces tolerate the flies that hug the lee sides—
out of the wind—but out of the little sun, too—
it's getting cloudy again, and cold, let alone later—
their faces have them forge deltas of their own shit
that has come of waiting: dumb conjecture,
their faces outlive the unreal, and eat the real,
and bow their heads to it, give their hunger over to it.

STEVE ORLEN

The Great Wheel

What ever became of the people from the 1960's?
What happened to the young man
From a well-off family in the east,
Who had tried college and found it wanting?
Each night waxing and polishing
The hallway floors of the English Department,
Where I was, and still am, teaching,
He looked very busy, all the labor
Concentrated in his narrow shoulders,
Trying to both control and let loose
The heavy polishing machine in its back and forth
Swathing across the linoleum, a hippy, long-haired,
An unlikely night maintenance man, making a mirror
Which would become dirty and blurred
Again in a week, and I deemed him purer,
More innocent than I.
                          Once, he rapped
At my office door and showed me his poem,
Hand-written, on the several lined sheets
Of a yellow legal pad. It was terrible stuff, more
Manifesto than poetry, full of
The powerful feelings of political expedience
In the guise of political commitment.
I suggested that he put a waterbed in one line,
And the roach of a marijuana cigarette
In another, and that tall, sensual, homely girl
We both knew from the bar
We all used to drink and play pool at, in another,
And to include the dark spaces between her teeth,
For which he thanked me profusely,

Thinking me an expert. Then I suggested
That he not use the world *revolution*
In its commonly-used sense
Of replacing the Government of Old Ideals
With the Government of New Ideals,
But as a word for change, as in *rotation*,
Like a fan belt, or a wheel:
How everything goes around and comes around,
As the working people he admired would say.
And although he looked hurt,
He thanked me for that, too.
I never saw him again, either in the English Department
Now called the Department of English, or in the bar
We hung out in, still called *The Shanty*,
At that time filled with the poets and painters,
The street people who arrived from everywhere in America
Just to hang out and *be*, and the few elderly pensioners
From the neighborhood who thought we were crazy
But loved it all, for the coursing energy
Fueled by the music, the drugs and the sex
You could almost smell it was so easy.

Tonight, I sit in my same office,
Hearing the same heavy, humming, *swish swish*
Of the polisher in the hallway outside my door.
Strange, how memory works, how it serves us
And doesn't serve us. Hopefully, the scientists
Will never lay bare the gears and pulleys of its chemistry.
Strange, also, poetry, how, as with memory,
You start with a first thought, a gist,
A ghost of a question, and you wonder
Where it's headed. For example, will that tall homely girl
Grow up to be a woman? Will she get her teeth fixed?
Will she remember us who secretly desired her,
Homeliness and all? How much of the brain's chemistry
Is narrative and how much imagination
Nudging narrative along? What is it
The poem is getting at? The nature of work
Or the nature of change? The transience of ideology
Or the poetry of transience?

Or memory itself, in the way it *constitutes*,
How a shape will rise
Up out of the electron stew
Into a noisy hallway and become
A young man again, with an iffy future,
Doing his labor so that I may do mine.

Onomastics & the Falling Snow

Most everything has a name except the falling snow,
　　By which I mean each flake, each one different,
As one spirit is different from another, and close up,
　　Under a microscope, crystalline, like a thing made
By a master watchmaker with a motor the size
　　Of a fingernail and an awl as fine as a hair.

Sillier men than I have tried to name the flakes of snow
　　While standing hatless at a bus stop, watching the snow
Fall on apple trees and oaks, making them all the same.
　　Did you know that among the ancient Hebrew tribes
Children were given two names at birth,
　　One sacred, one profane? The child wasn't told

The sacred one. So he walked around with two names,
　　One by which to be called in from the sheepfold
And the other intricate, mysterious, useless.
　　And in Norway, circa early twentieth century,
There were so few hereditary names to pass down
　　Everyone must have thought everyone else a cousin. Maybe

That's why they're so polite, so orderly, and why,
　　If it's snowing in Oslo, there will always be
A helpful soul standing beside you to offer space
　　The size of an umbrella while waiting for the bus.
In America a name means nothing—a marker to be called in,
　　A convenience: Mr. Weaver may not be at his loom,

Nor Mr. Lavender making soap. Nor does anyone remember
 Herr Gross, the fat man who stood in line waiting for
The greedy minions of the fanatic Empress Maria Theresa
 To take his money and bestow upon him a name
To be passed down to fat and skinny children alike.
 And if a man were even poorer, and as a mean joke,

He might be called the German equivalent of *Grease,*
 Or *Monkey Weed* or *Do Not Borrow From* or *Gallows Rope.*
In Russia, in 1802, to raise an army, Czar Alexander
 Sent out a ukase ordering each Jew to take a last name—
It must have been like writing a poem, mind-sprung
 And wholly inspired on first draft, then inscribing it

On the forehead of a neighbor, each one befitting:
 Eiseman, for *He Who Laughs,* or Mazal, *Lucky Man,*
Or Trubnic for *Chimney Sweep,* or Soroka *The Magpie,*
 Meaning *The Gossip.* And babies in those days
Were sometimes given ugly names to turn aside
 The assiduous, bureaucratic Angel of Death;

Or, in illness, a child was renamed to befuddle
 The same angel coming down with his empty sack
To collect for God's heavens. But naming the snow,
 Each flake, each deliquescing cryptic coat of arms,
That would be a game for only the most inventive,
 Hopeless man. For after all, the snowflakes

Are the soon-to-be-dead, those who float awhile
 Then fall and, merging, pile up like corpses
On some northern battlefield, and there melt, flow
 Down as water to the river that has one name only.
It so happens it's snowing where I'm standing now
 At a bus stop in Oslo, between one moment and the next,

Feeling nostalgic, homesick, trying to remember the names
    Of everyone I've ever known. Hopeless, of course.
So it worries me that my son, who is more like me
    Than I care to think about, could recite the names
Of each child in his kindergarten class after only one week
    Of sitting with his hands folded on his desk.

He wasn't praying, he told me. He was waiting
    For the names to sink in so one morning he could say,
Suddenly, to each one, *Hi*, because it's good
    To be remembered. By the time we are old
We can baptize each flake before the bus arrives.
    There are so many people to know by name,

So many . . . They grew away from me.
    They became snow, fuzzy at this distance,
Just beyond my reach, waiting to be called upon again.

GREGORY ORR

The Excavation

for my father, on his first dig at seventy

1

In this dry, stubble field
a thousand years ago,
a nameless tribe lived
where two rivers joined.

Now with sun pressed
to aching back
you dig through chalk
and marl.

       Then down
among the layers you crouch
with a tiny brush.
The shards you seek
no bigger than a thumb,
or bits of bone
to tell you what they ate.

2

To tell you what they ate
I'd have to take you back
to where they sat
at the table: your sons
and daughter.
       It might be
early morning, before
the schoolbus comes,

or evening with dark
pressing down on the fields.

Their mother's been dead
a year now—her presence
less than a whisper.
Your absence is the mystery
their lives close around
as a mouth might close
with a small stone
on the tongue, and so
it's already begun:
their journey to the other world.

3

Their journey to the other world
we might infer from the way
a skeleton's arranged
in a grave, but this
is where they lived
and signs of life
are what we'll find.

I think that dark spot
marks a hearth. I think
your children grew, then
grew apart and made
their isolate ways
into the world.

                    I think
you are an old man
searching for artifacts
and what they might reveal,
here where the hole you dug
gives shelter from an unrelenting sun
in this dry, stubble field.

If There's a God . . .

If there's a god of amphetamine, he's also the god of wrecked lives, and it's only he who can explain how my doctor father, with the gift of healing strangers and patients alike, left so many intimate dead in his wake.

If there's a god of amphetamine, he's also the god of recklessness, and I ask him to answer.

He's the god of thrills, the god of boys riding bikes down steep hills with their hands over their heads.

He's the god of holy and unholy chance, the god of soldiers crossing a field and to the right of you a man falls dead and to the left also and you are still standing.

If there's a god of amphetamine, he's the god of diet pills, who is the god of the Fifties housewife who vacuums all day and whose bathroom is spotless and now it is evening as she sits alone in the kitchen, polishing her chains.

He's the god of the rampant mind and the god of my father's long monologues by moonlight in the dark car driving over the dusty roads.

He's the god of tiny, manic orderings in the midst of chaos, the god of elaborate charts where Greg will do this chore on Monday and a different one on Tuesday and all the brothers are there on the chart and all the chores and all the days of the week in a minuscule script no one can read.

If there's a god of amphetamine, my father was his hopped-up acolyte who leapt out of bed one afternoon to chase a mouse through the house, shouting, firing his .38 repeatedly at the tiny beast scurrying along the wall while Jon wailed for help from the next room.

If there's a god of amphetamine, he's the god of subtle carnage and dubious gifts who lives in each small pill that tastes of electricity and dust.

If there's a god of amphetamine, my father was its high priest, praising it, preaching its gospel, lifting it like a host and intoning: "Here in my hand is the mystery—a god alive inside a tiny tablet. He is a high god, a god of highs—he eats the heart to juice the brain and mocks the havoc he makes, laughing at all who stumble. Put out your tongue and receive it."

The Talk

for my father

How many years we've circled round this date,
not that it might come, but as a dreaded day.
And now we'll talk, although our talk's too late.

We played our cards, holding back each ace
until your last hand showed the queen of spades.
How many years we've circled round this date.

So "cancer" is the word we cannot say,
and can't not say—it works both ways;
but now we'll talk, although our talk's too late.

What stood between us was never outright hate
but fear so deep it urged us to delay,
and so for years we've circled round this date.

You hobble toward your chair; your lessened weight
propped on a cane. I hold my ground in a daze.
We'll talk, and, talking, pray it's not too late

to change the way we've read our lives as fate.
We hid our love. Now we must hide dismay,
forget the years we've circled round this date,
and talk at last, though all our talk's too late.

JACQUELINE OSHEROW

Analfabeta

for Laura Dondoli, in Memory of Her Great-Grandfather

I have a friend whose great-grandfather learned to read
From an uncle blinded in battle under Garibaldi
Who wanted Dante read to him aloud

And the boy learned to distinguish our unwieldy
Signs as simply sketches from his world,
Each with an unalterable melody:

Did he see two mountains touching, side by side?
They initiated *Magic, Music, Mastery.*
A three-pronged pitchfork's unsupported head?

Excellence, Echo, Elasticity.
A half-moon? *Delusion.* A full moon? *O . . .*
And the boy, who was bright, apparently, as well as feisty,

Found out what he hadn't known there was to know:
That his own close-fisted, monotonous world
Would yield unmingled treasure, canto by canto—

That the unacknowledged mist inside his head
Could be converted to explicit rapture.
His uncle's illogical and graceless code

Could root out pervasive music anywhere,
A face one encounters always, once acquainted . . .
But am I wrong in also thinking he learned more

Than those of us for whom someone merely pointed
Uttering a too-fast string of monosyllables
(With one bright lingering *W*)? He circumvented

Our sullen lines and curves, random intangibles,
The shortest, quickest distances to sounds.
To him, markings on the page were parables:

Suns and stars were things a snake surrounds,
Vision started when a bird tried out its wings,
All imprinted words were loopy compounds

Of language's intent and actual things . . .
I envy him. For me, it's artifice,
But every time he read, his uncle's moorings—

Does it look like the rind of a devoured slice
Of melon turned upon its side? That's C—
Kept him dreamily in place . . .

Unless those early portraits fell away
And he, like the rest of us, just followed signs
Into the inner sanctum of what Dante—

Oblivious to his letters' prongs and wings and moons—
Required, simply, three strong rhymes to say.
My friend's grandmother remembered hearing lines—

Her father's favorites—almost every day.
He would read them, overcome, in the kitchen,
After which her mother would shrug and say

That the ravings of a drunkard or a madman
Would make more sense to her than all this poetry . . .
Still, he'd read out line after line

And what I want to know is, did every *Z*
Flash—as he read along—with sudden lightning?
Was there an awkward kiss in every *A*?

Was each *H* a ladder with one rung?
And did he see on that one rung—like the runaway
Who stole his only brother's only blessing—

A sudden envoy, winged and otherworldly?
If so, was it climbing or descending?
Did it disappear or did it stay?

Phantom Haiku/Silent Film

> Friends part
> forever—wild geese
> lost in cloud
>   —Basho

I don't write haiku. I'm no good at silence,
Which may be why I crave those movies so much,
Though someone told me it's the silver nitrate,
The way it so luxuriates in light
That anything relinquished to its lunar reach
Becomes a kind of parable of incandescence—
Take a scene in a night-club in war-torn France:
The smoke, the silverware, the sequined dress,
The bubbles orbiting a long-stemmed glass,

Who would interrupt them with a voice?
And then there's what happens to a face.
I wonder if I could get some silver nitrate
To take what I have to say and give it back
With a little of that luminescent silence . . .
Not that I'd show a close-up of my face
Or anything that might be used as evidence;
There's not a single thing I wouldn't leave out.
But in silent movies when the screen goes black

It still feels as if there's something there.
Maybe it's the pervading threat of fire.
That's why they don't use silver nitrate anymore—
It's so flammable—that, and the cost of silver—

But in this case, I'd want it to explode.
In fact, clumsy as it is, it's my metaphor.
I admire Basho, but I just can't buy
That bit about the wild geese and the cloud.
Unless he meant to float the possibility

That, after a season or two, the geese return.
It might even be implicit in the Japanese,
Which names a graceful but predictable species
Famous for going back to the same location.
You get to invent a poem in translation;
Only what isn't said is accurate.
For my haiku about friends that part,
I'd need the Japanese for *silver nitrate*,
A catch-all character for *luminous* and *burn*.

JAY PARINI

Ice

Already the lines are down in county after county,
      and it hasn't stopped:
the slantwise slur, the hiss and skitter.
         Lights went out at 4 p.m.
            and dusk is hazy
as a midnight summer's solstice walk
         around the pond. The pond
is black now, black ice
         floating over bubbled spring: another pond
         now moving like a prehistoric fish
in blinkers, blinded, deep as dream.

                              It is often
like this in the world at large, when
         surfaces will seem, seem something
            other, glitter-crystal, hard
                  unmoving as the face of History,
         all frozen-fire events (like war or famine)—
all that falls in one full decade
and becomes a bitter panorama at the decade's
         end: that moment when you look back
like dumb Orpheus and lose the lot.

A vision is so easily dislodged.
      There is no way not to look behind you, or to lose
exactly what you wanted most to gain,
         or thought you did.
      But think again: this pond,
its underworld of rippling wealth is well
beyond what can be told.

I was once as cold,
once standing at a decade's turn, in 1969,
    in the Cairngorms, Scotland.
                            Snow
was swirling over moor and mountain,
furze was brittle underfoot like glass. I climbed
    alone, where nobody that day could wish to follow.
        I was lost, unmapped,
a foreign body in a welter-white, pure drift,
a down-draft starfall blizzard of the wintering heart.

Too weirdly, I could only think of Balaclava,
        outer regions of another empire—
            visionary bluster run amok. The diaries
of Richard Kidd, a captain in the Guards, recorded this:
        "The ice extends beyond all seeing.
        I cannot discern the end of white, the other side."
He and his company were trapped for months
and lost the best and worst among them.

Only Kidd, at last, remembered what was summer:
"I was like a child in early May one day
        when sunlight hit the ice
like daffodils, so yellow. I was like a child."
Such yellow ice. I, too, remembered summer
        as I knelt that night in snow
            but not to pray.
                        I would not disturb
a God so foolish that he'd make a stone he could not lift.

Something that night inside my anorak
        was warm, was me: a pulse beyond lub-dub lub-dub.
        I listened calmly as I listen now,
putting my ear down hard against the ice, the pond's
        black lid, where nothing can be heard.
The world that matters can be heard by naked ear
        and can be seen by naked eye.

It's yellow, clustered, far away but close enough
       to find if only you can stand alone
              and long enough to let what happens
happen freely, fall what falls, find some dark way
beneath the covers, under lids, beyond the star-whorl,
falling snow, the fell of sky-flanks, stonelike ice
       that covers what is precious, cold, below.

The Trees Are Gone

Rebecca Avenue has lost its trees:
the willow that would brush against my window,
and the spruce that cooled our porch out back,
the ginko I would rake in mid-October,
with its matted leaves like Oriental fans.
Even the beech has been cut down,
that iron pillar of my mother's garden,
with its trunk so smooth against one's cheek.

The dirt I dug in has been spread
with blacktop: tar and oil. They've rolled it
blithely over sidewalk slate
where cracks once splintered into island tufts.
Even leafy hills beyond the town
have been developed, as they like to say:
those tinsel woods where I would rinse myself
in drizzle, in the pinwheel fall.

You can stand all day here without knowing
that it once knew trees: green over green
but gamely turning violet at dusk,
then black to blue-vermillion in the dawn.
It's sentimental, but I miss those trees.
I'd like to slip back through the decades
into deep, lush days and lose myself again
in leaves like hands, wet thrash of leaves.

LINDA PASTAN

Another Autumn

Another autumn, the dogwoods turning first,
their hard berries bright as drops of blood
in the oak woods where a wild fox limped past
just yesterday—a harsher bleeding, and the sound of hounds
came faint as a scent on the wind, barred I had thought
from this wilderness of suburbs. I looked out
my kitchen window this morning and saw a deer,
tame as some neighbor's dog, eating the rhododendrons,
and I listened for the small thunder of shotguns
to stop that beautiful, omnivorous mouth.

The cold will come on fast now. Last week
I emptied the closet of its summer dresses;
draped over my arms they were pale
and insubstantial as last spring's flowers,
and the wool sweaters and skirts I hung in their place
depressed me with their heaviness, their dull, nut colors.
This is the true start of the year; the Jewish calendar
knows it, the school calendar too. Maybe that's why
our old dreams come back to taunt us, hanging
before our faces like condensed breath on this chilly air.

My parents married in fall, a May/September union.
Now in the crystalline light of that anniversary
the same questions repeat their old refrains.
Was love enough, even then?
Will we survive another winter? I remember
how my mother in her middle age looked
at my father, knowing he would be the first to go,
and how I looked at her, the last autumn of her life,
wanting her to flee that ravished flesh
but willing her to stay.

Armonk

In sleep I summon it—dark green shutters
opening on my childhood, white clapboards
bathed in the purple shadows
of azaleas, the perfect 18th Century
farmhouse—"Armonk" we called it,
as if there were no village of that name.
How we loved the old, contorted apple trees
of Armonk, the revolutionary musket
in all its ornamental firepower hanging
over our mantel, the plain pine furniture
assembled from a more strictly crafted age.
It was as though we longed to be part
of a history that could replace our own
ancestors' broken nights in the shtetl
with the softly breaking light
of an American morning.

But what is history if not the imagination
of descendants, made almost flesh?
In old photographs, the cook holds high
a platter of Thanksgiving turkey,
an aunt waves from a mullioned window,
my mother, at her needle and thread, smiles
her understated smile. This
is my authentic childhood.
And my Orthodox grandfather, hunched
over a table, dealing out cards
in an endless game of pinochle,
straightens up for the camera.
Patriarch of the armchair, he could be
some early New England governor
posing for posterity in his starched
white shirt and dark cravat.

To Penelope

After Reading Cavafy's "Ithaca"

Let the days pass slowly, in Ithaca.
Let there be many summer days
with their lingering, lemony scents,
with all the perfumes of the sea
pricking your fine nostrils.
Your stuccoed walls, so cool to the touch
are much too thick for you to hear
the noisy suitors downstairs.
And without the mess and bother
of a man, the sheets of your bed will remain
as white as the morning sands
after the sea has smoothed them.
But never forget Odysseus.
Without him and his journey
the olive trees wouldn't seem bent
in a passion of longing; your loom
would have stayed unstrung, its music
lost on a wind that never was.

Let others applaud you
for what they call patience.
The sound of their hands clapping
will be no more than a small surf beating the shore,
and besides, you deserve applause.
For you are like a fine actress
who takes her bows modestly,
and no one would ever guess you were in love
with solitude. But again, remember:
though he must come back at last,
though you must open your arms
which have grown strong alone at their weaving,
without Odysseus and his journey
there would be no tapestried story.

CARL PHILLIPS

Interior: The Kill

The last time I gave my body up,

to you, I was minded
briefly what it is made of,
what yours is, that

I'd forgotten, the flesh
which always
I hold in plenty no

little sorrow for because—oh, do
but think on its predicament,
and weep.

We cleave most entirely
to what most we fear
losing. We fear loss

because we understand
the fact of it, its largeness, its
utter indifference to whether

we do, or don't,
ignore it. By then, you
were upon me, and then

in me, soon the tokens
I almost never can let go of, I'd
again begin to, and would not

miss them: the swan
unfolding
upward less on trust than

because, simply, that's
what it does; and the leaves,
leaving; a single arrow held

back in the merciless
patience which, in taking
aim, is everything; and last,

as from a grove in
flame toward any air
more clear, the stag, but

this time its bent
head a chandelier, rushing
for me, like some

undisavowable
distraction. I looked back,
and instead of you, saw

the soul-at-labor-to-break-its-bonds
that you'd become. I tensed
my bow:

one animal at attack,
the other—the other one
suffering, and love would

out all suffering—

Interior: Retreat

The sea and then, before it, the salted
meadow of sea-hay, the meadow
graven by narrow channels, the more

easy, once, to gain entry, farmers
sailoring into—to cut again down—
the meadow, to harvest the blue, the

green hay which is blond now, which
will for months stand for *Sleeping, Let
be,* the kind of abandon that is endurable

because its ending, if not yet visible,
is nevertheless sure, as much anyway
as all promises: believe them, or

don't believe them, and—then what?
That's history, about the farmers.
Come spring, then summer, the boats

that come instead will be for finding
pleasure because, simply, it's findable
here, and still free, even if, just now,

who will say so? Nobody's here. In
the narrow channels, no pleasuring
boats, either. A single and wooden

dock, yes, but opening out into a space
in which nothing drifts tethered and
waiting, unless memory—what some

plash of want or of need, idling briefly,
makes appear there—counts, waiting.
From inside the meadow, the fidget of

darkness that was, all along, birds
lifts abruptly, assembles: first a shield
thrown, too soon, too recklessly aloft,

then any door by a storm opened, in a
wind swinging, that someone—whom
nobody sees, whom nobody thinks,

therefore, to thank—passes, and—
not tenderly, just—responsibly, pulls
shut. The body first. Then the soul.

The Truth

And now,
the horse is entering
the sea, and the sea

        holds it.

Where are we?

Behind us,
the beach,
      yes, its
scrim,
    yes, of
        grass, dune, sky—Desire

goes by, and though
it's wind of course making
the grass bend,

      unbend, we say
it's desire again, passing
us by, souveniring us with
gospel the grass, turned
choir, leans into,

Coming—
Lord, soon.

Because
it still matters, to say something. Like:
the heart isn't

       really breakable,
not in the way you mean, anymore
than a life shatters,

       —which is what
dropped shells can do, or a bond sworn to,
remember, once

       couldn't, a wooden boat between
unmanageable wave and rock or,
as hard, the shore.

The wooden boat is
not the heart,
       the wave the flesh,
         the rock the soul—

and if we thought so, we have merely been
that long
mistaken.

       Also,
about the shore: it doesn't
mean all trespass
is forgiven, if nightly
the sand is cleared of
any sign
       we were here.

It doesn't equal that whether
we were here or not
matters,
doesn't—

　　　　　Waves, because
so little of the world, even
when we say that it has
shifted, has:

same voices,
ghosts, same
hungers come,
　　　　　　　stop coming—

Soon—

How far the land can be found to
be, and
of a sudden,
　　　　　　　sometimes. Now—
so far from rest,
should rest be needed—

Will it drown?

The horse, I mean.

And I—who do not ride, and
do not swim

And would that I had never climbed
its back

And love you too

ROBERT PINSKY

The Green Piano

Aeolian. Gratis. Great thunderer, half-ton infant of miracles
Torn free of charge from the universe by my mother's will.
You must have amazed that half-respectable street

Of triple-decker families and rooming-house housepainters
The day that the bole-ankled oversized hams of your legs
Bobbed in procession up the crazy-paved front walk

Embraced by the arms of Mr. Poppik the seltzer man
And Corydon his black-skinned helper, tendering your thighs
Thick as a man up our steps. We are not reptiles:

Even the male body bears nipples, as if to remind us
We are designed for dependence and nutriment, past
Into future. O Europe, they budged your case, its ponderous

Guts of iron and brass, ten kinds of hardwood and felt
Up those heel-pocked risers and treads splintering tinder.
Angelic nurse of clamor, yearner, tinkler, dominator—

O Elephant, you were for me! When the tuner Mr. Otto Van Brunt
Pronounced you excellent despite the cracked sounding board, we
Obeyed him and swabbed your ivories with hydrogen peroxide.

You blocked a doorway and filled most of the living room.
The sofa and chairs dwindled to a ram and ewes, cowering: now,
The colored neighbors could be positive we were crazy and rich,

As we thought the people were who gave you away for the moving
Out of their carriage house—they had painted you the color of pea soup.
The drunk man my mother hired never finished antiquing you

Ivory and umber, so you stood half-done, a throbbing mistreated noble,
Genuine—my mother's swollen livestock of love: lost one, unmastered:
You were the beast she led to the shrine of my genius, mistaken.

Endlessly I bonged according to my own chord system *Humoresque,*
The Talk of the Town, What'd I Say. Then one day they painted you pink.
Pink is how my sister remembers you the Saturday afternoon

When our mother fell on her head, dusty pink as I turn on the bench
In my sister's memory to see them carrying our mother up the last
Steps and into the living room, inaugurating the reign of our confusion.

They sued the builder of the house she fell in, with the settlement
They bought a house at last and one day when I came home from college
You were gone, mahogany breast, who nursed me through those

Years of the Concussion, and there was a crappy little Baldwin Acrosonic
In your place, gleaming, walnut shell. You were gone, despoiled one—
Pink one, forever-green one, white and gold one, comforter, a living soul.

The Haunted Ruin

Even your computer is a haunted ruin, as your
Blood leaves something of itself, warming
The tool in your hand.

From far off, down the billion corridors
Of the semiconductor, military
Pipes grieve at the junctures.

This too smells of the body, its heated
Polymers smell of breast milk
And worry-sweat.

Hum of so many cycles in current, voltage
Of the past. Sing, wires. Feel, hand. Eyes,
Watch and form

Legs and bellies of characters:
Beak and eye of A. Serpentine hiss
S of the foregoers, claw-tines

Of E and the claw hammer
You bought yesterday, its head
Tasting of light oil, the juice

Of dead striving—the haft
Of ash, for all its urethane varnish, is
Polished by body salts.

Pull, clawhead. Hold, shaft. Steel face,
Strike and relieve me. Voice
Of the maker locked in the baritone

Whine of the handsaw working.
Lost, lingerer like the dead souls of
Wilno, revenant. Machine-soul.

Ode to Meaning

Dire one and desired one,
Savior, sentencer—

In an old allegory you would carry
A chained alphabet of tokens:

Ankh Badge Cross.
Dragon,
Engraved figure guarding a hallowed intaglio,
Jasper kinema of legendary Mind,
Naked omphalos pierced
By quills of rhyme or sense, torah-like: unborn
Vein of will, xenophile
Yearning out of Zero.

Untrusting I court you. Wavering
I seek your face, I read
That Crusoe's knife
Reeked of you, that to defile you
The soldier makes the rabbi spit on the torah.
"I'll drown my book" says Shakespeare.

Drowned walker, revenant.
After my mother fell on her head, she became
More than ever your sworn enemy. She spoke
Sometimes like a poet or critic of forty years later.
Or she spoke of the world as Thersites spoke of the heroes,
"I think they have swallowed one another. I
Would laugh at that miracle."

You also in the laughter, warrior angel:
Your helmet the zodiac, rocket-plumed
Your spear the beggar's finger pointing to the mouth
Your heel planted on the serpent Formulation
Your face a vapor, the wreath of cigarette smoke crowning
Bogart as he winces through it.

You are not in the words, not even
Between the words, but a torsion,
A cleavage, a stirring.

You stirring even in the arctic ice,
Even at the dark ocean floor, even
In the cellular flesh of a stone.

Gas. Gossamer. My poker friends
Question your presence
In a poem by me, passing the magazine
One to another.

Not the stone and not the words, you
Like a veil over Arthur's headstone,
The passage from Proverbs he chose
While he was too ill to teach
And still well enough to read, *I was*
Beside the master craftsman
Delighting him day after day, ever
At play in his presence—you

A soothing veil of distraction playing over
Dying Arthur playing in the hospital,
Thumbing the Bible, fuzzy from medication,
Ever courting your presence.
And you the prognosis,
You in the cough.

Gesturer, when is your spur, your cloud?
You in the airport rituals of greeting and parting.
Indicter, who is your claimant?
Bell at the gate. Spiderweb iron bridge.
Cloak, video, aroma, rue, what is your
Elected silence, where was your seed?

What is Imagination
But your lost child born to give birth to you?

Dire one. Desired one.
Savior, sentencer—

Absence,
Or presence ever at play:
Let those scorn you who never
Starved in your dearth. If I
Dare to disparage
Your harp of shadows I taste
Wormwood and motor oil, I pour
Ashes on my head. You are the wound. You
Be the medicine.

To Television

Not a "window on the world"
But as we call you,
A box a tube

Terrarium of dreams and wonders.
Coffer of shades, ordained
Cotillion of phosphors
Or liquid crystal

Homey miracle, tub
Of acquiescence, vein of defiance.
Your patron in the pantheon would be Hermes

Raster dance,
Quick one, little thief, escort
Of the dying and comfort of the sick,

In a blue glow my father and little sister sat
Snuggled in one chair watching you
Their wife and mother was sick in the head
I scorned you and them as I scorned so much

Now I like you best in a hotel room,
Maybe minutes
Before I have to face an audience: behind
The doors of the armoire, box
Within a box—Tom & Jerry, or also brilliant
And reassuring, Oprah Winfrey.

Thank you, for I watched, I watched
Sid Caesar speaking French and Japanese not
Through knowledge but imagination,
His quickness, and Thank you, I watched live
Jackie Robinson stealing

Home, the image—O strung shell—enduring
Fleeter than light like these words we
Remember in: they too are winged
At the helmet and ankles.

STANLEY PLUMLY

Catbird Beginning with a Cardinal

for Larry Levis

First the all-red male arrives, in order to attract attention,
and once it's safe, the softer, buff-brown female.
They sit as a pair for less than the time it takes to see them.
Survival skills. None in the hand worth two in the tree.
And the mockers, even faster, split second by split second,
conspicuous as semaphore and flight-song.
Still, if you sing well enough, disappear enough,
and speak in a granular dove sort of gargle—and come alone—
the slate-gray, black-capped catbird, mewling along the arbor,
seems friendly, even catchable, if only captive,
or at least capable of being company,
since it isn't shy when it should be
and is susceptible to charm.
And trying to charm or catch one
wouldn't be an entirely alien if wild idea—
not so much to touch as to be proximate, in the presence of,
but close to the extent that if it let you
you might stroke its black felt cap or run a finger down a wing
or feed it suet or a berry from the holly
or talk to it as if it were the copy of the namesake of the cat
who sits outside the window in the rain like a ghost wanting in,
or, last resort, address it as a soul in transmigration,
one outsider to another, lost beaten locations—
though, on second thought, an old and flawed idea,
less because impossible than sentimental
in the worst domestic-garden-variety way,
failing to account for fundamental differences,
the obvious and not-so-clear genetics and odd genius,
the arrow of the tongue,

the nature of the eye and what we hear,
the sometime fever in the brain,
the hollowing of bone,
the graphite pencil-blue transparency of wings
opened like a greeting, then erased,
then quickly drawn again.

Cheer

Like the waxwings in the juniper,
a dozen at a time, divided, paired,
passing the berries back and forth, and by
nightfall, wobbling, piping, wounded with joy.

Or a party of redwings grazing what
falls—blossom and seed, nutmeat and fruit—
made light in the head and cut by the light,
swept from the ground, carried downwind, taken . . .

It's called wing-rowing, the wing-burdened arms
unbending, yielding, striking a balance,
walking the white invisible line drawn
just ahead in the air, first sign the slur,

the liquid notes too liquid, the heart in
the mouth melodious, too close, which starts
the chanting, the crooning, the long lyric
silences, the song of our undoing.

It's called side-step, head-forward, raised-crown, flap-
and-glide-flight aggression, though courtship is
the object, affection the compulsion,
love the overspill—the body nodding,

still standing, ready to fly straight out of
itself—or it's bill-tilt, wing-flash, topple-
over; wing-droop, bowing, tail-flick and drift;
back-ruffle, wing-spread, quiver and soar.

Someone is troubled, someone is trying,
in earnest, to explain; to speak without
swallowing the tongue; to find the perfect
word among so few or the too many—

to sing like the thrush from the deepest part
of the understory, territorial,
carnal, thorn-at-the-throat, or flutelike
in order to make one sobering sound.

Sound of the breath blown over the bottle,
sound of the reveler home at dawn, light of
the sun a warbler yellow, the sun in
song-flight, lopsided-pose. Be of good cheer,

my father says, lifting his glass to greet
a morning in which he's awake to be
with the birds: or up all night in the sleep
of the world, alive again, singing.

BIN RAMKE

A Little Ovid Late in the Day

It is late in the day
to outlive the words:
tales of incest, corruption,
any big, mythic vice
against the color of sun,
the sweetness of the time of day—
I know the story,
it is the light I care about.
The book falls from my hands
and I know all the stories,
I know better than that.
They glitter in the grass.
This is fun in the summer,
the sun descending onto my back,
the weight of eight light-minutes
warm there against skin.
Someone will read aloud to me
when I have forgotten the words,
the look they make against the page,
the kind of stain it is against the paper.

Livery of Seisin

the delivery of property into the corporal possession of a person; in the case of a
house, by giving him the ring, latch, or key of the door; in the case of land, by
delivering him a twig, a piece of turf, or the like

—OED

Of touch, the annoyance
That if I touch you you
Touch me—the affront it is and

Its reciprocal nature and it is
The basis of the lighter
Perversions, *frottage*, for instance which is

The secret joy of public
Touching it is, on a bus
To transport to touch the whole self

There is no stopping
It, if (there is no defense)
I touch you you touch me

If I touch (if not you)
The glamour of the stars
Oh the stars (famously beyond reach)

That such light touches
The eyes the retina, parts of the skin
The inevitable body (where we live no matter)

And too
The warm the sun striking out
But the stars softly at night (impossibly by day)

That we touch the stars
And that any light-
Emitting body (heat, and any radiation)

Is infinite in size or will be,
Caressing the universe
At a hundred eighty-six thousand

Miles per second
O love o sacred. To change,
To hold the house in your hand, the subject,

To expand infinitely to the end
Too terrible to think upon
Each man's life is but a breath (Psalm 39) A touch

A touching most intimate,
The breath a column still attached
To the warm wet lung, every leering man knows

What he's doing, dreary,
Perpendicular sounds flying past
Touch, extensive touch of someone's tongue,

Expensive,
O do talk less, give us
Room, give us air dry and drifting

Flowers inventing
Themselves on the tips
Of trees, reach out Nature reaches

Trees reach out like
Stars light their touch
And candor, all their own.

A Theory of Fantasy

The boy his hand the size of the bird
Brilliant into the window pane the bird
The same heartbeat beat at the boy's
Wrist the folded wings. The bird revived
To stare at the view the aspens the
Mountains beyond. The bird flew and
I said You saved him. This art
Of lying we found alluring.
Boy and father staring at the aspens the
Mountains beyond.

We looked up the name of the bird studied the colors
And ranges. He tried to read the Latin like
A summer language. He failed.
As if evil were useful
He continued to dwell in that body not
Diseased merely doomed. And play to the world. Snow
Lay under the limbs of trees. The leopard lay with the lamb.
Contingencies threatened. He read himself
To sleep he dreamed spotted animals slink
Brain sex and muscle under pelt. Snow
Gathered by night by morning the world wore
Its white brain through which some crocus
Might break small and bright a language.

ALBERTO RÍOS

Common Crows in a Winter Tree

The birds, they make this happen.
In the sky with nothing else to do, a Saturday,
The slow knee-bend of an afternoon, out there.

I have seen them myself.
The birds caw down a rain, tease it
To a hard ground of grass and flat and edge.

The birds, they cannot stop, they are birds.
They play when they do it, they don't mean it
When the rain reaches bottom.

But there is so much rain, and it listens
So well, who would not, like the birds,
Try other things, try to train this water

To tricks, and to laughter? Circus
Ringmaster to a thousand lions of water:
Rain do this: And again: And now this:

To get away from the birds rain tries a mask:
It becomes snow, a show of wings, the flakes
Drunk moths in an aimless, cool wander.

Then it is ice, a trick again, rain

Turning into tiny fists without skin.
Hailstones, each a clutch of finger bones,
Brittle, as much dry as wet. Rain to snow

Then ice, then bone. Then more,
To skulls, and teeth, breaking against the earth
In a white fireworks of cruelty.

The birds, they get carried away, they cannot
Do a small thing or make a quiet noise.
But the birds do not mean it, this

Teasing of the sky to tears. They are birds,
They caw at anything, at little boys
Walking, boys who will look up.

And a loud caw, it will draw the boys, lift them
A little, until they cry. The birds
Do not mean to frighten,

But neither do they mean not to frighten,
Not to lift a boy into a branch
The way boys will go, lift a boy to a second

Branch, higher. The boys will go.
They cry at first, but they rise.
They are boys, and these are birds.

And the rain is falling, it makes a sound
Until snow, which is itself a sound,
Bigger and smaller than the moment before.

The boys come down from climbing, the boys who were lifted
Into trees, the boys who were birds.
The birds make their noise again, at something else.

From the Life of Don Margarito

He was a serious man
But for one afternoon
Late in his life
With serious friends.
They adjourned to a bar
Away from the office
And its matters.
Something before dinner,
Something for the appetite
One of them had said,
And the three of them walked
In long sleeves
Into the *Molino Rojo*.
The cafe's twenty tables
Were pushed together
Almost entirely
Or pulled apart barely,
Giving not them
But the space between them
A dark and ragged shine
Amidst the white tablecloths.
And tables
And the spaces they made
Looked like the pieces
Of a child's puzzle
Almost done,
A continent breaking, something
From the beginning of time.
To get by them
Don Margarito had to walk
Sideways, and then sideways
Again, with arms outstretched
And up.
It was a good trick of the place
Conspiring with the music
To make the science
In this man's movement
Look like dance.

Los Voladores de Papantla

I saw the flying men of Papantla in the 1950s,
And then several times since,

The Tarascan Indians from inside Mexico
Playing flutes, some of them, the others answering

From the small platform at the top of a 50 foot pole,
Binding their ankles to the end of a rope.

It was the first time that stays with me,
Especially now. Today it's neat and clean—

The ropes are checked and insurance forms signed.
But the first time, people crowded right up to the pole,

And the men jumped without testing first.
Their ropes, anyone could see, were homemade.

These men were not putting on a show.
They were painted, but were not clowns.

Their ropes were like fuses
And their thin, reddened bodies

Like penny firecrackers.
They were faith-jumpers,

And it was religion we were in the middle of.
Religion with silver sweat and with yellow screams,

Whole audiences in thrall to blood that was real.
These were fireworks like any

But with the explosions, the green
And the blue, the rosettes of sparkle

Imagined, but easily, so clear was the next moment:
A man would jump.

At that moment in life and in the world anything could happen.
People clasped their hands together

In prayer, but as much in desperation.
With so many crowded in, it just sounded like applause.

DAVID RIVARD

Clarity

So long as the self accuses itself
it makes itself necessary & strikes at
shadow so long as it pretends
always to be what it is not so long
as you cannot touch who you are
and it is necessary for the pieces of
your puzzle, your great lucky story,
to be shoved deep in the lint-
packed corners of a jacket pocket,
so that the anchorage is gone
from which the ships were launched,
and there are no panties on the floor,
no cotton blouse, no husband & no
mountaintop, there is no belt buckle,
and at the airport no maze of lights,
and then the gifts go, at dusk, the boots
her husband wore in the garage, the car,
and then the dusk goes, a hell
the size of an apple seed, & there is no
slow ride across the lake, no diamond,
no cut-glass cat, & no cat gut
to sew the wound, no scissors
either, & no hair the blades
might hack, no earring, no bee's wax,
no glasses an old man could wipe
clear, & no sneer, indelicate,
the sand vanished, the bathwater drained,
gone, the same with the chimney
in need of pointing, the pit where
they changed the oil, the house lent

for a day, it is a pain in the neck,
a pain in the ass, but there is no
headwater for the Mississippi,
and no asp, not even a bee
wearing a cocked bosun's cap,
machinegun in one hand, hammer
in the other, there be no clouds
so swift & no sun so slow, so slow,
slow, & naturally, no loneliness
to make you grateful for having had
something or someone to serve.

The Favored

In the dream that repeats as certain
as dusk you walk with me
again as it happens strolling by

yards of quiet or clamoring families.
Affable street, & nothing accidental
here, so it makes sense

I like the people we pass by thinking
the sunglasses I wear
mean me a blind man.

Always you grip a white second-hand paperback.
I can almost smell the spine's
cracked glue as you read

aloud. Pulp—
narrated by a foolish minor princeling
or gypsy tinker, his eyes aquamarine,

squinting through venetian shades into
the bedroom of a scullery maid/dominatrix/police detective
who offers to straddle

the plantation master/diplomat/dope dealer's head
as he lies there on the floor,
the enticements of her taffeta, spandex, musk,

and blondness
quite clear, & if he submits—one
can only hope—he will, later, pray

to be part of the various
silver-green mosses & tendrils hanging from branches
over-hanging a river. In the dream we seem

the same man & woman who
each day step-out onto our porch.
Ourselves. Meat & potato-eaters,

but favored. We are ordinary,
glad
someone dares to tell our story.

Guests of the Wedding

Does it ever end? Sure, hard to say where tho, & naturally
the facts of the next thirty minutes or years
are not like tent pegs pounded into the earth,
not knowable because sharp & stationary.
But that morning walking beneath the tent—
a large tent—I saw
there was candlewax pooled on the starched white tablecloths,
proof of the pleasure
people had taken
circling & dancing & burning in the light
those candles threw the night before.
Thank you, gracious candles.
It was a wedding.
All of us, Michaela said, are really
animals, & she accepted that, glad.

And that morning
in the house belonging to Candice & Ed
next to the tent we met
the boy named Jake, a four-year-old, & his mother
with her tattoo designed by an unknown hand
to encircle like a wide bracelet her tanned upper arm,
a bracelet marked by totemic shapes & faces—
beaks, fins, talons, feathered tails, lidded eyes—
Kwakiutl if there were no Kwakiutl around to ask
the mother of Jake why & from where & who
did she think she was? Who was she
who had also had drawn across her back
shoulder blade to blade an unfurled pair of wings?
She was a lovely citizen & an employee of Ed
if the obvious can be counted on
sometimes in the sharp late-September sunlight.
Many things might happen to her
but those tattoos remain the same
or changed only slightly of course
by the fading of color,
slackened skin. Many things
would happen, her future—
months without jobs, & later,
success, against a backdrop of stables, success,
and then the night she would nearly be raped,
the rainy night she would fish
the beach with Brazilians, & on another shore
the morning she'd lick a pebble & laugh
to tell her as yet unborn daughter
I am Demosthenes & must practice my oration—
the future I invented for her,
and within which
I moved her from place to place.
To own another person, completely, in the imagination.
How else do you teach yourself
what you wish to become?
And isn't it
one after another after another after another
the many things men & women wish to be?

PETER SACKS

The Ocean, Naming It

Less than a mile out I was
exhausted.

Ghosting out of history;

it came again,
betrayal, so called,

spear-head.

And its eye
stared.

&

Excuses
horned around me, crescent, manifold.

&

Asleep on the dunes.

The moon came up so large I rolled aside.

Involuntary whiteness of the crests

spilled flashing for each generation.

Early stars hung low over the wake,

the future comes toward us.

Every word.

&

Traveling in the cage.

Not fully formed.
                         And there were
many cages.

The Tree

This was a different sound, repeated from the other side pressed to the disappearing throat, face, fingers, memory of.

The door blew wide on swells that shone back through the tree the ocean swung from, single leaf.

Branch by branch you climbed to where the voices rained.

You held up the song frayed to the whispered friction of grass when wind drops & the meadow whistles under a dipping finch,

the surf swept backward by a larger breath than you could draw till now.

Releasing everything, you climbed again among the others reaching through

to where the world, surprised by hearing pieces of its name, looks back into the crowd of those still vanishing. Who called?

IRA SADOFF

Honeymoon in Florence

As they putty up their frescos,
as they scrape and file, the artisans of Florence
think this church in the Year of Our Lord,
think nature is nature, they think the olive
is an olive. They think the sentence
is an unshamed body part. The sentence
"buried in rubble," does not expect
sex trauma, stretch marks, chest scars,
the quick cut of collage, salutes
to the fractional, where I come from.

In the past we had blue cedars and country roads
with full-throated thrushes
laying down a soundtrack of pure sentiment.
From here you can see the olive groves of Tuscany,
where a statue can replace a worry,
and idiot savants hold out their arms
as if to receive an angel. What they rescued
was a fallen plaster crucifix
the year my marriage was fill in the blank
and certain close friends were coughing away their cancers.

Something about me knocks keys off the vanity,
shouts from our hotel balcony: we're tired of trekking
through the mimetic woods to find some flower
to represent us, some psychic storm
to vanquish it. Underneath, in the shadow part,
the Tiepolos are swirling toward heaven
like a backwards flush of the toilet. Statues
die away at a very slow rate. Copperized monuments
are moldy with prattling, pecking sparrows.
Oh, I've been saved by love, but privately.

Long Island

I've spent the last few years with an eraser,
trying to uncover the masterpiece under the canvas,
scratching at the crusted-over surfaces:

were there windows? Certainly
there were gaping spaces and cherubim on bicycles
painted over with a dog and a few affairs . . .

The old subjects were the good subjects.
Love, greed, a stultifying awareness your arms
need replenishing. The paradise of shifting traumas

slivered into a chorus of bickering interior voices—
everyone had a defect, a mismatched seam, a flaw
you could see through, a pencil thin crack in the cup.

So whatever was distinct about us, bright or sensual,
became sordid, unworthy, a visit to the doctor
where the cancer's fastened to a rib, a series of periods

on an old piece of carbon paper. The twisted
machinations of childhood were nothing more
than a few coughs at the office, to be discounted later,

so while one was changing the channel,
another was soaking the dishes and the third
stood behind her, waiting to sexualize the moment.

Those who had maids understood slavery.
Those who had wives, bosses, those who decorated
according to magazines, those who sat in a chair

while a parent guided their pencil to the right answer,
the dead draped in flags, they also served.
While on the other side of town, on a more personal level

we didn't want to be no more nothing, so we slummed
at the chicken shack, where the dead flies on the counter
that looked like jewels were really roaches.

The Rapture

The tongue wagging, mumbling and moaning,
calling out, shouting instructions, legs buckling, scalding
where the flesh grinds against the flesh, the veil

of seduction dropped, the quick and shallow breathing
(outside, truck tires whistling, a child on a bike,
but muffled, as if the gagged world were boiled down

to liquid, capped, pharmaceutical, a store
where sickness is soothed), then the acquired things:
this borrowed from what she did with someone else,

that from what he once saw, this from magazines,
the once shamed and detonated flesh now truculent
and delectable, then the seizure, the moment

nothing more than rapid eye movement,
mere transparency, followed by declarations
and a snail-like withdrawal, the dreaded afterwards,

the schism and the questions, the heart
beginning to stutter and calm, space coming back
into focus, coming back too quickly:

the night table, the book, the clock,
everything that refuses to change pulsing with solidity.
Then it's back: the anonymous clutter of the avenue,

ravenous looks reflected in every storefront
so nothing's left but a flash of body part,
a sensation dimly lit, scored like film and fluttering.

DAVID ST. JOHN

Another Kiss

It is instead the echo of a kiss
The vibration of the air surrounding
The moment before the collision
Of lips with lips

It is the certain solemnity of the tongue
Arriving without thought
But with enormous & admirable determination
& special drive

It is the hunger & the bark of hope
It is soul lifting the apple to its lips
It is the melting of the bones of the face
Into the bones of another's face

It is the robes of despair let fall
It is the pressed silence of the usual lie
Held just under the tongue like
A penny for passage to the land of the dead

It is the bowl of ragged scarlet tulips
Suddenly lifted in the sunlight
Like champagne flutes
To toast the simple rags of tenderness

Scattered everywhere upon the air

Fragment

My soul *is* envy & for that very reason
I delight in dressing in the faintest
Fatal green most often
A green like Key Lime so fresh & delicate

It seems simply a gossamer glint
Of fragile wings or gills or scales
Pulled from nature to decorate
What is unnatural

By which I mean myself & my
Disgust at your simple happiness ah yes
But perhaps I have it all wrong
Perhaps in my dazzling silks of envy

I am more lost & alluring even
More alarming than I might
Ever have become as myself alone
Naked as the lonely knife of nothing

Sheer as the cliff-face of your own appalling life

Her Painting

In her painting called "The Tree
Of Life" (I know, I know) my friend Solange
Had placed a clear self-portrait of
Herself at seventeen cocooned in rough

Bark ribbons & draped like some peculiar
Fruit upon the lower & clearly
Deformed branches of her autobiographical
L'arbre & when I asked if that was really

The way she'd always seen herself
A waif of chance a petrified baby owl
Some cold blossom of preliminary nascence
She just looked up at me from her coffee

& said Some of us take what we can get
& some of us recognize the facts of our own fates
& those who like you can't are simply sentenced
To being death's tiny decorations

Those minute ornaments of pleasures almost past

ALAN SHAPIRO

The Beach Chair

for David Ferry

The leaves drift in a clatter and dry hiss
over the beach chair left out in the yard
since summer: its symmetries and surfaces,
the taut green fabric of its back and seat,
the dull sheen of its frame, are aswarm with leaves
that fall all afternoon into the shadows
of leaves that haven't fallen yet and now
seem almost to be rising from within
the form they float on up to what's falling down.
It is as if by holding still, it holds
each instant's omen and its memory,
omens of altering, and memories
of having altered, as the leaves, brittle
as coral, reticulating through the air
in swirls and drifts, fall toward the shadowy sway
of leaves about to fall along the planes
and angles of what happens to be there.

Feet

Feet he can't lift, feet padding with a toddler's half-
step, sh-sh-sh, down the carpeted hall, feet swollen,
purple, with minuscule white cracks between the toes,
along the sides, the heel, sore feet he's asking me,
if it's, you know, no bother, will I rub with cream?

dry feet I gingerly cup and lift into my lap,
feet of the stockyard, feet of the slaughterhouse, factory,
showroom floor, my fingers working the moisturizer
down into the parched soles, the rinds of calluses,
over the bunched skin rough as braille above the heel bone,

the instep whitening under the pressure of my touch,
then darkening again, whitening then darkening,
lifted and let down, feet of the love bed, feet of we had
a few good years before the war, before you children,
feet of I never cheated on her, I never beat her,

what the hell else does she want? First one and then the other,
cupped in my hand, cupped even as I let them down
so slowly that the weight, the gravity, the pulling
from the earth's core for a moment's mine, not theirs, then theirs
again, half-stepping sh-sh-sh down the carpeted hall.

The Singer

The way you sang, half dozing as I drove,
the radio on; the way your hovering
so near sleep, unaware of me, appeared
to purify your shyness, not free you from it;
the way you needed even then to sing
without appearing to, your hushed voice lagging
with a furtive clumsiness behind the singer's,
each syllable only half formed on your lips
before the next one and the next arrived;
the way you happily seemed to falter after
what was always half a syllable beyond,
was not the least accomplished of your many
unknowingly disclosed when most disguised
most accidental flashings of a presence
that's not for yours but other people's eyes.

Thrush in Summer

Aged as Hardy's thrush, frail, gaunt, but silent,
not flitting away, or even flinching there
in the azalea when I pull back branches
and lean in, my face just inches from you now.
The eye you eye me with is a drop of tar,
glassy and blank; the bent twig of your beak
is shut; your grey-brown plumage ragged, blast-
beruffled, though the day is calm, though there
is only a calm morning's drift of pale
and dark green shadows rippling the air,
with every moment now a different sound
of bird song high up in the trees, throughout
the understory, everywhere around us,
it seems, the day is singing in its shapes
and sounds and colors the full-hearted song
you sang once in another century,
another season, while beyond the poem,
mutely, your body sings the song you sang
against, of frost and wind, the shrunken pulse,
the weakening eye of day that this new day
is singing over, blessedly unaware.

JANE SHORE

Happiness

My friend Joyce opens her antique silk-covered box
and we shuffle twelve dozen ebony tiles
face-down on my kitchen table.
Joyce calls this the "Twittering of the Sparrows."
She's teaching my daughter, Emma, and me
how to play mah-jongg, the game
all the Jewish mothers played, except mine.

It's way past Emma's bedtime,
the harvest moon having risen hours ago
round and full as the one dot
on its tile of worn ebony.
After we've stacked the tiles
and built a square Great Wall of China,
Joyce hands Emma a tiny box carved from bone,
which holds two tiny ivory dice,
small as her baby teeth I tucked away
in an envelope in my keepsake drawer.

This is weird. My generation of women
wouldn't be caught dead playing mah-jongg,
the game all the Jewish mothers played
summers at Applebaum's Bungalow Colony,
red fingernails clicking against the tiles.

Joyce's friend, Susan, taught her mah-jongg;
and like a big sister,
Joyce wanted to teach me.
Her favorite bakelite bracelets
clunking noisily around her wrist,
she consults her tattered mimeographed sheets,
reading the rules out loud as we go along.
Beginners, we are not yet ready
to gamble with real money.
We lay our tiles face-up on the table,
exposing our hands, so everyone can see.

At Applebaum's, my mother would watch
the other mothers playing mah-jongg—
but she wouldn't sit down and join them.
Even when she took the summer off,
my mother was not about playing.

I roll the highest score on the dice,
so I am the East Wind, the dealer.
But I'm sitting at the foot of the table,
where the south, on a map, would be.
It's not the normal geography.
The South Wind sits to the left of me
clunking her bracelets,
and Emma's the North Wind, on my right.
Joyce tells us a little trick to remember
the clockwise order of play—
"Eat Soy With Noodles,"
(East, South, West, North)—
and to remind us who'll be the East Wind next.

Oh how I love the sound of the tiles
clicking together, the sound our nails make
clicking against the tiles,
the sound the ebony tiles make
scraping the oak table, the sound the dice make
bouncing softly on the wood,
the sound my mouth makes calling out
"eight crack" and "five bamboo" as I discard them,
the sounds the ivory counting sticks make
when we add up our scores,
and the names of the hands we have scored,
syllables of pure pleasure:

combinations of Pungs, Chows, Kongs,
and pillows, pairs of East Winds or Red Dragons,
making a Dragon's Tail, Windfall, LillyPilly,
Seven Brothers, Three Sisters, Heavenly Twins,
making a Green Jade, Royal Ruby, White Opal,
Red Lantern, and Gates of Heaven . . .

Why did my mother deny herself?
Once when I asked her, she confessed
that she never really enjoyed business.
I think that my mother
didn't much like mothering, either.
It scared her, too, the closeness of every day.
It was easier to fold my clothes
than to touch me. Even as she was dying,
she shut me out, preferring to be alone.
Now, she's like the West Wind in the empty chair
opposite me, the absent one we skip over
because we are playing with only three.

Emma shouts "mah-jongg!"—she's won her first game.
Joyce is so thrilled, she forgets
we're not playing for money.
Rummaging in her purse, she pulls out
a dollar bill and crushes it into Emma's hand.
Emma flushes with pleasure, delighted
to be playing with the grown-ups,
happy to be considered "one of the girls."

We reshuffle the tiles. Twitter the sparrows—
all peacocks, dragons, flowers, seasons
hide under their black blankets of night.
Reflecting us, the dark window blurs our hands
then brightens into the all other hands I saw
around card tables set up under shade trees
during those long hot afternoons
in Rockland Lake, New York.
Babies napping, husbands away at work—
all the other mothers playing—
happy, sipping their iced drinks,
happy, smoking their cigarettes.

A Reminder

My husband gets a postcard in the mail
from Temple Beth Israel,
forwarded from our last address: it asks him

to light a yartzeit memorial candle
for his ("beloved father Larry")
on the evening of ("January 14")—
the blanks for the name and date, in parentheses,
filled in with blue ball-point ink.

I don't want to see my husband's face
when he reads it.

I never met my father-in-law.
He never met our daughter,
his granddaughter.

It's been a year since he died,
a year since my husband flew
to Ohio, to attend the funeral,
drove a rentalcar to his uncle's house,
and sat shiva with the rabbi
and curious cousins and aunts—
people he'd never met before—
and his father's friends
and business associates, and the buddies
his father played poker with
every Friday night for the last twenty years.

When his father first got sick,
my husband deliberated for months
about whether or not to visit him
and say good-bye.
He died before my husband could decide.

Tomorrow's the 14th.
There's not a candle in the house.
My husband's out of town, working.
I'll have to go to the Grand Union,
to the Jewish shelf
where they keep the matzoh meal and kasha,
and buy a yartzeit candle, just in case.

He'll be home in plenty of time
to light the candle at sundown.
But he's ambivalent.
Guilty if he lights it.
Guilty if he doesn't.

When his father walked out
on his wife of thirty years, my husband's mother,
he took all the family savings, cleaned out
the safety deposit box, and disappeared
to another state for twenty years,
his whereabouts a blank.

But during those twenty years,
he found a girlfriend, a house, a job,
another life.

He ate breakfast at McDonald's
with his best friend, Sol,
every morning for the last ten years.

Sol told my husband,
"You could have knocked me over with a feather.
In the whole time I knew him,
your father never once mentioned
that he had a son."

Four sons. My husband's brothers
all kept in the dark, all
written out of their father's will.

A week after the funeral,
someone sent us the obituary
clipped from the newspaper:
The deceased has no immediate survivors.

Now, this reminder—
my husband has to live with it.
Remembering, while he struggles to forget.
Deciding whether he should light a candle,
or not, every year when the day comes around.

JEFFREY SKINNER

Play Dead

Like the black D.J. in New Orleans
who declared his own wake on the air
and the resurrection to follow—five bucks
admission, with the promise of a hundred
to anyone who caught him breathing.
One woman pulled up a chair
before the open casket, and fastened
her eyes on his chest for six hours,
the roar of blues and whiskey all around.
I don't know if she got the hundred;
arriving at my meeting of drunks
before the story's end, I clicked off
the radio with the engine. One man
was missing from our group, the story
on him an old one: he went out
and booked a cheap hotel to drink
undisturbed, telling no one. Then finished
the job with a twelve-gauge. We
spoke in turn, each of us careful to say,
with the precision of a soldier cleaning
his weapon in the night, just how
the story cut. *Play dead:* we were familiar
with that command. We had risen once.

Stay

A clearance sale banner has broken free and risen
momentarily into clouds: *Everything Goes.* Cool air,
Canadian import, silvers the look of grass
and branch, each leaf a tuning fork set humming,
each shadow exact, razor-cut. Across the street
Frank rakes his hosta bed: the scritch
of tines jerks up my dog's head briefly. But it's
a known sound, and she sinks back
into the furred rumple of dream. My daughters
have entered their teens intact, whole shells, rarely
found, waiting to be lifted and filled with a new
element, air breathers now. Everyone alive
is arrayed. I don't say joyous, I say singular
constellation. And I want everything
to stay as it is: stay, cloud pinned
over the slaughterhouse on Market Street,
stay voices of men laying concrete on Mossrose.
Stay Sarah, whose body has sifted mine fifteen years.
Stay sober mind, stay necessary delusions.
Stay shadows, air, rake, dog. Good stay. Good.

TOM SLEIGH

The Invasion

Above highways mutating endlessly,
beyond sodium lamps adrift
in parking lots where rainbows
flare in the mouths of sewer grates;

past construction lamps haloing hard hats
and freeway interchanges knotting
into asphalt crowns, they hear
the cadences of Marine recruits at dawn:

—What are they, standing there, not flesh, not fog, faces swarming
in the shine misting over blacktop? Remembrance
of race track, bettors' voices shredding
into frenzy, cartops sweating in Grand Avenue's body shops:

Wisps of speech swirl through insubstantial mouths,
"The deal is . . . cash out . . . load it up . . . don't give me that!"
Both sexes, all conditions, all colors of flesh
line up in their troop: Some are in uniforms,

some wrapped in leather and chains, some in party clothes,   .
business suits, ratty jeans, johnnies,
mumus, cut-offs and sandals, wetsuits, jams.
—And some have windpipes whistling like birds

in dreams, two loud notes, one soft,
feathers moulting to patches of raw skin . . .
Now they smell eucalyptus hills, ghosts of hills and valleys
under these hills and valleys, September's

desert wind touching confused faces.
Neon sidewalks wincing MR MOJO HAMMERHEAD XXX
flush their brains
with light so that they almost know, almost grasp it:

Have they risen from ether,
from Persephone's
palm court rustling in the dark?
Wherever they look everything is sign!

(See how that one's and that one's faces,
hungover with jungle war, keep their heads
down, exploding shell-casings of thought
littering what's left of their minds' DMZ.)

—Oh work your way into roots of iceplant, bougainvillea,
clutch at retaining walls as if to tear them down,
stare mesmerized by white lines racing to the merge,
be fumes torn piecemeal and dragged under wheels.

Shimmer of ectoplasm dripping in too steady sun, those feet
could be yours edging out into the Void along
the surfboards' rails, foam racing back over the wave's collapsing
lip smothered in the next wave and the next.

Minutely scintillant, you grasp
at transparence hovering in the blue,
your faces fleshed and grinning
dissolving in the flare of a tossed match jackknifed in the air.

Joy on a Sunday

Pulsing there like a wound in the air
    Turning to a mouth that sings what
My parents in their thirty-fourth year
    So loved to hear in her throat—

There are so many reasons one could offer:
                    The delayed pain of war
                              In the bedroom,
The sorrow that "many boys didn't come home . . ."
                    Joy on a Sunday
Morning to hear her voice, palpable, throaty,
                    Enjoying the immense
          Obstacles overcome the way love,
                    Abrasive and intense
Even when it hungers in shadows
          Dissatisfied, breasts bulwarks of
                              Lips and eyes.
Mother, Father, they're downstairs listening
                    To Judy Garland sing,
          Zing went the strings of my heart
          Clang clang clang went the trolley
                    The man who got away . . .
How unendurably sweet and perfect
                              Is her tone!—
Though the undertones are raw, raw to the bone
What she did to herself, her voice shredding
          Into rags she wore like finery,
                    Casting off the old Judy
                    And no reason
                    Or cliché about war can
                              Suffice.
Mother, Father, and Judy together,
                    United in their
                    Momentary rapture
Above all that happens and will happen
                    And keeps on
          Happening once they're gone.

Spring Morning

Hierarchies are coming unstrung. Whoever I am at this moment,
Whoever I might be at the next is suddenly in abeyance:
I've stepped sideways out of cascading white water hesitating
At the waterfall's backward scrambling, horrified-of-falling
Reversal at the instant of the plunge.
                                        A siren cuts through the quiet.
The dog next door barks and barks. The walls between rooms
Grow more and more transparent, there's a buzz and blur
Of spring's first bees before my window.
                                        A sweet sensation
Of feeling myself for this moment immortal is giving way to
An equally intense gravitational pull casually and impartially
Pulling everything into it.
                            Inside my mood I am on a battlefield
In a square of infantry, the first row kneeling to fire,
Then falling back as the next row steps forward, kneels, fires,
Our square helplessly advancing no matter that the man
Next to us falls, no matter that our volleys can't be heard
In the void of the battlefield we're slowly crossing.
The smoke is clearing from my eyes.
                                    The developer who planted
Trees in the backyard is out there on a bench reading
The newspaper. He's promised the neighborhood this house is
The house he'll live in forever, but even as he sits, moving men
Carry his rugs and kitchen stuff out the door.
                                        Who knows
What it is that's keeping the trees from appearing to us
The way they appear to the lifelong blind stricken
Unexpectedly with sight, blots and flashes of scarifying
Green burning into retinas that see disordered
"A vast vacuity . . . the womb of nature . . . neither sea,
nor shore, nor air, nor fire,/ But all these in their pregnant
causes mixed/ Confusedly, and which thus must ever fight"
To make green adhere to the leaves' shadowy dip and toss.

ARTHUR SMITH

"Come Back, or Send Somebody"

Brush-painted as though yesterday
Red and wet and running

Down the whitewashed sheet of plywood,
Those letters have been alone

With the weather of northern Texas
For a long time, as has

The frame house they lean against,
Its porch- and floor-boards

Shot through
With a few weedy saplings.

For a moment, you might not know
If it were north or south

The bus headed, or why you were on it,
If one afternoon between Dallas and Waco you woke

And the first thing you saw was how little lasted,
And how long—

Though if you had been alone
With the weather anywhere

You'd know the house plowed
Newly up to and around,

And the scrub oaks bony in the wind,
And the way the wind points through them.

You'd know who left, and who stayed, and what happened next,
And why the bus drives on.

Lights from a Pier

From here, I can see many things at night
Sitting out long enough
If I am willing to.
I can see all the way to heaven
And how indistinguishable it is
From the sea and its darkness
Except as the whitewash rubs
A little of it away.

I can see lights from the pier
Where the sinks are, for cleaning fish,
And a few ropes for tethering crab-traps,
Where I stood earlier
As the high-pitched children kicked
At the casual waves, and I can still see
The long white sleep-blown hair of the old
As they walked below me.

Merest of light on a sheen,
Just when I think there is nothing
Beyond you, from behind me I hear a sound
Something like my love brushing her hair
She washed the sea from
Only minutes earlier,
The sea winds whipping a bit,
Helping to dry and make it shine.

My Mother's Name in English

My mother going
Back door to front
Shadows a frailty
All the way from
Her kitchen to
This small wooden
Desk I'm watching
Her from tonight.

Back door to front,
The two ports
Swinging on darkness,
Swinging on light,
The winter-insistent
Bermuda not even
Knitted back through
Her daughter's grave.

Wiping her hands,
Back door to front,
Pursuing a note
No one can hear,
Though her name
In English means
"Iris," though
She is not brave.

She would rather
Not go back
Door to front,
From before knowing
Begins, to after
Knowing matters,
Over and over
Everything between.

I can't even
Call it brutal,
Given the given
Between, my mother
Going back
Door to front,
And no one at either,
No one at either.

DAVE SMITH

Black Silhouettes of Shrimpers

Grand Isle, Louisiana

Along the flat sand the cupped torsos of trash fish
arch to seek the sun, but the eyes
glaze with thick gray, death's touch
already drifting these jeweled darters.

Back and forth against the horizon slow trawlers
gulp in their bags whatever rises
here with the shrimp they come for.
Boys on deck shovel the fish off

like the clothes of their fathers out of attics.
Who knows what tides beached them,
what lives were lived to arrive just here?
I walk without stepping on any

dead, though it is hard, the sun's many blazes
spattering and blinding the way ahead
where the wildness of water coils
dark in small swamps and smells fiercely of flesh.

If a cloud shadows everything for a moment, cool,
welcome, there is still no end in sight,
body after body, stench, jewels
nothing will wear, roar and fade of engines.

Mussel Work

What I like about it is the free fall
into depths you don't see coming,
walls of the discrete thing shown up
at last so foreign you'd never think
I am was always there, waiting, humped

mussel on a swamp-sunken log: you
hunch down close, near-sighted,
steady living dazzles you, the glue
of work in tides that wash and dry
this small house, horizon, and none

shows self-scrutiny's busted confidence,
no angst, no ambition for promotion,
not even night-classes hot to express
all the dreams they will never know.
This work is pure being, until dead,

a sort of compact flesh has with will.
I'm ok, you're ok. No questions asked.
Except the one at out-tide, discovery
you're alone, not swept off like the rest,
why me? when you were nothing's memory.

St. Augustine's Goldfinch

Did he have one? Who can say without doubt.
He liked to sit in the late afternoon sun,
cats, calico or the white, both long past sex,
pooled in his heavy robe, and the young woman's

breast just visible then, his fingertip slipped it more
to his liking, her shift parted, her tinted cheek
held to the last of the world's light.
He liked to tell her he had enjoyed temptations,

suffered ambitions, loved wine, gambled, made a child,
but above all things he adored women, had prayed
many hours to stay off the soft skin's road,
but each fluttery morning there he found himself.

It could be a room where wind whistled under a door
hardly more than a locked slab, his belly
bubbling, a squawking in each ear, so he might
bite a stone to empty what was in him.

Always flying into his tales, as he lifted her breast,
the goldfinch yellower than her hair, bird
of no use, inedible, its song too quick, too brief,
as he said, like the pears of his youth.

His words, she thought, were like straws.
They trailed around her nipple but went only so far
and she wanted to ask what stopped him, what
of the children he claimed? And what future had she—

only he hardly stopped to breathe, the black hole
where a tooth had once held whistling its tune.
How could she know he would make good,
that lover of a butter-puff of a bird?

In tea-rooms she said, I always knew his passion.
She produced notes, a definitive study.
Later, when she had conceived by another,
she uncovered herself in his poems. I am his goldfinch,

her announcement cried. When times got very tough
she exposed her breast in the main mud-road,
crying this was the one he had abused, it was
there you might hear the saint's goldfinch singing

its wish to be only part of God's beauty. A small charge.
A wish she was given, of course. As years passed
the memory of his brooding face was called
winter, and much lamented. Often in the fire pit

some yellow thing flamed, a whistle of something gold.
One of us would say spring was near, you mustn't
deny the saint's goldfinch, the one so sweetly
asking for more log, and wasn't it always given?

MARCIA SOUTHWICK

A Portrait of Larry with Trogons

At first you can't spot a red & green trogon against
a background of deep green leaves & red berries.
It's also difficult to find the exact right words for poetry
when they're camouflaged against the background of speech,
newspapers, and T.V. If you were to see the trogon
against a white wall, you'd be dazzled by its brilliance. The same
goes for the right words when they're taken out of conversation
& placed into the unnatural habitat of poetry. If you train yourself,
you'll eventually see the trogons when nobody else can . . .
Sorry, I'm too tired for this right now. It's midnight & my
18-year-old son took off for the East Coast today from our house
in Colorado, & he didn't take enough money or food.
He just finally called to say he's briefly stopped at a Ramada,
not to spend the night, but to use their hot-tub. He *also* told me
he's borrowed my credit card. I worry like crazy when he does
things like that! He'll probably get caught in the hot-tub and call me
in trouble with the desk clerk or he'll lose the credit card.
I can't blame him. He's sad right now because his dad,
the poet Larry Levis, has died. When someone you love passes away,
it's almost impossible to grasp the sheer darkness of it
against the solid blackness of death itself. Nick & I feel Larry
slipping away into the habitat of history, where too many names and faces
go blank. We've got to get him back. We've got to lock him forever here,
like a trogon, in the cage of our hearts, where he stands out.
But a trogon's natural instinct is to sit on a branch, deep inside
the green-leafed tree with the berries & hold perfectly still & upright—
its long slaty tail wavering ever so slightly in the breeze. Or
to rise & flap against a backdrop of white sky, where just as you try
to grasp the brilliant & quick presence of it, it disappears.

A Saturday Night at the Flying Dog

I was drinking Stoli with Helen & a young guy
tried to hustle me big-time. Really he'd just hitch-hiked
from Glenwood Springs and needed a place to stay.
No *way* anybody was going to follow me back to my place.
He was lot meaner & scruffier than I'd thought—around midnight
I started to sober up and could see it. When I split,
he did too. He "walked me" about half-way home,
and even though I told him over & over I was just *fine*
he wouldn't turn back. Finally I got scared & said:
"You know how wolves are territorial and pee everywhere
to set their boundaries? If you cross this line, you're *dead*."
I pointed to my feet, then bolted. I didn't want him to see a middle-aged
woman slip off her shoes & run like hell, but the moon was out.
I could feel him see me disappear, my purse and skirt flapping,
into a wall of spruces. I ran through an alley & no matter how
familiarly blue the columbines were, they froze in fear.
And aspen trunks looked fluorescent as if exposed to a blacklight.
The next day, Murray came back from New York.
After his shower, he put on his aqua & white-striped bathrobe.
His hair was white & curly as always, and his face had the usual tan.
He's got a little gold filling, a speck on a canine tooth that shimmers
when he smiles. I've never been so glad to see anybody in my life!
Today I've got to get to work dead-heading flowers. I've got to pick
the last few sprigs of thyme before the dog gets them—our Lab
also eats chives and he's splashing around, biting the water,
in his plastic swimming pool. I'm about to get up from the lawnchair,
when six evening grosbeaks flurry out of nowhere, a whirlwind
of yellow and gray surrounding the feeder. They're migrating
down valley! After a few seconds they take off—
And floating down from the upstairs window is Murray's voice
saying, Marcia? Marcia! Where's the . . . I look up, see his face & know
that *this* is it, our little territory of happiness, our wolf country.

ELIZABETH SPIRES

1999

to Gerald Howard

In a hundred years, we won't be here,
replaced by the unimaginable, a flash,
a whir, as forests fall, rise up again,
and houses that we lived in disappear.
Changing our form, will we come back then?
Or stay underground, quiet and companionable?

Will poems be written then?
Whose hand will write them?
Will someone stand, time's ghost,
as I do now, in a peeling gazebo with antique
posts and scrollwork, here on the edge
of a lake, the edge of time so close?

To the west, the mountains are immovable,
a sheer cliff face that no one can climb.
Shadows play on the lake's surface
as clouds race by, seeded and shining,
a wind from the north whipping the water
into waves, unreadable to the eye.

In a hundred years, will the mountains
exhaust themselves? Will the lake move on?
Will my hand, severed from mind, lie fallow
forever? For a week or two, summer is endless.
Then we fall back into lives that rush forward
with terrible speed, our future glimpsed in dreams:

the gazebo gone, the dusty road paved over,
its blind curves straightened out, leading
nowhere we want to go, the sun and moon
whirling brightly above the figure of a tree,
its branches black as char, where no bird
sings and no wind blows through ever.

Once, all flesh and shadow, we prayed
for our own permanence. Now we stand
in the center of a vacancy that is the center
of the new, asking what will be left
when each thing goes. Our answer an echo—
The singing. Only the singing.

"In Heaven It Is Always Autumn"

—John Donne

In heaven it is always autumn. The leaves are always near
to falling there but never fall, and pairs of souls out walking
heaven's paths no longer feel the weight of years upon them.
Safe in heaven's calm, they take each other's arm,
the light shining through them, all joy and terror gone.
But we are far from heaven here, in a garden ragged and unkept
as Eden would be with the walls knocked down, the paths littered
with the unswept leaves of many years, bright keepsakes
for children of the Fall. The light is gold, the sun pulling
the long shadow soul out of each thing, disclosing an outcome.
The last roses of the year nod their frail heads,
like listeners listening to all that's said, to ask,
What brought us here? What seed? What rain? What light?
What forced us upward through dark earth? What made us bloom?
What wind shall take us soon, sweeping the garden bare?
Their voiceless voices hang there, as ours might,
if we were roses, too. Their beds are blanketed with leaves,
tended by an absent gardener whose life is elsewhere.
It is the last of many last days. Is it enough?
To rest in this moment? To turn our faces to the sun?

To watch the lineaments of a world passing?
To feel the metal of a black iron chair, cool and eternal,
press against our skin? To apprehend a chill as clouds pass
overhead, turning us to shivering shade and shadow?
And then to be restored, small miracle, the sun shining brightly
as before? We go on, you leading the way, a figure
leaning on a cane that leaves its mark on the earth.
My friend, you have led me farther than I have ever been.
To a garden in autumn. To a heaven of impermanence
where the final falling off is slow, a slow and radiant happening.
The light is gold. And while we're here, I think it must be heaven.

Two Chairs on a Hillside

"Look up. And tell me what you see."

> "I see two chairs on a hillside.
> What are they doing there?"

"Through good days and bad, two sat there
having a conversation. Flowers grew up around them,
vines twined around their chairs. They didn't seem to care,
but moved the chairs higher or lower to adjust the view
of rushing streams and valleys, a town that they both knew.
Autumn approached, the hillside changing color,
and still they stayed, feeling the change within themselves.
Their talk was a thread unspooling, leading them where it would.
Sometimes one lost the thread, her mind for a moment
blank, and then she'd find herself, again pick up the thread.
With the first chill wind, their bare hands touched,
as if to reassure. They braced themselves, pulling their coats
closer, as snow fell through the air, whitening all they said."

> "And so they stayed all winter?"

"They did. Shivering and skeletal, they preferred frost
to interruption. They wintered out the worst with words
until their rags thawed out. Spring came again.
Green shoots, some from the heart, sprang up.
They felt themselves anew. Each had a story to tell.
The first recalled an island where summer lasted year
to year. South, she flew south, pulled by a dream
of herself unlike the northern dream she knew.
Like the first face one sees on waking, she loved that place.
One year she lost its whereabouts, the next, that face,
and suddenly she found herself alone and ancient
on a hillside looking down. The view inspired a poem.
The second came up and found her there, white pages
blowing down the hillside. Each was surprised
to find a compatriot. That's how it all began."

"And the second?"

"The second is harder to speak of.
She moved in extremes of ice and fire,
swinging from hate to love. Her passion
took her up the hillside, away from the town.
Once there, she would have liked to stay,
climbing higher than mid-range. I can't say
more than that. That's all that I can say."

"Don't then. You've said enough."

"Have I? I've only told part of it.
You've heard how poets stand in fields and pray
for lightning on the bluest day? They never had.
They weren't that crazy. And yet, one day it struck
between them, the ground parting for an instant,
then closing up, taking the first somewhere dark.
The second wasn't surprised, and yet she was.
She sat there grieving, stunned. As some will talk
to a grave, she talked to the chair's vacancy,
believing she was heard—"

"Perhaps she was."

"—Then she came down to where we're standing.
She stood where I stand now. Stars wheeled
around her, the night sky streamed and blurred,
the scene seen as if through tears. Then all was quiet,
the sky as fixed and deep and measureless as before.
Each night I stand here looking up. The chairs are proof
of what I've told you. Can you see them up there?
Two empty chairs no element can change, as fixed
in their relation as any starry constellation—"

        "As we are?"

"No, as we will be someday. We aren't complete
in what we are yet. We're in the middle of a story
we'll tell twice over, each in our own slant way.
We've written half the pages, but half remain.
To be done, if at all, out of love—"

        "How do you know all this?
        Who told you?"

"I was one of the two."

GERALD STERN

About Women

Trying to find out about women I realized
it was glasses was the key to everything,
and watching one with huge white comic frames
belittling her nose I realized my life had passed
in ignorance.
       And when she picked her flower
and she was dragged into hell I knew I'd have to
think about it for fifty years and sit there
on the edge of my sofa with my thick wool
melton shirt and wool socks figuring out
the path in and the path out, especially now—
more than a while ago—that I was doing
so many final things.
       Seeing her go,
or going before her, I was humiliated
first by the mud, then by the trees; and it was
morbid leaving the road for we had to walk
through almost a forest of vines; and it was foolish
being philosophical while she screamed in
my ear or cut up food in her tiny kitchen,
either holding a book near my eye or glaring
back at the sun since there was no stick to carry
or silk to tie.
       When we climbed down the hill
we hung on to the bushes, and when we walked
beside the shallow river it was her dog
made peace between us.

It may have been only loosestrife
between the rocks, or tiger lilies; the trees
may have been ruined by too much salt, and water
may have reversed the channel unless the tide
moved it back and forth, but it was easy
going across and neither of us wanted to look
for there was only darkness, given the time
of the year, and it was cold in spite of the bright
new scarves she worked on during the summer, the orange
I always called yellow, the blue I always called green,
they were so unembellished, and how it was windy
and even noisy and how we had to yell.

Larry Levis Visits Easton, Pa., During a November Freeze

I said "Dear Larry" as I put down his book, *Elegy*,
across the street from the Home Energy Center

and its two embellished secular Christmas trees
and its two red wreaths over red ribbon crosses

enshrining a thirty inch stove in one of its windows
and a fifty gallon water heater in the other,

knowing how wise he would have been with the parking lot
and the tree that refused against all odds and all

sane agreements and codicils to let its dead leaves
for God's sake fall in some kind of trivial decency

and how he would have stopped with me always beside him
to watch a girl in a white fur parka and boots

build the first snowball on Northampton Street she collected
from the hood of a Ford Fairlane underneath that tree

and throw it she thought at a small speed limit sign
although it landed with a fluff just shy of the twin

painted center lines inducing the three of us,
her lover, Larry, and I to make our own snowballs

from the hoods and fenders of our own Fairlanes although
she threw like none of us and to add to it

she was left-handed, so bless her, may she have
a good job and children and always be free of cancer

and may the two of us scrape some roofs before the
rain relieves us, and may we find gloves for our labor.

Last Blue

You want to get the color blue right,
just drink some blue milk from a blue cup;
wait for the blue light of morning
or evening with its blue aftermath.

You want to understand,
look at the parking lines outside my window,
the neon moon outside Jabberwocky's.

And funk! You have to know funk.
A touch of blue at the base of the spine;
long threads going into your heart;
a steaming fountain you pour into your own bowl.

My dead sister's eyes!
Those of her porcelain twin at the Lambertville Flea,
twenty dollars a day for the small table,
all the merde you need to get you across the river.

And one kind of blue for a robin's egg;
and one kind of blue for a bottle of ink.
Two minds to fathom the difference.

Your earrings which as far as I can see
are there as much to play with as to look at.
Your blue pencil
which makes your eyes Egyptian. Blue bells, bluebirds,

from Austin, Texas, the dead hackster
who drank potassium, Governor Bush
who drank Milk of Magnesia; a chorus of saints
from Wylie Avenue and one kind of blue

for my first prayer shawl and one kind of blue for the robe
Fra Lippo gave to Mary. Blue from Mexico
and blue from Greece, that's where the difference lay
between them, in the blues; a roomful of scholars,

in Montreal one year, in New York another,
that is blue, blue was their speech, blue
were their male and female neckties, their food was blue,
their cars were rented, Christmas lights

were in the lobby, one of the bars had peanuts
in all the urns and on the upper floors
the hospitality rooms were crowded with livid
sapphire cobalt faces—I was blue

going into the tunnel, I am blue every night
at three or four o'clock; our herring was blue,
we ate it with Russian Rye and boiled potatoes,
and in the summer fresh tomatoes, and coffee

mixed with sugar and milk; I sat in a chair
so close to Sonny Terry I could hear
him mumble, the criticism he made
of his own sorrow, but I was that close to Pablo

Casals in 1950, talk about blue, and
though I left it a thousand times I stood—
since I didn't have a seat—in front of an open
window of Beth Israel in Philadelphia

to hear the sobbing, such a voice, a dog
came up to me that night out of the blue
and put his muzzle in my hand nor would he
leave me for a minute, he would have stayed

with me forever and followed me up to my house
which butted onto the woods in back of the synagogue
and sat outside my door; or blue on the street
outside a Parlour near the Port Authority—

my seed inside—or blue in Ocean Grove
where sky and sea combined and walking the boardwalk
into the wind and blue in a shrink's small parking lot
watching the clock and blue in my mother's arms

always comforting her and blue with my daughter
starving herself and blue with my wife all day
playing solitaire or drawing houses and blue,
though smiling, when I came into the world, they called me

Jess Willard, thirteen pounds, and I had just hammered
Jack Dempsey into the ropes and I was shouting—
in a tinny voice—it sounded like someone weeping—
it always sounded like that—everything living.

SUSAN STEWART

Apple

If I could come back from the dead, I would come back
for an apple, and just for the first bite, the first
break, and the cold sweet grain
against the roof of the mouth, as plain
and clear as water.

Some apple names are almost forgotten
and the apples themselves are gone. The smokehouse,
winesap and York imperial, the striped
summer rambo and the winter banana, the little
Rome with its squat rotunda and the pound apple

that pulled the boughs to the ground.
The sheep's nose with its three-pointed snout,
the blue Pearmain, speckled and sugared.
Grime's golden, cortland, and stayman.
If an apple's called "delicious," it's not.

Water has no substance
and soil has no shell,
sun is all process
and rain cannot rise.
The apple's core carries

a birth and a poison.
Stem and skin, and flesh,
and seed, the apple's name,
no matter, is work
and the work of death.

If you wait for the apple, you wait
for one ripe moment. And should
you sleep, or should you dream, or
should you stare too hard in the daylight
or come into the dark to see

what can't be seen, you will drop
from the edge, going over into
coarse, or rot, or damping off.
You will wake to yourself, regretful,
in a grove of papery leaves.

You need a hillside, a small and steady wind,
a killing frost, and, later, honey-bees.
You need a shovel, and shears, and a ladder

and the balance to come back down again.
You will have fears of codling moths
and railroad worms, and aphids.

Scale and maggots and beetles
will come to do their undoing.
Forests will trap the air

and valleys will bend to gales—
cedars will bring on rust, so keep them
far in the distance. Paradise,

of course, was easy, but you and I live
in this world, and "the fruit of the tree
in the midst of the garden"

says nothing specific about apples;
the "apples of gold" in *Proverbs*
are probably oranges instead.

And so are the fruits
Milanion threw down:
an apple does not glitter.

If you're interested in immortality
it's best to plant a tree, and even
then you can't be sure that form

will last under weather.
The tree can break apart in a storm
or be torqued into pieces over many

years from the weight of its ruddy labor.
The state won't let you burn the wood
in the open air; the smoke is too dense

for breathing. But apple-wood
makes a lovely fire, with excellent
heat and aroma.

Fire will take in whatever it can
and heat will draw back
into earth. "Here is the fruit,
your reward and penalty
at once," said the god

to the waiting figures.
Unbearable, the world
that broke into time.
Unbearable, the just-born
certainty of distance.

You can roast late apples
in the ashes. You can run
them in slices on a stick.
You can turn the stem to
find the letter of your love

or chase them down with
your chin in a tub.
If you count the seeds to tell
the future, your heart will
sense more than your

tongue can say. A body
has a season, though
it may not know it
and damage will bloom
in beauty's seed.

If I could come back from the dead, I would—
I'd come back for an apple,
and just for one bite, one break,
and the cold sweet grain on the tongue.
There is so little difference between

an apple and a kiss, between desire
and the taste of desire.
Anyone who tells you other-
wise is a liar, as bad
as a snake in the quiet grass.

You can watch out for the snake and the lie.
But the grass, the green green wave
of it, there below the shadows of the black
and twisted boughs, will not be
what you thought it would be.

Bees

after Virgil

That the bees were born in the corpse of the injured animal.
That the bees came forth out of the corrupted flesh.

That a small room was chosen, made narrow just for this
and the animal was led beneath the low roof and cramped walls

and that the four winds came through the four windows
and that the morning fell upon the small

and heavy head, its horns curving out
from the whorled medallion of the forehead.

That the hot nostrils and the breathing mouth were stopped
and the flesh was beaten, pounded to a pulp,
beneath the unbroken hide.

        He lies on his side on the broken apple-boughs. He lies on a bed
     of fragrant thyme and the cassia is laid in sprays about him
and the sweetness of the fields surrounds him.

Do this when the west winds blow. Do this when the meadows
are alive with poppies. Do this when the swallow hangs her pendulous

nest and the dew is warm and the days grow long.
And all the living fluids will swirl within the hide, and the bones

will dissolve like bread in water.
And a being will be born, and another, and then a thousand

and a thousand thousand swarming without limbs or form.
And that the wings will grow from atoms. And that the stirring wings

will find their way into the air. And that a thousand stirring wings
will come forth into the day like a storm of arrows made of wind

and light. And the flesh will fall back into the earth, and the horror
into sweetness and the dark into the sun and the bees
thus born.

MARK STRAND

Here

The sun that silvers all the buildings here
Has slid behind a cloud, and left the once bright air
Something less than blue. Yet everything is clear.
Across the road, some dead plants dangle down from rooms
Unoccupied for months, two empty streets converge
On a central square, and on a nearby hill some tombs,
Half buried in a drift of wild grass, appear to merge
With houses at the edge of town. A breeze
Stirs up some dust, turns up a page or two, then dies.
All the boulevards are lined with leafless trees.
There are no dogs nosing around, no birds, no buzzing flies.
Dust gathers everywhere—on stools and bottles in the bars,
On shelves and racks of clothing in department stores,
On the blistered dashboards of abandoned cars.
Within the church, whose massive, rotting doors
Stay open, it is cool, so if a visitor should wander in
He could easily relax, kneel and pray,
Or watch the dirty light pour through the baldachin,
Or think about the heat outside that does not go away,
Which might be why there are no people there—who knows—
Or about the dragon that he saw when he arrived,
Curled up before its cave in saurian repose,
And about how good it is to be survived.

I Will Love the Twenty-First Century

Dinner was getting cold. The guests, hoping for quick,
Impersonal, random encounters of the usual sort, were sprawled
In the bedrooms. The potatoes were hard, the beans soft, the meat—
There was no meat. The winter sun had turned the elms and houses yellow;
Deer were moving down the road like refugees; and in the driveway, cats
Were warming themselves on the hood of a car. Then a man turned
And said to me: "Although I love the past, the dark of it,
The weight of it teaching us nothing, the loss of it, the all
Of it asking for nothing, I will love the twenty-first century more,
For in it I see someone in bathrobe and slippers, brown-eyed and poor,
Walking through snow without leaving so much as a footprint behind."
    "Oh," I said, putting my hat on, "Oh."

JAMES TATE

An Afternoon Stroll

You don't know if you are being followed,
so you dip into a department store,
and, disguising yourself as a shopper,
you buy several expensive items.
On the next streetcorner you stop a policeman
and ask him, "Are you also a Nature poet?"
He smiles and nods yes indeed he is.
You invite him to join your secret club
and he is delighted. "See you Saturday!"
A day which started off rather dismally
turns a sharp right and there up ahead
is the prospect of something sweet with
an officer of the law, who is now following you.
So you slip into the cigar store,
and, though you have never been a smoker,
you stock up on some very fine stogies.
Miles on a bench beckoned me and I sat
half-expecting paradise to attack.
A pigeon blinked at my feet, and my head
spun around in search of a tail.
No one conspicuous was on my case,
or maybe I'm just losing my edge.
I sat there blowing smoke into
the wee hunger of nothing's eye.
My pajamas were as blue as the ocean,
and choppy, too. They were very choppy.

Scattered Reflections

I cabled my lawyer about the incident,
then returned to the hotel bar
and ordered a whiskey. The dame
sitting next to me was tight
but not as tight as her sweater.
Later, I helped her catch a taxi
and gave her some money for the ride home.
God knows I like the ladies but
I like to think I'm a gentleman
and wouldn't take advantage of one
when she's down on her luck.
I've been down too often myself.
And only myself to blame—love,
booze, stupidity, mix 'em up
and you find yourself babbling
to God in Arabic about a demonic cat
living in your head next to the
fiery urinal. I've been there
and back more times than I care
to remember. When I was young
I thought respectable meant dead.
I liked the dark side of life,
the hoods, fast girls, and nights
that told a thousand stories.
And then at some invisible point
you realize it is the same story
told over and over, and that's
when you either move on or die.
I went out west and worked on a ranch
for a couple of years, learned to ride,
brand, you name it. I was a cowboy
and loved every minute of it.
I missed the women, but there was
no time for that, so I visited them
in my dreams. I'd fall in bed after dinner
and pick an old favorite and call
her up, dancing, kissing, all of it.

We never fought, had no problems.
Sometimes in the morning I would be
surprised to find myself alone in bed.
As I said, I like the work, but I
also knew that this was not my real life.
I had no idea what my real life was,
but I knew I had to look for it.
So one day I packed my car and took off.
I drove the whole country, examining
homes, stores, businesses, streets,
people, like a crazed inspector general,
when all I was looking for was me.
I concluded that there was no me,
just flutterings, shudderings and shadows.
I think most people feel the same way,
and it isn't bad, floating under the stars
at night like fireflies sending signals.

The Workforce

Do you have adequate oxen for the job?
No, my oxen are inadequate.
Well, how many oxen would it take to do an adequate job?
I would need ten more oxen to do the job adequately.
I'll see if I can get them for you.
I'd be obliged if you could do that for me.
Certainly. And do you have sufficient fishcakes for the men?
We have fifty fishcakes, which is less than sufficient.
Would fifty more fishcakes be sufficient?
Fifty more fishcakes would be precisely sufficient.
I'll have them delivered on the morrow.
Do you need maps of the mountains and the underworld?
We have maps of the mountains but we lack maps of the underworld.
Of course you lack maps of the underworld,
there are no maps of the underworld.
And, besides, you don't want to go there, it's stuffy.
I had no intention of going there, or anywhere for that matter.

It's just that you asked me if I needed maps . . .
Yes, yes, it's my fault, I got carried away.
What do you need then, you tell me?
We need seeds, we need plows, we need scythes, chickens,
pigs, cows, buckets and women.
Women?
We have no women.
You're a sorry lot then.
We are a sorry lot, sir.
Well, I can't get you women.
I assumed as much, sir.
What are you going to do without women, then?
We will suffer, sir. And then we'll die out one by one.
Can any of you sing?
Yes, sir, we have many fine singers among us.
Order them to begin singing immediately.
Either women will find you this way or you will die
comforted. Meanwhile busy yourselves
with the meaningful tasks you have set for yourselves.
Sir, we will not rest until the babes arrive.

HENRY TAYLOR

Commuter Marriage: Homecoming

One more arrival. Parking in the drive
of our house that too much of the time is yours,
I think of an evening down at Holbrook's Wharf
when I glanced up from supper to speak to you,
but stopped my breath as a motor launch slid in
to kiss the dock below the dining pier.
One passenger, almost astride the gunwale,
leaning but propped for the recoil ahead,
reached out to grab the shock he would absorb,
prepared to take in and stave off at once,
then to make fast, with just that touch of slack.

For William Matthews

If nothing ever happens more than once,
we still think we know enough to entitle us
to a few expectations, and to love

those moments when anticipated pleasures
strike us sweetly numb. How many times
you felt and spoke the exact way it was

to be in a room where musicians worked
toward those rare and swiftly fleeting
convergences of everything there is,

the world honed down to what vibrated
between your glass and the cone of light
in smoky air where sorcery kicked in

often enough to keep you coming back.
One time in Washington, it was you
the light picked out at an elevated podium,

your head tilted a little to one side
as if you were listening and speaking at once,
eyes sometimes closed, the soft voice

grazing carefully over lines and sentences,
and it came to me that if I had the power
to keep you around and turn you off and on

at will, as if you were a radio,
I would have all I need of what I get
from writing poems, and could quit.

It might be so. Slavery's illegal,
and now you are gone. I still like telling it,
bringing back the realization of that moment

to meet the disbelief or faith it might arouse.
I believe it. Like the tunes you wrote about,
your poems don't so much bring back a time

as lift us out of this one toward another
that has never been, not yet, no matter
how hard we might wish it had been, however
much about it comes just close enough.

ARTHUR VOGELSANG

The Line

What am I, suppose I am,
A cliff of flowers grabbed and shook
Like a large light blanket across a bed
Across a beach and into the Pacific Ocean?
Like a lure such tall flowers
Are arranged on a steel hook curving a half mile.
What is the motion of the blanket,
Creases chasing waves
In the interior air of the bedroom? The shaft
Of the hook is a sandy road one mile long
With oyster shells and crows,
Big lean ones, blue black and afraid,
Fleeing over the hairy yellow flowers.
The black animals fly inland over two fields
Where there will be a house of ballet
In the future. It is a place of hints and rain
Now, like whispers during a slight slap of flesh.
Other birds were like birds
Free in a house which fly excitedly
But always near the humans.
Though he's on one stage,
A dancer is making brief perches
In other rooms, you said, and that's most like you.
The doors an hour from the water, inland.

Liquids in Quantities

Not twice a day but half a time or once, a tide
On the sun is a tide. In the hideous person Jackson Pollock's brain
About that frequently a bay of enzymes or a gulf of sea water
Or a sea of pee receded on a beach
And of course bulged on another beach being a tide or
On another day a joke with no punch line but a nice middle
Brought a minor smile to his face as when the sun smiles.
If you don't think the sun smiles, look at the moon would you
And deny the infectious planetary humor,
One big ochre organ setting off spasms in the liquid or the dust of the other
That lasts a day or a half day or a day and a half.

When another massive body calls to the sun come
Its incandescent sauce shifts like our salty water.
There is actually a bulge in the water off Delaware
When there is actually a concavity or long shallow crater in it off Spain.
Places on the sun are not places
Due to so many places there being purple gas
That changes to disappearing dry white relish
Like a surf of only pebbles and no water
Or that explodes as if it were its job
Which it is to explode as much as possible.
All the words on the sun are for explosion.
You could think of a sun joke like over there is the Sea of Ruth
But it would never smile because as soon as you said "over" it would explode.
How may it have tides? then and how may those tides
Be approximately like something that went on in Jackson's dreadful brain?
Settle this first: as the sun is one of a kind around here
It smiles to itself alone so it doesn't need a punch line, yes?
A man in the street would say that's ok, let it do it, yes?
A woman about whom many have said what an eminently just piece of work
    that gorgeous
Little weasel is if asked in the street with her mind on her next trial
Would say "it is fine for the sun to laugh or even explode
At something with no demonstrably absurd point."
I said to the moon which would not answer
I said to it as it thought of the answer to another question

Suppose tides on the sun
Is just a shot at a beautiful idea or something which is like something
And not really boiling methane that's a big surf,
And if the sun actually saw on itself waves like that it would explode them
But the one appearance would be the beginning of the end what do you think?
The moon called to the Atlantic and to the Pacific by turning like the moon.

Which Way?

We dreamed as we swam.
The surf was a radio fading off its signal.
In the back of our minds and in back of us
Were naked bathers,
Each one big as a palm on a small thin beach.
Wet Paris and wet Africa
Filled each bather's mind.

We thought as we swam
That we did not need our brains,
That we would not use them.
It was our desire.
We would float, in our ardent wish.
The universe was out to sea.
Crazy to believe it had an end.
It was limitless, of course,
A concept that solved a lot,
And all were insane who had a metaphor for it.

We would float and pretend
A limb would flake off
And dissolve into grains before it hit bottom.

Our bodies of blood,
In the entire universe one other liquid like it,
Which was the water in which we swam.

Someone must have been on the inland road
Staring at the bathers on the beach.
It would be tempting.
Most of the time they were the normal size
Of ripe older teenagers nude on a beach.

Beyond the inland road was all existence.
Pianos, bananas, printing presses, aspirin.
Our desire to float conscious as salt
Was as good a reason as any to turn and swim
And swim and swim.

ELLEN BRYANT VOIGT

The Art of Distance, I

Wrinkle coming toward me in the grass—no,
fatter than that, rick-rack, or the scallops a ruffle makes,
down to about the eleventh vertebra. The rest of it: rod
instead of a coil.
              So I'd been wrong the afternoon before
when the dog, curious, eager to play and bored with me
as I harvested the edge of the raspberry thicket,
stalked it from the back stoop to the lip
of the bank and grabbed the tip
in her mouth and tossed it—
sudden vertical shudder
shoulder-level—
              wrong
to read survival in its cursive
spiraling back to the cellar window-well
where it had gathered fieldmice like a cat.
And now, if it meant to be heading for the brook,
it veered off-course, its blunt head raised
like a swimmer's in distress.
              The functioning part
gave out just short of me, inside the shade
but not the bush; the damaged part,
two fingers thick, was torqued
pale belly up, sunstruck.
I left it where it was,
took the dog in, and for hours
watched, from the kitchen window, what seemed
a peeled stick, the supple upper body that had dragged it
now pointed away and occluded by the shade,
the uncut grass.

                My strict father
would have been appalled: not to dispatch
a uselessly suffering thing made me the same, he'd say,
as the man who, seeing a toad,
catatonic Buddha in its niche, wedged
within the vise of a snake's efficient mouth
clamped open for, then closing slowly down and over it,
bludgeoned them both with the flat side of a hoe.

For once I will accept my father's judgment.
But this had been my yard, my snake, old enemy
resident at the back side of the house. For hours,
the pent dog panting and begging, I watched
from the window, as from a tower wall,
until it vanished: reluctant arrow
aimed at where the berries
ripened and fell.

Plaza del Sol

This is a veterans' ward, here by the pool
in Florida, where every chaise is taken, every frame
stretched out to full extension, the bodies just removed
from cold storage, exposing to light and air
the wound, the scar, the birthmark's crushed grape,
contiguous chins undisguised by pearls,
pitted shoulders plumped or scapular, flesh
pleated under an upper arm, a vast loaf rising
out of the bathing bra, or chest collapsed
and belly preeminent, spine a trough
or a knotted vine climbing the broad cliff-wall.
Down from this pelvic arch five children came;
that suspicious mole, his mother kissed;
but who will finger such calves, their rosaries?
Here's a brace of ankles like water-balloons;
here's a set of toes shingled with horn.
Here is the man, prone, whose back is a pelt,

and the supine woman whose limbs are tinkertoys,
and the man whose tattooed eagle looks crucified,
and his brother with breasts, and his wife with none—
a woman tanned already, dried fruit arranged on a towel—
and her pale sister, seated, bosom piled in her lap,
oiling the lunar landscape of her thighs.
The hot eye over them all does not turn away
from bodies marooned inside loose colorful rags
or bursting their bandages there at the lip of the cave—
from ropy arms, or the heavy sack at the groin,
or the stone of the head—bodies mapped
and marbled, rutted, harrowed, warmed at last,
while everyone else has gone off into the sea.

What I Remember of Larry's Dream of Yeats

A roomful of writers, three on the couch a cat
had pissed on, others clustered like animated trees,
Shahid benched at the melodiophobic piano
Reg had played while Deb and Karen sang;
and centered, under the fixture overhead, Larry,
pleated around a straight-backed chair, not drinking
then, not doing dope, his face above the mustache open
for company—although I heard him tell the dream
in North Carolina, after he moved to Virginia,

he'd dreamed it long before in Salt Lake City.
"Things not going very well," he summarized,
hurrying to what would make us laugh: him alone
and broke and barely hanging on, Strand advising
"'Buy silk sheets.'" I've forgotten whether or not
he did, whether or not the stained mattress
had been sheathed in silk, because he so expertly
buried for us that bed in papers, notebooks, volumes
underlined, low mound of the written word

as erudite, disheveled as Larry was,
taking a turn in the light of our attention, T-shirt
even though it was winter, distressed gray hair.
"In the midst of this" (here he lit another smoke),
"I'd been preparing for my class on Yeats," days, nights
on guided tours of the Variorum and *A Vision*;
also in the layers, the *L.A. Times*, manuscripts of poems
(his students' and his own), clean and dirty laundry,
letters, bills, an opened bag of chips.

Both white feet splayed flat on the splintered floor,
forearms on his knees, he leaned forward, maybe
to give this part some shoring-up, since labor
ran counter to his irony, his off-the-cuff,
his disaffected style—but didn't he know we knew
an intelligence as restless and large as his
needs feeding from time to time? (What did Dobyns say:
a billion who ought to die before Larry did?) Besides,
he looked so much like a caught thief coming clean,

none of us doubted he had read it all,
everything on Yeats, and fell asleep, and Yeats
stopped by, wearing a white suit. He'd come to retrieve
a last still-undiscovered poem, which he happened to keep
in Utah, in a locked drawer in Larry's room—just then
the kitchen howled and hooted, as if Larry
had also been in *there*, doing Justice, teacher
he loved, as an ice-cream man. Here's when Dr. Orlen
entered the room, stirring a short Scotch-rocks,

and Larry double-stitched: "Yeats in white,
pointing at my notes: 'Why do you bother with that?'"
Pause. Larry stared at Tony, next at me, the three of us
sharing the one ashtray, his eyebrows up, accents
acute et grave, like facing, aggressive bears:
"'Passion,' Yeats said, 'is all that matters in poetry.'"
Trawling the line to see if we would bite,
he leaned back in the chair, chair on its hind legs,
his legs straight out, his mouth a puckered seam.

In the dream Yeats turned away, as we ourselves
were starting to turn away now from the dream, to reach
for another fistful of chips or Oreos, another humiliation
from the Poetry Wars, another sensual or shapely thing
to throw at loneliness or grief, like what I'll hear
from Mary Flinn, how, when Richmond's ROBINSON'S REMOVAL
came for the body, days still undiscovered on the floor,
to wrestle it like a sodden log out to the hearse,
they swaddled it first in a scarlet velvet tarp,

then aimed for the stairs, headlong, the tapered end
under the arm of a ravaged small thin old black man
(that's Robinson), his doughy-bosomed lieutenant at the helm,
and Mary, foot of the stairs and looking up, expecting
Larry to break loose any minute, tumble forward—
the kind of punchline we were avid for
that evening in Swannanoa with good friends
(was Heather there? was Lux fanning the fire?) when Larry
pulled himself upright and dropped his voice

as Yeats paused at the door in a white silk suit:
ancient, graveled, this was the voice of the caged sibyl,
shriveled the size of a flea, when he read, from his long poem,
her song, "I want to die;" and saying now, as Yeats, "'Passion
is also all that matters in life.'"
                                        So weren't the dream,
and the telling of the dream, more lanky shrewd inclusive
Levis poems, like those in his books, those he left
in the drawer? If he comes back to get them, let him come
in his usual disguise: bare feet, black clothes.

DIANE WAKOSKI

The French Toy

A little machine, the size of a
matchbox, with a perforated drum
and a crank that when you turn it plays Beethoven's
"Für Elise," how can Sean
turn his car around, how
can Josh park it,
how can Jo-Ann take her old fat
horse to a rodeo in
Oklahoma, and how can Jason be a good father?
How can Carly or Heather find men who
are their equals, such beautiful girls
like moths, such talented ones
like little raccoons who already know how
to peel a piece of fruit.

And this little machine tinkles at whatever speed
I crank it, like Leslie Caron in her best movie,
the sound of windy days and running in the park, the
sound of pine trees at Christmas, the light
of Jon learning about sex in a parked car
and Tom playing computer games when the magazine
goes to bed, or Bryon buying me the best cheese I have eaten
in two years, and Chris coming back from Paris
feeling he's failed, when he's swimming for the gold.

The French toy that Linda gave me
after I delicately squeezed her stuffed gorilla
and made it sigh, works like a player piano, or the
barrel organ, organ grinders grind. It's sitting upstairs
in my velvet jewelry box right now, while I watch a purple finch;
no, censor that. Snow melts too fast for this race;
the Korean martial arts suit that Christian wears
is often hung up neatly in his narrow closet
as he sits in a tea shop writing letters.
Hello, hello, I crank the French toy's handle.
Judith is tagging owls, Ella is cultivating Moon Flowers,
Holly is wearing broken ballet shoes.
Nobody's fault. The French toy
plays over and over the same tune,
and yes I once played it on the piano,
and yes, I have finally reached the stage where I can hardly
look at the keyboard of a piano without wanting to
touch it. Just like sex, there is no place to go,
there is no way to make a complete story,
there are so many people to tell it,
so many different versions.

Silver Shoes

If this were a tap-dance studio
and I wore a green veil
my mother's sequin bra and my father's navy hat,
I'd put on silver tap shoes, and I'd find
a way. I'd find the ocean
off the alley, I'd find the sounds
of silver dollars. I'd find
a sea shell so big that I could sleep
in it with green feathers, and silver eyes
would watch me as I slept.
The shoes
tied with silver ribbons
would let me rest

until I felt as if I could tap all the way
across the world. I'd never
take them off. I'd offer anyone
who wanted to, a chance
to listen to the silver wheat of Kansas
that Dorothy felt drawing her,
but I would not return,
ever,
to the midwest. I'd find
a tap-dance studio in the middle
of the ocean,
find my father's submarine
or WW II aircraft carrier,
telephone the man
with all the keys,
and wait for the moon to slide down
and tap dance, tap dance, tap
her name all around me every time I'd sleep.

ROSANNA WARREN

E.R.

Your purpled, parchment forearm
lodges an IV needle and valve;
your chest sprouts EKG wires;
your counts and pulses swarm

in tendrils over your head
on a gemmed screen: oxygen,
heart-rate, lung power, temp
root you to the bed—

Magna Mater, querulous, frail,
turned numerological vine
whose every brilliant surge
convolutes the tale,

translates you to a life
shining beyond our own:
Come back to the world
we know the texture of—

demand your glasses back,
struggle into your clothes,
lean on me as you walk
into the summer dark

where you'll find once more your breath
and scold the wasted night.
Above us, satellites vastly wink.
Laugh. Come forth.

Island in the Charles

> By being scholar first of that new night.
> —Richard Crashaw

Taking the well-worn path in the mind though dusk encroaches
upon the mind, taking back alleys careful step by step
past parked cars and trash containers, three blocks to the concrete ramp
of the footbridge spanning the highway with its rivering, four-lane
unstaunchable traffic, treading on shadow and slant broken light,

my mother finds her way. By beer bottles, over smeared
Trojans, across leaf muck, she follows the track, clutching her
jacket close. The footbridge lofts her over the flashing cars
and sets her down, gently, among trees, where she is a child
in the weave of boughs, and leaf shapes plait the breeze.

She fingers silver-green blades of the crack willow, she tests dark grooves
of crack-willow bark. The tree has a secret. Its branches pour
themselves back toward earth, and my mother pauses, dredging a breath
up out of her sluggish lungs. The blade leaves scratch
her fingertips, the corrugated bark

releases a privacy darker than cataract veils.
But slashed and ribboned, glimpsed through fronds,
the river hauls its cargo of argent light
and she advances, past basswood and crab-apple clumps
along the tarmac where cyclists, joggers, rollerbladers

entranced in their varying orbits swoop
around her progress. With method, she reaches her bench,
she stations there. She sits columnular, fastened
to her difficult breath, and faces the river in late afternoon.
Behind her, voices. Before her, the current casts its glimmering

seine to a shore so distant no boundary scars
her retina, and only occasional sculls or sailboats flick
across her vision as quickened, condensing light.
There she sits, poised, while the fluent transitive Charles
draws off to the harbor and, farther, to the unseen sea

until evening settles, and takes her in its arms.

L'Oiseau de nuit

I wanted to read to you
    Colette's story about her mother calling
and calling her children in
    the lush, half-ruined garden in Burgundy
while the children hid in pine
    trees and the hay loft and roamed in swamp and field:

so we sat at the scarred oak
    table Pa had glued, pegged, sanded and varnished
forty-odd years earlier
    and let Colette's wisteria seize on us
(*la glycine centenaire,*
    she called it) as it had seized and wrenched the old

iron garden gate in that
    story where everything tumbles but resists—
gate, stone wall, sagging massive
    lilac bush, the children bruised, scratched, bleeding but
free—we sat in the after-
    -noon, and her words, *glycine, buanderie, pourpre,*

led us. Two years ago you
    still could follow prose. Colette's mother kept on
calling as evening fell
    in that garden, "Where are the children?" Their one
sin, says Colette, was silence.
    Her mother's arms were flour-whitened; she shook

blood-stained butcher paper to
    lure her cats as she called; when she knew she was
dying, she ordered a robe
    for burial—long, hooded, lace-collared—(that
is not in the story) and
    wrote her daughter, "To think I could die without

seeing you again." We drank
>tea, we looked up *buanderie* (wash-house), we
closed the book leaving Colette's
>mother still crying, "*Où sont les enfants?*" and
made our sort of peace with dusk
>as it gathered in the arbor vitae hedge:

I peeled the carrots, you had
>your glass of wine, my children came tramping in—
noisy, not bleeding, hungry—
>and Colette dancing "L'Oiseau de nuit" at Le
Bataclan Club did not and did
>not visit Sido (her mother) whose heart lapsed

and persistently lapsed yet
>lurched along; nor did you understand when I
tried the garden story a-
>-gain this spring. Never mind. At least we sat to-
-gether as yet another
>twilight sifted down and softened our voices,

and, in late August, Colette
>did leave lover, theater, writing desk and cats,
"three whole days," for Sido, whose
>heart, three weeks later, halted flat. No daughter
at her funeral, nor did
>Colette wear black. Those children are still roaming

loose, wild, hurting themselves, and
>I sit here stubbornly miles from you in my
own garden by the arbor
>vitae wrenched wide open by last winter's snow,
remembering Colette, and
>once again hold a book up between us: "The

house and garden still live, I
>know, but for what, if their magic is gone, if
the secret is lost which o-
>-pened—sunlight, odors, harmony of trees and birds,
murmur of voices now quelled
>by death—a world which I no longer deserve?"

C. K. WILLIAMS

Depths

I'm on a parapet looking down
into a deep cleft in the earth
at minuscule people and cars
moving along its narrow bottom.
Though my father's arms are around me
I feel how far it would be to fall,
how perilous: I cringe back,
my father holds me more tightly.
Was there ever such a crevice?
No, I realized much, much later
we were on an ordinary building
looking down into a city street.

A picture-book: desert sunlight,
a man and woman clad in sandals,
pastel robes, loose burnooses,
plying a material like dough,
the man kneading in a trough,
the woman throwing at a wheel.
Somehow I come to think they're angels,
in heaven, fashioning human beings.
Was there ever such a story?
No, the book, at Sunday school,
showed daily life in the bible,
the people were making jars, just jars.

Just jars, and yet those coils of clay,
tinted light to dark like skin,
swelled beneath the woman's hands
as I knew already flesh should swell,

and as I'd know it later, when,
alone with someone in the dark,
I'd close my eyes, move my hands
across her, and my mouth across her,
trying to experience an ideal,
to participate in radiances
I passionately believed existed,
and not only in imagination.

Or, with love itself, the love
that came to me so readily, so
intensely, so convincingly each time,
and each time ravaged me
when it spoiled and failed, and left
me only memories of its promise.
Could real love ever come to me?
Would I distort it if it did?
Even now I feel a frost of fear
to think I might not have found you,
my love, or not believed in you,
and still be reeling on another roof.

The Lie

As one would praise a child or dog, or punish it,
as one would chastise it, or hit it, *hit* it;
as one would say, *sit, sit down, be still:*
so don't we discipline ourselves, disparage,
do as thoughtlessly unto ourselves?

As one would tell a lie, a faithless lie,
not with good intention, to obviate a harm,
but just to have one's way, to win, *prevail:*
so don't we deceive ourselves,
and not even know we are?

A self which by definition cannot tell
itself untruths, yet lies, which, wanting
to tell itself untruths, isn't able to, not then,
and would like sometimes not to know
it's lied, but can't deny it has, not then.

And our righteousness before ourselves
how we're so barbarous towards ourselves,
so mercilessly violate ourselves;
as one would never, with a loved one, harm,
never, with a dear one, strike, not *strike.*

As one would with an enemy, implacable,
as one would with an animal, intractable,
as one would with a self which savagely resists:
this amputating, this assailing, this self-slashing.
As one would lie, as one so fervently would lie.

Shoe

A pair of battered white shoes has been left out all night on a sill across the
    way.
One, the right, has its toe propped against the pane so that it tilts oddly
    upwards,
and there's an abandon in its attitude, an elevation, that reminds me of a satyr
    on a vase.

A fleece of summer ivy casts the scene into deep relief, and I see the creature
    perfectly:
surrounded by his tribe of admiring women, he glances coolly down at his
    own lifted foot,
caught exactly at the outset of the frenzied leaping which will lift all of them
    to rapture.

The erotic will diffused directly into matter: you can sense his menacing
    lasciviousness,
his sensual glaze, his delight in being flagrant, so confidently more than merely
    mortal,
separate from though hypercritically aware of earthly care, of our so
    amusingly earthly woe.

All that carnal scorn which in his dimension is a fitting emblem for his energy
    and grace,
but which in our meager world would be hubris, arrogance, compensation for
    some lack or loss,
or for that passion to be other than we are that with a shock of longing takes
    me once again.

Tree

One vast segment of the tree, the very topmost, bows ceremoniously against a
    breath of breeze,
patient, sagacious, apparently possessing the wisdom such a union of space,
    light and matter should.

Just beneath, though grazed by the same barely perceptible zephyr, a knot of
    leaves quakes hectically,
as though trying to convince that more pacific presence above it of its anxieties,
    its dire forebodings.

Now some of the individual spreads that make up the higher, ponderous, stoic
    portion, are caught, too,
by a more insistent pressure: their unity disrupted, they sway irrationally; do
    they, too, sense danger?

Harried, quaking, they seem to wonder whether some untoward response will
    be demanded of them,
whether they'll ever graze again upon the ichor with which such benign exis-
    tences sustain themselves.

A calming now, a more solid, gel-like weight of heat in the air, in the tree a
     tense, tremulous subsiding;
the last swelling and flattening of the thousand glittering armadas of sunlight
     passing through the branches.

The tree's negative volume defines it now; the space it contains contained in
     turn by the unmoving warmth,
by duration breathlessly suspended, and, for me, by a languorous sense of being
     all at once pacified, quelled.

DAVID WOJAHN

After Propertius

(IV.7, Sunt aliquid Manes: letum non omnia finit)

Ghosts do exist. Ash & bone-stubble, we left her pyre
    smoldering, libations
where the flames contusioned skyward. We piled the battered
    red thesaurus, & then

her jewelry, her father's bee books. Toga-shroud & camphorwood, Cynthia
    now was shade, slithering colorless from smoke.
& on my bed I'd mourn each night before I slept—brass four-poster
    where we groaned delirious fucks.

& it was here her phantom swayed above me in my dream. *Wake up*
    Propertius, wake up, you shit
& look upon your Cynthia. Asleep already? The hair, her eyes—
    exactly as they'd been upon her shroud:

three years ago to this day. Patchouli-smell, lapis ring afloat
    before me, fire-gnawed & battered.
Wrist-bones clicking, humeri a-rattle. *How goes the poetry,*
    loverboy? Did I give good subject matter?

Don't think I haven't heard your three-year keening. & now it's given you—
    I've given you—another little book.
Yes, I've read it; not much else to do in Hades' endless cellblocks
    but unscroll papyri; nobody here shoots up,

wine's beside the point, & fucking means nada to a crew with coins
    so heavy on their ectoplasmic tongues.
Desire is for amateurs, & shame. Imagine it, Propertius, that I
    of all people am beyond

such things: though you, I see, have hardly changed at all: Mr. Legendary
     Piss & Moan. Give me a break.
How loose the mourning-toga hung upon her bones, & her turban,
     shot-through with golden thread,

floated glistening & unscorched, as did her eyes, gunmetal blue—
     flaring with the gaze that always shone
on me & with the same prodigious rage. *It's time, Propertius,*
     for a little travelogue.

Outside the Trailways station you'll find Cerberus asleep; he's mangy,
     a toothless shepherd-boxer mix,
jaws always working while he dreams of prey—waterfront rats
     most likely. & Styx?

Think Boston & the Combat Zone, but before it a shit-oozing smell
     from the flooded street, where Charon
(aka "Dr. Nods," aka "Tugboat") pulls the fillings from your mouth
     with pliers (though there is no pain),

& with his gold tooth shining, his 'fro sprawling beachball-size, he leads
     you on the steppingstones
he's made of carhoods, dumpster covers. & now you'll hover on
     The Other Side, floating along

the mentholed air, past "25 Cent Movies," GIRLS! GIRLS! GIRLS!
     ADONIS THEATRE *preening its neon.*
& suddenly you know Hart Crane is here, Chet Baker, Clytemnestra,
     Emily & Medea. & then

before you, dear Propertius, looms your S.R.O., its TRANSIENTS
     WELCOME *pulsing & its lobby*
sporting zoot-suits, eye-patches, hot-panted legs uncrossing, gang
     tattoos; arm-pit stink & every eye

fixed maybe on the Zenith with its sound turned down, maybe on
     the umbrella stand, bristling with canes,
prosthetic legs. The desk clerk's been expecting you. One milky eye,
     & his pinky-ringed hand holds out your key.

"With tears in death we ratify life's loves," he says. (At least
the sense of irony remains
intact.) The elevator's broken; you can use the stairs. Begin
your climb, Propertius. Begin.

Word Horde Against the Gnostics

Into error so often lead. Founded in error, as it is written
in *The Gospel of Truth,*
The Paraphrase of Shem, The Second Apocalypse of James. Father
Creator lost, shrouded in mist,

& these gods who are Gods of Error, who have founded (so it
is written)
this day, which is the carlot phone across Norwood, stuttering
loud enough to rattle

my windowpanes, the summer asphalt asmoulder. Which is the blind man
being lead by his son along
the fenders & grease pencil tractates pocking windshields: WOW
& BEAUT & FACTORY AIR.

And Anguish grew solid like a fog, so that no one was able to see,
Which is lawnsprinkler's cat hiss,
gelignite, ebola, battering ram, the influenza outbreak of '18,
& a hand working up

the antenna, over black lacquer grilles of 'stangs & Z-28s
Something for his boy
to make him one with & one with. Flap of pennants which he hears
& the boy ignores,

& my own hands fumbling the keyboard at my window, spendthrift
also in their error, which is,
which is, which is. *For this reason Error grew powerful,*
not having known the truth.

It fashioned its own matter, and Error did grow enraged at Him
     and He was nailed
to a tree . . . Which is attack dog, labyrinth, applause, stuck pig
     dangling from its feet on the trolley

of the Armour & Co. aerial railway, Dreiser by the "red-headed
     giant" butcher dodging blood,
the senile ex-President all smiles besides the actors in three-
     cornered hats, the cameras agog.

Sorrowful wheel. "Word horde," you jotted still living on
     the inside cover of Hart Crane,
for me to unearth this morning two years beyond. But say we can
     love this error, the one with

& the one with, book aslant on the desktop & flecked with
     your cursive, the imitation
leather seat, hand on the shiftknob & the powertop creaking down,
     salesman adjusting & glint

of the blindman's shades. Soon the check written out by the boy
     who will guide his father's hand to sign.
& soon the laser scanning the true-leather voice of Joey Ramone—
     Didn't you love that?—until

the speakers throb, how *Needles a-a-and pins hurt . . .* spendthrift
     in their error. Then segue
to the silken lamentations of Sam Cooke, begging *to just touch . . .*
     the hem of His garment . . . O say

we love this spendthrift error, this want, this lack, this key now
     jazzing the ignition,
top down & the deal made. *Tarnish, apples, tabloid, x-ray.*
     My hands along the keyboard & swirl

of hairpin turns. *Hyacinth, shoulders, tango, leotard, Grand Hotel,*
   perfected, invisible ink.
Shades off & the wind against the eyes, useless & holy & beautiful
   error lets out the clutch, three chords

slithering their sacred din. O founded powers hear me:
   look you now upon these wonders.

C. D. WRIGHT

Cervical Jazz: A Girlfriend Poem

for lida

In his worsted socks she followed

the clocks on their dissenting rounds
        of the Watertown apartment.

There is not a cat nor is the fire lit.

The way the vitrine absorbs the blue light.

Softly, into a cordless phone:
        "Have you ever tried tiger balm."

The left ear follows the churn
        of a not-so-distant engine.

Nor a mirror on a wall.

A glass of wine at six, aerogram from
        the sister in Hungary:

Furious holograph on life in the glove factory.

It was a blind street.

A bowl of paperwhites . . .

Holiness only in living;
        this the tablecloth knows,

the pillowcase makes it so.

Girlfriends

We make our own chairs and shoes and fix hair
                        Every other wednesday
staticky sheets get snatched from the dryer
                        The Childe
wants to know who invented talking
                        Once we buy sugar corn
we see silver queen further on down the road
                        The Childe
wants to know if one earth worm heart stops
do all five stop
                        The Childe
has to know where did the letter Y
get its name
Like a butterfly stretching its tips

                        All the children we know
nap under a covered bridge
The ant lion leads them down
into his suite of dreams
                        where he begins to tell stories

Already it's the day before yesterday

We are horny and not long on speeches
or ruins

On her highly simplified horse
Iona arrives
                        The butterflies open up
She agrees on one condition
will she be their docent
                        The children insist
she not speak to the police
with paper in her mouth
                        The widower discovers
his carbons are in backwards

with Brecht Wright Gander

The Revolving House *or* or Another Girlfriend Poem

The sitting women are sitting there
they are admiring what is there to admire

That whistling whistle in the breath
of the child as it escapes the child's oneric head

Slowly they begin to shift ever-so-slowly in motion

And swear they will tell no one of the things they see

So wandersome has been their ride so gladly they arrive

The visions they would limn of arches visions
of ladders and other lofty animate things

The waving women are waving they wave at you and I

They watch themselves in the water and the water
watches back waving at every other passerby

Spring Street Girlfriend

for carole

in the snug harbors helicopters and electric eel
blink like stringlight in the pathetic exhaust-resistant trees
there has to be one more night like this and then
peace and prosperity will reign for an even minute
the vendor's hands don't look very clean but we knew
it was a dirty city the chestnuts smell deceptively good we're
hungry even though they're mealy and then
she comes down in her otis elevator holding a cricket cage
she purposely wears the purple terricloth robe of nobility
the music scarcely changes up until now and then
with the tiniest monogrammed scissors we snip
a ribbon of undergraduate hair

she offers the food of her breasts
she does not give a fig about our depression
glass she's not into collectibles
she does not rust or crack up to this point
we know no more than two of the names under which she wrote
nor her intellectual milieu the buddha
in the take-out emanates an unknown strain of mercy
and then we get suddenly scared and tell the driver
we want transfers to the real world
where the fish smell like fish and the cheese like cheese

CHARLES WRIGHT

The Appalachian Book of the Dead VI

Last page, The Appalachian Book of the Dead,

full moon,

No one in anyone's arms, no lip to ear, cloud bank
And boyish soprano out of the east edge of things.
Ball-whomp and rig-grind stage right,
Expectancy, quivering needle, at north-northwest.

And here comes the angel with her drum and wings. Some
    wings.
Lost days, as Meng Chiao says, a little window of words
We peer through darkly. Darkly,
Moon stopped in cloud bank, light slick for the chute and long
    slide,
No lip, no ear.

Distant murmur of women's voices.

I hear that the verb is facilitate. To facilitate.
Azure. To rise. To rise through the azure. Illegible joy.
No second heaven. No first.
I think I'll lie here like this awhile, my back flat on the floor.
I hear that days bleed.

I hear that the right word will take your breath away.

Opus Posthumous III

Mid-August meltdown, Assurbanipal in the west,
Scorched cloud-towers, crumbling thrones—
The ancients knew to expect a balance at the end of things,
The burning heart against the burning feather of truth.
                                        Sweet-mouthed,
Big ibis-eyed, in the maple's hieroglyphs, I write it down.

All my life I've looked for this slow light, this smallish light
Starting to seep, coppery blue,
                    out of the upper right-hand corner of things,
Down through the trees and off the back yard,
Rising and falling at the same time, now rising, now falling,
Inside the lapis lazuli of late afternoon.

Until the clouds stop, and hush.
Until the left hedge and the right hedge,
                                the insects and short dogs,
The back porch and barn swallows grain-out and disappear.
Until the by-pass is blown with silence, until the grass grieves.
Until there is nothing else.

Sky Diving

Clear night after four days' rain,
                    moon brushed and blanched, three-quarters full.
Arterial pulse of ground lights and constellations.

I've talked about one thing for thirty years,
                                and said it time and again,
Wind like big sticks in the trees—
I mean the still, small point at the point where all things meet;
I mean the form that moves the sun and the other stars.

What a sidereal jones we have!
                              Immensity fills us
Like moonrise across the night sky, the dark disappears,
Worlds snuff, nothing acquits us,
And still we stand outside and look up,
                              look up at the heavens and think,

Such sidebars, such extra-celestial drowning pools
To swallow us.
                    Let's lie down together. Let's open our mouths.

St. Augustine and the Arctic Bear

China moon in the northeast, egg-like, 9:10 pm.
There is no story here, only the moon
                              and a few script-stars,
Everything headed due west on its way through heaven,
Constellations like silver combs with their shell inlays,
Darkness like a sweet drink on the tongue.

No story, perhaps, but something's trying to get told,
Though not by me.
                    Augustine said that neither future
Nor past exists, as one is memory, the other expectation.
When expectation becomes memory, I'd hasten to add,
We'll live in the past, a cold house on a dark street.

However, he also said,
None fall who will lift their eyes.
And said that time, in essence, remains a body without form.
On the other hand, the arctic bear,
Like time invisible in its element,
                              has form to burn,

But does not do so, and keeps his eyes
                                    fixed on the black water.
As I do, wherever I find it,
Bubba's bateau and his long pole
                              always at my back,
A lap and a noisome breeze.
Formless and timeless, he wears my heart on his hard sleeve.

Contributor Notes

Agha Shahid Ali is the author, most recently, of *The Country Without a Post Office* (W. W. Norton, 1997). He is an "All-American Shiite-Muslim Kashmiri." He teaches at the University of Massachusetts.

David Baker has published five books of poems, most recently *The Truth About Small Towns* (University of Arkansas Press, 1998). He edited *Meter in English* (University of Arkansas Press, 1996), and he serves as poetry editor of *The Kenyon Review.*

Marvin Bell's sixteen books include *Ardor* (Copper Canyon, 1997) and the illustrated *Poetry for a Midsummer's Night* (Seventy Fourth Street Productions, 1998). Bell teaches at the Writers' Workshop of the University of Iowa.

Stephen Berg is the author of numerous volumes of poetry, including *The Steel Cricket: Versions 1958–1997* (Copper Canyon Press, 1997) and *In It* (University of Illinois Press, 1986). He is the founder and coeditor of *The American Poetry Review.*

Frank Bidart was born in Bakersfield, California, in 1939. He was educated at the University of California, Riverside, and Harvard University. His fifth book, *Desire* (Farrar, Straus, Giroux), appeared in 1997.

Linda Bierds is the recipient of fellowships from the National Endowment for the Arts, the Guggenheim Foundation, and the John D. and Catherine T. MacArthur Foundation. Her most recent book is *The Profile Makers* (Henry Holt & Co., 1997).

Lucille Clifton, poet and children's book author, teaches at St. Mary's College in St. Mary's County, Maryland. Clifton's poetry has been nominated for the Pulitzer Prize and the National Book Award, among others.

Alfred Corn is the author of seven books of poetry, including *Present* (Counterpoint, 1997), a collection of critical essays entitled *The Metamorphoses of*

Metaphor (Viking 1987), and a study of prosody, *The Poem's Heartbeat* (Story Line, 1997).

Peter Davison recently retired as consulting editor to Houghton Mifflin Co. and is currently poetry editor of *Atlantic Monthly*. Davison is the author of numerous volumes of poetry and prose, including *The Poems of Peter Davison, 1957–1995* (Knopf, 1995).

Deborah Digges teaches at Tufts University. Her most recent collection, *Rough Music* (Knopf, 1995), won the Kingsley Tufts award.

Stuart Dischell is the author of *Good Hope Road* (Viking/Penguin, 1993) and *Evenings & Avenues* (Penguin, 1996). He teaches in the Master of Fine Arts Program in Creative Writing at the University of North Carolina at Greensboro.

Wayne Dodd is Distinguished Professor of English at Ohio University. His most recent books are *The Blue Salvages* (1998) and *Of Desire & Disorder* (1994), both of which are from Carnegie-Mellon University Press.

Mark Doty has published five books of poetry, most recently *Sweet Machine* (Harper Flamingo, 1998), and the memoirs, *Heaven's Coast* (Harper-Collins, 1996) and *Firebird*. He teaches at the University of Houston.

Rita Dove is former United States Poet Laureate. Her poetry books include the Pulitzer Prize-winning *Thomas and Beulah* (Carnegie-Mellon Press, 1986), *Mother Love* (W. W. Norton, 1995), and *On the Bus with Rosa Parks* (W. W. Norton, 1999).

Cornelius Eady's second book, *Victims of the Latest Dance Craze* (Omnation Press, 1986), won the Lamont Poetry Prize from the Academy of American Poets. His later books include *You Don't Miss Your Water* (Henry Holt & Co., 1995).

Nancy Eimers is the author of *Destroying Angel* (Wesleyan University Press, 1991) and *No Moon* (Purdue University Press, 1997). She is the recipient of a Whiting Writers Award for 1998. Eimers teaches at Western Michigan University and Vermont College.

Roland Flint has published six books and three chapbooks of poems, as well as three books of translations from Bulgarian. He recently published *Easy* (Louisiana State University Press, 1999).

Carol Frost teaches at Hartwick College. She recently published *Love and Scorn: New and Selected Poems* (TriQuarterly Books, 1999). Her earlier volumes include *Venus and Don Juan* (TriQuarterly Books, 1996) and *Pure* (TriQuarterly Books, 1994).

Tess Gallagher writes in Sky House, the house she designed and built in Port Angeles, Washington. Her most recent books are *At the Owl Woman Saloon* (Scribner, 1997) and *Portable Kisses* (Bloodaxe Books, 1996). Gallagher won the Lyndhurst Prize in 1993.

Forrest Gander is the editor of *Mouth to Mouth* (Milkweed Editions, 1993), a bilingual anthology of contemporary Mexican women poets. Gander has written four books, the most recent of which is *Science and Steepleflower* (New Directions, 1998).

Louise Glück's most recent volume of poetry is *Vita Nova* (Ecco Press, 1999). She is the author of *Meadowlands* (Ecco Press, 1996) and *Wild Iris* (Ecco Press, 1992), which won the Pulitzer Prize for poetry.

Linda Gregerson's *The Woman Who Died in Her Sleep* was published by Houghton Mifflin in 1996. Gregerson teaches Renaissance literature and directs the MFA Program in Creative Writing at the University of Michigan.

Marilyn Hacker's *Winter Numbers* (W. W. Norton, 1994) received the Academy of American Poets/*The Nation* Lenore Marshall Prize, as well as a Lambda Literary Award (both in 1995). Her most recent book is *Scars on Paper* (W. W. Norton, 1999).

Daniel Hall has published two collections of poetry, *Hermit with Landscape* (Yale University Press, 1989) and *Strange Relation* (Penguin 1996). He is the recipient of a 1998 Whiting Writers Award. He lives in Northampton, Massachusetts.

Daniel Halpern is the author of eight collections of poetry, including *Selected Poems* (Knopf, 1994), *Foreign Neon* (Knopf, 1991), and *Tango* (Viking/Penguin, 1987).

Michael S. Harper is coeditor of *Every Shut-Eye Ain't Asleep* (Little, Brown, 1994) and *Songlines in Michael Tree* (University of Illinois Press, forthcoming). His awards include the Robert Hayden Poetry Award (1990).

Jeffrey Harrison has written two books of poems: *The Singing Underneath* (Dutton, 1998) and *Signs of Arrival* (Copper Beach, 1996). He currently serves as writer-in-residence at Phillips Academy in Andover, Massachusetts.

Brenda Hillman's five collections of poetry from Wesleyan University Press include *Death Tractates* (1992), *Bright Existence* (1993), and *Loose Sugar* (1997). She teaches at St. Mary's College in Moraga, California.

Edward Hirsch has published five books of poems, most recently *On Love* (Knopf, 1998). He was awarded a MacArthur Fellowship, and he teaches in the Creative Writing program at the University of Houston.

Richard Jackson is the author of three books of poems, including *Alive All Day* (Cleveland State University Press, 1992). A winner of four Pushcart Prizes, NEA, NEH, and Witter-Bynner fellowships, Jackson was a Fulbright Poet to the former Yugoslavia.

Mark Jarman's latest collection of poetry, *Questions for Ecclesiastes* (Story Line, 1997), was a finalist for the 1997 National Book Critics Circle Award. His next collection, *Unholy Sonnets*, is forthcoming from Story Line.

Brigit Pegeen Kelly teaches in the creative writing program at the University of Illinois, Urbana-Champaign. She has published two volumes of poetry, *To the Place of Trumpets* (Yale University Press, 1988) and *Song* (BOA Editions, Ltd., 1995).

Galway Kinnell is a former MacArthur Fellow. In 1982 his *Selected Poems* (Houghton Mifflin, 1982) won the Pulitzer Prize and the National Book Award. He teaches at New York University. His latest book is *Imperfect Thirst* (Houghton Mifflin, 1994).

Yusef Komunyakaa has written ten volumes of poetry, including *Thieves of Paradise* (Wesleyan University Press, 1998) and *Neon Vernacular* (Wesleyan University Press, 1993), winner of the Kingsley-Tufts Poetry Award and the Pulitzer Prize. He teaches at Princeton University.

Li-Young Lee is the author of two books of poems: *Rose* (1986) and *The City in Which I Love You* (1990), both by BOA Editions, Ltd. In addition, Lee has written a book-length prose poem *The Winged Seed* (Hungry Mind Press, 1995).

Phillis Levin has published *The Afterimage* (Copper Beech Press, 1995) and *Temples and Fields* (University of Georgia Press, 1988), a Norma Farber First Book Award winner. She teaches at the University of Maryland and the Unterberg Poetry Center in New York.

Philip Levine has seventeen books of poems, including his most recent, *The Mercy* (Knopf, 1999). Levine won National Book Awards for *Ashes* (Atheneum, 1979) and *What Work Is* (Knopf, 1991) and a Pulitzer Prize for *The Simple Truth* (Knopf, 1994).

Larry Levis's posthumous *Elegy* was published by the University of Pittsburgh Press in 1997.

Thomas Lux teaches at Sarah Lawrence College. His most recent book is *New and Selected Poems 1975–1995* (Houghton Mifflin, 1997).

Campbell McGrath teaches creative writing at Florida International University. His most recent book is *Spring Comes to Chicago* (Ecco, 1997). McGrath lives with his family in Miami Beach.

Heather McHugh is the University of Washington's Milliman Distinguished Writer-in-Residence. She teaches part-time as well at the MFA Program for Writers at Warren Wilson College. Her web page is at http://weber.u.washington.edu/~amanuen.

James McMichael's most recent book is *The World at Large: New and Selected Poems, 1971–1996* (University of Chicago Press, 1996).

William Matthews' posthumous *After All: Last Poems* was published by Houghton Mifflin Company in 1998.

W. S. Merwin, who lives in Hawaii, has written numerous volumes of poetry, including *The Folding Cliffs* (1998), *The Vixen* (1996), *Travels* (1993), and *The Lost Upland* (1992), all from Knopf.

Carol Muske is the author of six books of poems, two novels, and a book of critical essays, *Women and Poetry* (University of Michigan Press, 1997). Her most recent book is *An Octave Above Thunder: New and Selected Poems* (Penguin, 1997).

Marilyn Nelson's *The Homeplace* (Louisiana State University Press, 1991) and *The Fields of Praise: New and Selected Poems* (Louisiana State University Press, 1997) were finalists for the National Book Award in 1991 and 1997, respectively. She teaches at the University of Connecticut.

William Olsen's most recent book of poems is *Vision of a Storm Cloud* (Tri-Quarterly Books, 1996). He teaches at Western Michigan University and the MFA Program of Writing at Vermont College.

Steve Orlen is the author, most recently, of *Kisses* (Miami University Press, 1997). He teaches at the University of Arizona and in the low-residency MFA Program at Warren Wilson College.

Gregory Orr has published six collections of poetry, the most recent of which is *City of Salt* (University of Pittsburgh Press, 1995). He has been a recipient of Guggenheim and NEA fellowships. Orr is the poetry editor of *Virginia Quarterly Review*.

Jacqueline Osherow is the author of *Looking for Angels in New York* (Princeton University Press, 1988), *Conversations with Survivors* (University of Georgia Press, 1994), and *With a Moon in Transit* (Grove, 1996). She teaches at the University of Utah.

Jay Parini, a poet and novelist, teaches at Middlebury College. His books of poetry include *Anthracite Country* (Random House, 1982) and *House of Days* (Henry Holt & Co., 1998).

Linda Pastan served as the Poet Laureate of Maryland from 1991 to 1995. Her tenth book of poems is *Carnival Evening: New and Selected Poems* (W. W. Norton, 1998).

Carl Phillips is the author of *From the Devotions* (Graywolf, 1998), *Cortege* (Graywolf, 1995), and *In the Blood* (Northeastern University Press, 1992). He has received awards and fellowships from the Guggenheim Foundation and the Academy of American Poets.

Robert Pinsky is Poet Laureate of the United States. His *The Figured Wheel: New and Collected Poems (1966–1996)* (Farrar, Straus, Giroux, 1997) was nominated for the Pulitzer Prize. His translation of *The Inferno* (Farrar, Straus, Giroux) appeared in 1994.

Bin Ramke edits the *Denver Quarterly* and the University of Georgia Press poetry series. His sixth book of poems is *Wake* (University of Iowa Press, 1999). His first book won the Yale Younger Poets Award in 1977.

Alberto Ríos is the author of seven books and chapbooks of poetry, including *Teodoro Luna's Two Kisses* (W. W. Norton, 1990), and two collections of short stories, including *Pig Kisses* (Chronicle Books, 1990). He has won Guggenheim and NEA fellowships.

David Rivard's *Wise Poison* (Graywolf, 1996) won the James Laughlin Prize from the Academy of American Poets and was a finalist for the 1996 *Los Angeles Times* Book Prize. Rivard teaches at Tufts University and the MFA Program of Vermont College.

Peter Sacks is the author of *The English Elegy* (Johns Hopkins University Press, 1985) and four books of poems, most recently *Natal Command* (University of Chicago Press, 1998) and *O Wheel* (University of Georgia Press, forthcoming). He teaches at Harvard University.

Ira Sadoff teaches at Colby College and the MFA Program at Warren Wilson College. He is the author of *Grazing* (University of Illinois Press, 1998), *Emotional Traffic* (Godine, 1990), and *The Ira Sadoff Reader* (University Press of New England, 1992).

David St. John's most recent collections of poetry are *The Red Leaves of Night* (HarperCollins, 1999) and *In the Pines: Lost Poems, 1972–1997* (White Pine, 1999).

Alan Shapiro's new book of poems, *The Dead Alive and Busy* (University of Chicago Press), will appear in spring 2000. Shapiro teaches at the University of North Carolina in Chapel Hill.

Jane Shore has published four books of poems, including *Music Minus One* (Picador USA, 1996), a finalist for the National Book Critics Circle Award, and *Happy Family* (Picador USA, 1999). She teaches at George Washington University.

Jeffrey Skinner was the 1997 Frost House Poet-in-Residence. His most recent collection is *The Company of Heaven* (University of Pittsburgh Press, 1992). Skinner is coeditor of *Last Call: Poems on Alcoholism, Addiction, and Deliverance* (Sarabande, 1996).

Tom Sleigh is the author of *Waking* (1990), *The Chain* (1996), and *The Dreamhouse* (forthcoming), all from the University of Chicago Press. His translation of Euripides' *Heracles* is forthcoming from Oxford University Press.

Arthur Smith teaches at the University of Tennessee in Knoxville. His most recent book of poetry is *Orders of Affection* (Carnegie Mellon University Press, 1996).

Dave Smith, Boyd Professor of English at Louisiana State University, edits *The Southern Review*. He is coeditor of *The William Morrow Anthology of Younger American Poets* (1985) and the author of *Fate's Kite: Poems 1991–1995* (Louisiana State University Press, 1996).

Marcia Southwick is the author of *Why the River Disappears* (Carnegie Mellon University Press, 1990). Her *A Saturday Night at the Flying Dog and Other Poems* won the 1998 Field Poetry Prize of the Oberlin College Press.

Elizabeth Spires has written four collections of poetry, *Globe* (Wesleyan University Press 1982), *Swan's Island* (Henry Holt & Co., 1985), *Annonciade* (Viking/Penguin, 1989), and *Worldling* (Norton, 1995). Spires is a Guggenheim Fellowship and Whiting Award recipient.

Gerald Stern's most recent books of poems include *Bread Without Sugar* (1992), *Odd Mercy* (1995), and *This Time: New and Selected Poems* (1998) winner of the National Book Award, all from W. W. Norton.

Susan Stewart is the author of three books of poems: *Yellow Stars and Ice* (Princeton University Press, 1981), *The Hive* (University of Georgia Press, 1988), and most recently, *The Forest* (University of Chicago Press, 1997). She teaches at the University of Pennsylvania.

Mark Strand is former Poet Laureate of the United States (1990). His most recent book is *Blizzard of One* (Knopf, 1998). Strand currently teaches at the Committee on Social Thought at the University of Chicago.

James Tate received the Pulitzer Prize and the William Carlos Williams Award for *Selected Poems* (Wesleyan University Press, 1991) and the National Book Award for *Worshipful Company of Fletchers* (Ecco Press, 1994).

Henry Taylor teaches at American University in Washington, D.C. His most recent collection is *Understanding Fiction: Poems 1986–1996* (Louisiana State University Press, 1996). His previous collection, *The Flying Change* (Louisiana State University Press, 1986), won the Pulitzer Prize.

Arthur Vogelsang received the Juniper Prize for his latest book of poetry, *Cities and Towns* (University of Massachusetts Press, 1996). He is an editor of *The American Poetry Review*.

Ellen Bryant Voigt's fifth volume of poems, *Kyrie* (W. W. Norton, 1995), was a National Book Critics Circle Award finalist and the winner of the Teasdale Award. Voigt coedited *Poets Teaching Poets* (University of Michigan Press, 1996) with Gregory Orr.

Diane Wakoski is Writer-in-Residence at Michigan State University and the author of *Argonaut Rose* (Black Sparrow Press, 1998). *Emerald Ice* (Black Sparrow Press, 1998) won the William Carlos Williams Prize from the Poetry Society of America in 1989.

Rosanna Warren, associate professor of comparative literature at Boston University, is the author of *Each Leaf Shines Separate* (W. W. Norton, 1984) and *Stained Glass* (W. W. Norton, 1993).

C. K. Williams' book of poems, *The Vigil* (Farrar, Straus, Giroux), was published in 1997. His recent books include *Repair* (Farrar, Straus, Giroux, 1998) and a selection of essays, *Poetry and Consciousness* (University of Michigan Press, 1998).

David Wojahn teaches at Indiana University and in the MFA in Writing Program at Vermont College. He is the author of *The Falling Hour* (1997), *Late Empire* (1994), and *Mystery Train* (1990), all from the University of Pittsburgh Press.

C. D. Wright is the author of *Deepstep Come Shining* (Copper Canyon Press, 1998) and *Tremble* (Ecco Press, 1996). She teaches at Brown University.

Charles Wright teaches at the University of Virginia. Wright has "dabbled in the occult and is still trying to break into show business." He is the winner of the 1998 Pulitzer Prize and National Book Critics Circle Award for poetry.

Editor Notes

Michael Collier is the director of the Bread Loaf Writers' Conference and codirector of the Creative Writing Program at the University of Maryland. His most recent book of poems is *The Neighbor* (University of Chicago Press, 1995).

Stanley Plumly is a Distinguished University Professor at the University of Maryland. His most recent book of poems, *The Marriage in the Trees* (Ecco Press), was published in 1997.

continued from page iv

Points, The Georgia Review, The Gettysburg Review, The Hamline Journal, The Harvard Review, Indiana Review, Kenyon Review, Luna, Maine Times, Meridian, Mid American Review, Michigan Quarterly Review, Nest: A Magazine of Interiors, The New Criterion, New Virginia Review, New England Review, The New Republic, The New Yorker, Nightsun, Orion, The Paris Review, Parnassus, Ploughshares, Poetry, Poetry Review, Prairie Schooner, Provincetown Arts, Quarterly West, Raritan, Salt Hill Journal, River City, Slate, Third Coast, The Threepenny Review, Trafika, TriQuarterly, Virginia Quarterly, Washington Post Magazine, The Yale Review.

We are grateful for the help and guidance provided by the staff at University Press of New England, and the enthusiastic support of the project by Middlebury College. We are also deeply indebted to Kellie Tabor, whose assistance in every aspect of the anthology's creation has been invaluable.

Library of Congress Cataloguing-in-Publication Data

The new Bread Loaf anthology of contemporary American poetry / Michael
Collier and Stanley Plumly, editors.

     p.   cm. — (A Bread Loaf anthology)

    ISBN 0 – 87451– 949 –7 (cl. : alk. paper). — ISBN 0 – 87451– 950 – 0 (pa. :
alk. paper)]

    1. American poetry—20th century.   I. Collier, Michael, 1953 –
II. Plumly, Stanley.   III. Bread Loaf Writers' Conference of
Middlebury College.   IV. Series.

PS615 N385   1999

811' 5408—dc21   99 –20942